GETTING DIVORCED
WITHOUT
RUINING YOUR LIFE

Sam Margulies, Ph.D., J.D.

A Fireside Book

Published By Simon & Schuster
New York London Toronto Sydney Tokyo Singapore

FIRESIDE

Rockefeller Center
1230 Avenue of the Americas
New York, New York 10020

Copyright © 1992 by Sam Margulies

FIRESIDE and colophon are registered trademarks of Simon
& Schuster Inc.

Designed by Chris Welch
Manufactured in the United States of America

10 9 8 7 6

Library of Congress Cataloging-in-Publication Data
Margulies, Sam.
Getting divorced without ruining your life/ Sam Margulies.
p. cm.
"A Fireside book."
Includes bibliographical references (p.   ).
1. Divorce—United States.   2. Divorce mediation—United
States.
3. Divorce—Law and legislation—United States.   I. Title.
HQ834.M28   1992
306.89—dc20   92-7045
CIP

ISBN: 0-671-72826-1

TO SARI

ACKNOWLEDGMENTS

This book would have been difficult to write without the encouragement and assistance of numerous friends and colleagues. Joyce Ochs and Ken Parkinson were invaluable in helping me organize the book and in editing draft after draft. Kathy Emery displayed the patience of a saint deciphering my abominable handwriting, and along with Gus Essig, helping me unravel the mysteries of my computer. I want to thank my agent Faith Hamlin and my editors at Simon and Schuster, Julie Merberg and Sheridan Hay. I also want to thank Jan Woititz, Jim Boskey, Linda Mortenson, and Ron Brown, for their helpful critiques of the manuscript.

CONTENTS

FOREWORD

The dissolution of a marriage is difficult for all concerned. It is stressful at best and devastating at worst, regardless of who wants out.

The adversary system more often than not exacerbates the difficulties and both parties end up at an impasse with the only beneficiary being the lawyers. All too often children become pawns in this drama and the damage to their emotional well being is long lasting.

I first met Sam Margulies about fifteen years ago when he was doing some pro bono work with a local women's shelter. We had many discussions about the necessity for folks in crisis and/or transition to be protected both legally and emotionally at the same time. To this end we worked conjointly on several cases with good results.

Sam founded The New Jersey Counsel on Divorce Mediation and brought together a group of counselors and lawyers to train to work in this area. It gave the counselors the opportunity to work with lawyers, use that perspective in their work, and offered the lawyers the counseling perspective, the goal being to offer divorcing couples a more benign way through this difficult process.

As a professional, Sam uses both these perspectives and brings them to his practice and to this book. Anyone who is contemplating or is in the process of a divorce needs to have this book at his or her night stand. The information presented is thorough and easy to read, and the approach can save a lot of grief. I urge you to put the material presented here to constructive use.

—Janet G. Woititz, Ed.D.

PREFACE

This is a book I've wanted to write for a long time. After thirteen years as a divorce lawyer and divorce mediator, I've seen hundreds of couples through their divorces. Several hundred of those cases I observed from the perspective of an adversary litigator. That is, I represented either the wife or the husband, while another lawyer was my adversary. After a year or two (or three)—depending on how acrimonious things got—we would almost always settle the case before it went to trial. A few did go to trial, but not many. Several hundred other couples were my clients in mediation. Here I represented neither spouse. In mediation, I helped the couple negotiate a resolution of all the issues about children and money that have to be resolved in order to get an uncontested divorce.

Being both a litigator and a mediator gives me a unique perspective. Lawyers generally see a case only through the eyes of one client, but mediators see the case through the eyes of both husband and wife. Mediating has taught me how distorted the perspective of the adversary lawyer can be, and it has shown me how much unnecessary damage can be done by the adversary process. In this book I want to share what I have learned with divorcing couples so that they can avoid the worst aspects of adversary divorce and move on to new lives as quickly as possible.

Soon after I graduated from law school, I decided to special-
ize in divorce law. After a few years, it became apparent to me
that when families turned to the legal system to resolve familial
disputes, the system didn't work. For example, the performance of the system in regard to family violence has been dis-
graceful. After a great deal of prodding, judges and family
lawyers are just beginning to get serious about protecting
women from violent men and protecting children from violent
adults. The performance of the divorce courts and divorce
lawyers on the issue of child support has been equally dis-
graceful. Again, reform in the state courts has come only as a
product of federal legislation mandating child support guidelines in all states. Divorced women with children are still the
largest group in America living below the poverty line.

With certain noticeable exceptions, several conclusions
emerge when you look hard at the system:

- Women get the kids but not enough of the money.
- Men get more of the money but too little of their kids.
- The kids lose big. They don't get the money, and many of
  them, for all practical purposes, lose their fathers. Too
  many of them end up with broke and overwhelmed mothers
  and an abiding sense of anger.

It is simply impossible to look at the products of this system
and not conclude that something is terribly wrong.

By my third year of practice I began to feel, with some sense
of urgency, that there had to be a better way to deal with
divorce. With all the expense, delay, and posturing, the legal
system settles about 97 percent of all divorce cases before trial.
If only 3 percent go to trial and 97 percent get settled prior to
trial, then by and large the entire adversarial system must be
defined as a system for *settling*—not trying—cases. As a system, it is a grossly inefficient, unfair, and costly way to resolve
divorces.

During the early years of my practice I developed a referral network among psychologists, psychiatrists, and other professionals who treated couples and families. Because I had a Ph.D. in the social sciences, I had a perspective on emotional processes not shared by most lawyers, and I had good rapport with therapists. As I consulted with them and represented their clients, I was struck by the almost unanimous view they had of the adversarial divorce system. By and large, mental health professionals regard American legal divorce as an appallingly insensitive and destructive way to end marital relationships.

In the late 1970s and early 1980s, a few lawyers and therapists in the United States started experimenting with a new way to settle divorces. Instead of two lawyers negotiating on behalf of clients against a background of actual or threatened court action, couples were encouraged and assisted in negotiating directly with each other by a specially trained mediator. The mediator's role was to keep the discussions on track, help set the agenda, and provide an environment in which divorcing couples could thrash out the economic and parenting issues without having to endure a draining adversarial contest.

In 1980, I became intrigued with this concept. I already had felt, during many negotiations, that if I could get my adversary out of the room, I could settle the case quickly and fairly for both my client and his. I attended a training seminar with O. J. Coogler, one of the early pioneers in the field, and returned eager to try out what I'd learned.

But when I started looking for cases to mediate, I ran into a buzz saw of angry opposition from my colleagues. Just the idea of divorce mediation made most divorce lawyers furious. They claimed it was unethical for a lawyer to mediate because it meant he was representing two clients with conflicting interests. My explanation that mediation was a process essentially different from representation fell on deaf ears and closed minds. During the first three years of my mediation practice,

I spent (and perhaps wasted) a lot of time trying to convince other lawyers to support the process. By and large, the local bar remained hostile and resistant.

Most referrals to my mediation practice came from therapists who had seen the couple in marriage counseling. Over time, satisfied clients referred friends and family, and within two years almost half my practice was devoted to mediation. Today, I no longer accept clients for adversarial divorce. But the years I spent doing both kinds of work were instructive and provided the basis for this book.

Having now watched hundreds of couples go through divorce, I have seen many who have done well and many who have done poorly. By doing well, I mean that the divorce ended an unhappy relationship and launched the couple back into the world as individuals equipped to cope and to build something new. The couples who did poorly are the ones who did not succeed in ending an unhappy relationship but simply found a new way to relate destructively to each other. To an interminable marriage they added an interminable divorce—a divorce which became the primary influence in their lives and the lives of their children.

When I compare the couples who mediated their way to settlement with those who took a conventional route, the percentage of those who did well is dramatically greater among those who mediated. The post-judgment litigation rate—that is, the couples who went back to court after the divorce was over—was about 3 percent among those who mediated and about 30 percent among those who used the adversarial process. I regard mediation as clearly superior.

However, mediation alone is not the whole story; many couples who used a conventional adversary system also did well. We have to look at these couples, too, to find out why some get divorced successfully and why others get divorced dreadfully.

Over the years, I have learned a great deal from my clients.

I learned that most people, even those in very great emotional pain, are capable of making responsible choices when information is presented so that they can hear it. I learned that most people suffer from major misconceptions about divorce and about how they should behave during a divorce. In fact, I came to believe that most of what people do "instinctively" when faced with a divorce is wrong. On the other hand, couples can be taught to behave differently and, for the most part, can avoid self-destructive behavior when provided with adequate professional leadership. I also learned that even though divorce can bring out the absolute worst in most people, divorcing couples are motivated to retain as much dignity as they can.

Consequently, I do not agree that bad divorces are simply caused by vengeful people, although there are people who are so self-destructive that they will make a mess of it, no matter who tries to help them. I have seen many cases where bad divorces were caused by bad lawyers. Many of those I regard as bad lawyers are considered competent by their peers because they exhibit the most aggressive postures and are "tough" negotiators. But they are bad lawyers because they pursue a mindless advocacy that exaggerates the worst in their clients and feeds the flames of anger and recrimination.

Many bad divorces are caused by the nature of the legal adversary system. I have seen numerous cases where strategic interventions by a mediator or an attorney avoided what was sure to be a bloody war. And I have seen many protracted battles that could have been avoided but for the lack of sensitivity of one or both attorneys. All the carnage cannot be explained away by blaming the clients. Some of the blame must rest on the system itself.

I decided to write this book because I think that many more couples can divorce decently if they understand how to maintain control over their divorce. I also believe that people do not learn this from their lawyers. Although the organized bar includes many fine and decent people, many lawyers have little understanding of the psychological and philosophical prerequisites of decent divorce.

In summary, your chances of getting what you really need are not very good if you simply rely on your lawyers. The purpose of this book is to empower you to make your divorce suit your purpose and to help you spare yourselves and your children unnecessary grief. Although I believe that mediation is a superior way to negotiate a settlement, it is not the only way. Nor is this book meant only for people who use mediation. Whether you negotiate with a mediator or through your lawyers, the principles remain the same:

- You can make choices that help rather than hurt you.
- You can keep control of the process, if you are determined.
- You can accomplish your goals instead of defeating yourself.

In this book, I will tell you how to do that.

Part One

GETTING
READY

Chapter One

MAKING CHOICES

PAUL AND LIZ

*P*aul and Liz *have* been married for nineteen years. After taking off fourteen years from work, Liz recently resumed her career as a supervisor in a bank. The couple's children, ages fourteen and twelve, no longer required Liz's full-time attention and she was bored staying at home. Liz liked having a life of her own again and enjoyed the new friends she made at work.

Paul was unhappy with the change. He had just been promoted to a top administrative position in the insurance company where he worked and a large pay increase came with the promotion. At last he felt able to give up the extra job he had long held to make ends meet, and to spend more time with his family. But now that he had time to spend with Liz, she had neither the desire nor the time to be with him. He was furious. He resented being excluded from her new friendships and didn't like it when Liz went out after hours with her colleagues. He was also angry that she spent her income as she pleased. Paul, who had always had a hot temper, frequently ended up in a rage when he fought with Liz. Over time, Liz responded by growing ever more remote, while Paul became even more sullen.

After a year of this unhappiness they consulted a therapist suggested by one of Liz's friends. At the first session Liz told Paul and the therapist that she really wanted a divorce. "I've been unhappy for years with Paul but have never felt that I could do anything about it. When the kids were younger and I couldn't work, I couldn't even think of divorce. But now I'm enjoying life for the first time in years and I realize how unhappy I've been. I'm tired of Paul's rages and I'm tired of Paul always having to have his way about everything. He's a bully, and I've had enough. He belittles me and my friends, he belittles the kids. The only way is Paul's way. I don't care any longer what he thinks, I've had enough and I want out."

Paul was stunned by Liz's outburst. He thought they were coming to counseling to improve their marriage. He had hoped the therapist would help Liz see how her new life was hurting the marriage and help restore things to the way they were before. He certainly didn't want a divorce. All of a sudden the whole thing seemed like a big setup. Liz had never intended to fix things. She had lured him to counseling just to make it easier for her to break the news to him. He felt betrayed and he was furious. "You lying bitch," he screamed, "all you've ever done is lead me on. Do you think you can walk out on twenty years just like that? Well, I'm going to fight you all the way. This is all because of your new friends. See if they'll help you now." Although the therapist tried to calm him down, Paul was so agitated that he just walked out.

For two days Paul brooded, refusing to talk to Liz. She tried to talk to him. She suggested that they try a separation to see if being apart improved things. When Paul asked what she had in mind, she suggested that he move out temporarily. "Maybe if we were apart for a while, I might change my mind." He immediately concluded that this was another ruse and that she was just trying to get rid of him. Once he was out of the house he knew there would be no getting back in. If she wanted to leave she could, but she wasn't going to get rid of him like that. Liz responded that she was responsible for their two daughters and that he could never cope. She felt that the obviously sensible decision was for him to leave so she could stay in the house with the kids. "So I'm just supposed to leave my family and my home and move into some flea-bitten apartment while you keep everything and live on my money? How stupid do you think I am?" he replied. "I'm not going anywhere."

Paul and Liz are almost certainly headed for divorce. The events leading to Liz's decision to divorce are not unusual. One partner invariably reaches the decision before the other, but there are many variations on the theme. In this case Paul is surprised, even though the warning signs were there for a long time. The outcome would not be much different if they had spent six months in counseling before Liz declared that she wanted out. It would not even be much different if Liz were having an affair, or if it turned out that Paul had had an affair years ago and that Liz had suspected or discovered it. Or Paul might have been bored with the marriage and stayed because of inertia. There are a hundred ways that couples reach the decision to divorce.

If you're reading this book, you have probably decided that you are getting divorced. Maybe the decision is yours, maybe it is your spouse's, or maybe you reached the decision together. The important fact is that you are going to divorce, and, like Paul and Liz, you have some important choices to make.

CHOICES

The choices concern the manner in which you will divorce. Will it be bitter or civilized? Will you have an intense adversarial divorce, or will you have a cooperative, even amicable, divorce? Will you attempt to vindicate the past or will you use your resources to build your separate futures? Will your children suffer emotionally or will you minimize the impact on them? Will your divorce be a mess or will it be a transition to new and better lives for you both? In other words, will you choose a good or a bad divorce?

Many people will argue that you do not have such choices. It's a matter of luck, they say. They will tell you that divorce causes so much bad feelings and anger that there is no way to keep it under control. Its just something that you have to survive and if you're lucky, you will not be too hurt by it. On the other hand, it could ruin your life. However, good divorce or bad divorce is *not* a matter of luck: The outcome is very much subject to the choices you are about to make.

COUPLES DECIDE AND COUPLES DIVORCE

This book will help you and your spouse make the decisions required to prevent your divorce from ruining your lives. Your divorce does not have to be a disaster. Painful though it is, successful divorce can help both of you to begin new lives that offer a second chance at successful relationships. You are ending a relationship because, in some critical ways, it has not succeeded for at least one of you. There will be new relationships and new opportunities ahead. You can enhance these opportunities or you can destroy them. You can use your economic and emotional resources for the benefit of yourselves and your children or you can squander them in battles in which, ultimately, you all lose. You can help your children come out of this difficult period with two effective parents or you can turn them into emotional orphans.

You will make these choices as a couple. Remember, until you are successfully divorced, you are still a couple. Legal ties make you a couple. Economic ties and—yes—even emotional ties make you a couple. Do not believe that because there is anger or distrust or sadness you are not emotionally connected. Fighting is often a way of staying together. Some people remain connected through fighting for years after a divorce.

You are about to begin the final task of the marriage: negotiating a decent end of your relationship. How well you perform this difficult task in large part will determine how the divorce turns out.

Divorce is a process, not an event. During the process of getting divorced you can choose to treat yourselves respectfully or you can choose to treat yourselves with contempt. The important thing about these choices is that you can only make them as a couple. Couples get divorced, not individuals. One of you can choose a bad divorce; but only both of you can choose a "good" divorce.

If one of you engages in war, it is very difficult for the other not to retaliate. In divorce, few partners "turn the other cheek." One of you may want an amicable divorce but may believe (correctly or not) that the other is too angry or too vindictive to make it possible. This is a particularly trying time because you are separated and single on one level, but still married and together. In this time of confused and mixed signals, it is easy to offend each other.

You are neither clearly together nor clearly apart. If you were capable of unlimited cooperation, you would probably stay married. But you **are** capable of *limited* cooperation, and this is enough to get divorced decently. It is this residual capacity that enables you to choose, as a couple, the manner in which to end your marriage.

WHO SHOULD READ THIS BOOK?

Ideally, both husbands and wives will read this book simultaneously. Certainly, if you are going to negotiate a settlement agreement along the lines suggested in it, you both need to read it.

However, this book is also intended for husbands and wives separately. The probability is good that if you are the one who bought the book, you are also the one who is initiating the divorce. As we will see later on, there is a great difference between the way the initiator and the non-initiator approach the tasks of divorce.

One of the most critical issues in shaping a good divorce is timing. It may be that your spouse will benefit from this book and will actually read it. But right now he or she may not be ready. If the book accomplishes nothing more than to give you a realistic sense of timing, it will have been worth reading. So do not be discouraged if your wife or husband is not yet ready to join you in cooperative problem solving as you work toward a divorce. What you learn here may provide you with the patience to wait the few months that might be necessary before your spouse is also ready.

WHO THIS BOOK IS FOR

Most of the couples at risk for difficult divorce either have children, have been married for a long time, or both. Although the problems associated with children are an important part of this book, the chapters on emotional issues will still be useful even if your children are grown. This book assumes that you, the reader, belong to the economic middle class. The very poor do not have complex divorces, although they do tend to have terrible divorces. For the very rich, the economic problems that shape the middle-class divorce are not present. Much of the book focuses on ways to master the problems associated with the economic retrenchment required by middle-class divorce. If money is not an issue in your divorce, the discussions of emotions and parenting issues will be relevant and useful, but the discussions of budgeting and support will not be applicable. I have written this book essentially for people who are not so fortunate that they can disregard economics.

IS GOOD DIVORCE POSSIBLE?

Perhaps it seems strange to talk about "good" divorce. Isn't all divorce bad? Historically, divorce has been viewed as socially deviant behavior and therefore a bad thing. It is generally regarded as an unfortunate event that leads to negative results like "broken homes."

But social attitudes have changed substantially in the past twenty years. Although no one feels that divorce is desirable in itself, we are witnessing a wide-ranging reassessment of divorce, stemming partly from its pervasiveness. Half of all marriages that occur this year will end in divorce. About 80 percent of the people who get divorced remarry and about 60 percent of the second marriages end in divorce. This means that about half our population experiences one divorce, and about a quarter will live through two.

In view of a phenomenon that involves so many, it is no longer accurate to refer to divorce as "deviant" behavior. Serial marriages have become as much a norm as marriages until "death do us part."

In fact, some family therapists suggest that we need a new way of looking at the family, one that recognizes divorce as a change that occurs to the entire family. The task, then, is to help all the family members through the divorce process as a family, not as isolated individuals each dealing separately with the changes of divorce. Divorced spouses would be counseled to accept their past experiences as a part of their personal histories. Divorced parents would be encouraged to use the divorce agreement to work out a way to cooperate in parenting, even though their personal lives will be separate.[1]

I won't quibble over the validity of the term "good" divorce. What I am talking about, and what I believe you as a couple can choose, is a divorce that achieves legitimate and constructive goals for yourselves and your children.

A good divorce accomplishes three objectives:

- A **legal divorce** that ends the marriage within a reasonable time of the decision to divorce—without huge legal fees that drain the family's finances, and with a minimum of acrimony and fighting.
- An **economic divorce** that separates the marital partners into two distinct economic units so that assets and income are fairly distributed and economic sacrifice equally shared. (In this economic divorce, all members of the family will begin anew with about the same standard of living.)
- An **emotional divorce** that allows both partners to mourn the end of the marriage so that each can move on to new relationships. Properly completed, the emotional divorce leaves the former partners capable of cooperating as parents, behaving decently and respectfully toward each other, and embarking on new relationships without destructive baggage from the previous marriage.

A good divorce requires completing all three objectives. Of course, all three are interrelated and each step affects the others.

Paul and Liz, like all divorcing couples, will make their choices. They have a difficult road ahead and can easily make damaging choices. Liz must choose whether she will wait the additional months it will take Paul to come to terms with the divorce and to share the responsibility for it. Paul is just beginning the process of emotional divorce while Liz is well along the way. Each will have to choose whether or not to forgo the innumerable provocations that are temporarily gratifying but that make it impossible to negotiate, and each will have to choose whether or not to let the provocation pass when the other instigates it. Each will have to give higher priority to the emotional comfort of the children than to himself or herself. They will choose whether to fight a legal war of attrition or to negotiate an equitable settlement. Paul will have a harder time than Liz because he is not yet motivated to cooperate. But if he chooses to pursue his interests instead of his hurt feelings, he can succeed. There are no guarantees for this couple, as there are none for any divorcing couple. But they are by no means doomed to an ugly and vengeful divorce. If they make the right choices they can each achieve satisfying new lives within a few years.

NEW LIVES—SECOND CHANCES

The ultimate goal of divorce and the ultimate measure of how well you get divorced is the ability of all family members to move on to satisfying and productive new lives.

From the perspective of your children, your ability to cooperate as parents is the most important influence on their ability to adjust. Of course there are other factors, but without this, the children are in trouble from the beginning. If your children do not cope well, they in turn will make it difficult for you when you try to build a relationship with a new mate. Stepparenting is a challenge in the best of circumstances. But children still caught up in your unresolved divorce are guaranteed to wreck your next marriage.

On the other hand, if the two of you retain the ability to parent well, available research suggests that you maximize your children's ability to adjust in time. Judith Wallerstein's *Second Chances* documents the long-term difficulty of children's adjusting to their parents' divorces but states that parental cooperation is a critical factor in helping children overcome the devastation of divorce.[2] Your cooperation is not required only for the "children's sake." It is the key to your own adjustment to the divorce.

Finally, if you divorce well, you give yourself the ability to understand what went wrong and how you contributed to the process. Santayana's dictum that "Those who cannot remember the past are condemned to repeat it" applies to marriage and remarriage. I have seen many people lay the foundation of their second divorces during their first. Bad divorces breed bad second marriages.

CHOOSING THE WAY YOU DIVORCE

Movies like *Kramer Versus Kramer* or the more recent *War of the Roses* that show divorcing couples battling it out in court reflect popular misconceptions about divorce. This image of divorce as an inevitable battle is based on an erroneous assumption: that divorcing partners are too angry and distrustful to divorce in a nonadversarial manner. Both our legal system, which is based on the assumption of opposing positions, and its practitioners present this as the only possible alternative. There is another choice.

Though there was a time when most divorces were resolved in court, and the only grounds for divorce were based on "fault," grounds like adultery or desertion, this is no longer true. Although the legal system continues to operate as an adversary system in which lawyers, as advocates, struggle to advance the cause of their respective clients, there is growing consensus that this adversarial system and the behaviors it encourages are not very useful for most divorcing couples. In fact, there is reason to believe that the current system of divorce survives more because it fits the cultural biases and economic interests of lawyers than because it fits the needs of divorcing families.

So you can follow convention and choose an adversarial divorce in which you surrender your future to a system that may or may not meet your needs—or you can do what was once unconventional but is now gaining popularity, by holding on to that control in pursuit of a nonadversarial divorce.

This choice is the greatest problem for Paul and Liz. Because he is hurt and frightened, Paul is inclined to make choices that will embroil them in war.

Adversarial divorce may seem more comfortable or "normal" in the beginning, but it is likely to be more damaging in the long run. Staying in control of your divorce leaves you in much better shape to live your life after the divorce. It may be more difficult in the beginning because it requires you to forgo much of the hostile behavior that usually occurs in the early stages of divorce: You must avoid much of what you want to do reflexively—like getting even—and concentrate on the difficult tasks of building a new life for yourself and your children.

What is important to keep in mind is that the choices you make now will determine the way your divorce turns out. As a couple, you can choose to control the extent to which you behave as adversaries. The fact that you are angry, sad, distrustful, or anxious does not prevent you from choosing.

I do not propose that you behave in a saintly or selfless manner. To the contrary, the most self-serving thing you can do is to choose to stay in control of a process that can defeat and hurt you when it is out of control.

NEGOTIATION AS CONTROL

In most cases, the product of the divorce is a negotiated contract called a "property settlement agreement" (sometimes called a "settlement agreement" or "property agreement"). This contract, signed by both spouses, reflects your agreement on economic issues like support and property division and child-related issues like parenting (traditionally referred to as custody and visitation). At best, the settlement agreement can be negotiated by the two of you with a minimal amount of professional help. I say *minimal* with great caution. You need help to understand the issues, gather and assimilate the pertinent facts, learn the applicable law, and negotiate fairly to resolution. Professional help may include the advice and help of lawyers, a mediator, accountants, appraisers, and psychotherapists. More help than is minimally necessary simply removes you from control and increases the chance that this will become someone else's agreement—not yours.

The other extreme is a settlement agreement that is hammered out at the courtroom door hours before your trial. You understand little of what goes into the agreement or why. You listen to your lawyer who's the "expert" and because it is his/her opinion you are paying for. In this setting, you are passive and dependent, like a child. You are the **subject** of the agreement, not its **author.**

The more active you are, the more the agreement will reflect your needs. The more active you are, the less you depend on your lawyer, and the lower your legal fees will be.

Remember, there is almost always a settlement agreement in the end. What varies is your role, what it costs you emotionally and financially, the time it takes to get there, the quality of the agreement, and its impact on your life after divorce. The greater your role, the more you are in control. The more you know and the better you negotiate, the better will be your agreement. If it is negotiated well, it will reflect your needs, your partner's needs, and your children's needs. It will be fair, it will use the available resources most efficiently, and it will maximize your chances of success in your new life.

The key to a good divorce is the quality of negotiation. Effective negotiation means you made choices that made it possible. The following choices must be made as a couple:

- Be active, not passive
- Acquire knowledge rather than depend exclusively on professionals
- Base your positions on need, not fault
- Negotiate in good faith, not bad faith
- Experience and express your anger rather than act it out.

This book will help you, as husband and wife, to negotiate an effective separation agreement by providing you with the information and the strategies you need to put that information to work.

UNDERSTANDING THE LEGAL SYSTEM

In chapters 5 and 6, I will explain the law governing divorce and the system in which it operates. By understanding the basic legal issues and the applicable laws, you increase your competence and control.

Divorce law is a creature of state government, so we have fifty different sets of statutes in the United States. However, while there are some important variations, state laws have quite a lot in common. Your first job is to become sufficiently acquainted with the law to ask questions and get answers from your lawyers and other experts. This is not as difficult as it sounds—remember, the object is not to make you a lawyer, but to help you use a lawyer's advice without giving up control. You also need to learn how to choose the lawyer who is right for you and, having made your choice, how to hold your lawyer accountable. I'll walk you through these processes in later chapters.

Learning about divorce law will also give you an understanding of how the adversary legal system works and the specific procedures that occur. You will understand where such things as pleadings and motions and grounds, etc., fit into the legal process. You will be able to tackle without anxiety potentially explosive concepts like custody because you will know what they mean.

Most people want to understand their rights and obligations so they will know what to expect. You will learn that these rights and obligations are often not precisely defined and can take many forms. The important thing to know is that when you approach them as a couple, you will shape the agreement you want according to your needs, and the legal system will be more than content to go along with you.

FAMILY ECONOMICS AND FINANCE

The second area of information you need concerns the money issues that are the subject of the agreement. The chapters ahead discuss economics from two perspectives. First, you'll see how to assess your family's economic resources and how to analyze income. You will examine both past and future income potential. You must identify and value the family assets so you can divide them. You must also understand the tax and legal issues that affect the division of assets and income.

I shall also address some of the larger economic issues that affect divorce, such as fairness in support and the impact on careers of time spent as homemakers. I'll talk about what money means in this society and how your feelings about money must be identified for successful negotiation.

UNDERSTANDING THE EMOTIONAL PROCESS

The third task of this book is to help you deal with the intense feelings that accompany the divorce. If you are like most couples, one of you wants the divorce more than the other. There is anger—even rage at times. You may feel depressed and humiliated, or you may feel a sense of relief that things long suppressed are now out in the open. It's a sure bet that husband and wife do not feel the same thing at the same time, and you may be very uncomfortable in each other's presence.

All these feelings and problems are normal. For most people, divorce is the most stressful time of their lives. The question you have to answer is: How you are going to let these feelings affect your ability to negotiate your settlement agreement? In time, anger diminishes. But the results of angry acts live on.

GENDER DIFFERENCES

Men and women experience divorce differently. They tend to have different emotional styles, different ways of coping with emotionally intense challenges.

Whereas women are more likely to acknowledge and talk about fears and feelings of vulnerability, men are more likely to deny or bury such fears. They feel that they must be strong, invulnerable, and impervious to pain. This means that men and women will often behave differently in response to similar problems. We shall look more closely at these differences later on. We shall also examine the different challenges faced by men and women as they attempt to adapt to the changes in living patterns that divorce requires.

It will be helpful to understand these differences. The more you understand about what you are feeling *and* what your spouse is feeling, the better choices you will make. If you don't understand, you can't make effective decisions.

HOW TO NEGOTIATE THE AGREEMENT

The first half of this book informs, equips, and empowers you to negotiate; the second half takes you through the process. First I will show you a strategic approach to help you meet your future needs by negotiating.

You will negotiate your agreement in stages, resolving each set of issues in turn, and you'll find that you are in agreement on more issues than you think.

It will be work. You must do your research, ask questions, get answers, and come to the negotiation prepared to solve problems. Along the way you will learn how to find effective assistance—lawyers to advise you, a divorce mediator to facilitate negotiations, an accountant, an appraiser or a good therapist—at the lowest possible cost.

If you stay with the work and stay in control of the process, your divorce will help you both get on with your lives. It is not an easy task. Divorce presents a complex set of problems, and constructive solutions require intense work. There are no easy solutions—only the illusion of easy solutions. You and your spouse can take control—or you can lose control. The choice is yours.

What about Liz and Paul? As you will see from the many couples described in the following chapters, it is possible for angry couples to choose decent, self-preserving divorce. The couples we will discuss are all real people, from real divorces, and I think you will know people just like them. They all had to struggle with the same issues you face now, and most of them did it successfully. I hope you will recognize many of your own feelings in the couples I have described and that you will realize that like them, you can choose a decent divorce.

Chapter Two

WHY DIVORCES GO BAD

To work toward a good divorce, you need to understand the reasons that divorces go bad. There are two related aspects of a bad divorce: The first is the *nature of the divorce process* itself, and we will identify the characteristics of the legal system that combine with the behavior of divorcing partners to produce bitter fights. Second are the *products of bad divorce*—settlement agreements that are unfair and unworkable and the feelings of bitterness and injustice that arise from them. When your settlement agreement is complete, it is important that both of you feel that it is fair. If you do not, it will be difficult for you to get on with your new lives. Such feelings of abiding bitterness continue to interfere with readjustment, growth, and new relationships. Defective settlements can bring you and your ex-spouse back to court again and again so that the continuing battle contaminates and ruins your new lives.

From a statistical perspective, divorce is a disaster in America. About half of all fathers default entirely on their child-support obligations, while only a quarter pay their full obligation.[3] Average visitation between divorced fathers and their children is less than once a month. Divorced women with children constitute the fastest-growing segment of Americans living below the poverty line.[4] The statistics point to systematic defects in the American approach to divorce and should serve as a warning to any divorcing couple. A terrible series of tradeoffs is typical of divorce in America: The mother loses the money and gets the kids. The father gets more money, but for all practical purposes loses the kids and, one might argue, a large part of himself. The children lose at least one parent, and perhaps two, because the parent who is left is frequently too tired and worried to meet their needs. This is not the exceptional horror story. It is the norm.

The divorce disaster is a product of the feelings that accompany divorce (anger and vengeance) and the legal system itself, which is based on opposition, not cooperation. There is a bad fit between the needs of the divorcing family and the American legal system, so before you are drawn into it, you need to understand how it functions and why it functions that way.

THE ADVERSARY LEGAL SYSTEM

The adversary process lies at the heart of the American legal system. It has a long and deeply embedded history. The primary assumption is that a judge or jury acting as fact finder will find the "truth" based on the evidence presented in the conflict by the lawyer-advocates of the opposing (adversary) parties. This assumption shapes the entire legal system and culture, including the training of lawyers, the nature of our courts, and the way we resolve our conflicts.

The job of the lawyer is to present the client's case in the best possible light. This central premise of the legal system assumes that the trial is the final act of the play. That is, the decision of the jury overcomes the dangers and distortions created when two adversary lawyers present two radically different versions of the truth. Now here is the problem: In about 97 percent of all divorces, the case never goes to trial! Less than 3 percent actually culminate in a trial resulting in a judgment by a judge. (Juries are rare in divorce trials.) The overwhelming majority of cases are resolved by a negotiated settlement prior to trial.

This is a dramatic inconsistency. The entire system is designed for trial and, indeed, depends on the trial to find the truth. But the primary product of the adversary system in divorce are settlements, not trials.

Is this reliance on trials the most efficient means of producing settlements? The answer, of course, is no. It is an inefficient way to negotiate the settlement of a conflict and it is exceptionally wasteful to put couples through the expensive, exhausting and lengthy process of preparing for trial when in fact everyone knows they will settle before trial.

FAULT: WHO DONE WRONG?

Another contradiction concerns the issue of fault. One of the primary purposes of the adversary system is not simply to find the truth but also to answer the question "Who is guilty?"

Fifty years ago, this system applied to divorce, too. The plaintiff had to prove that the behavior of the defendant spouse was so vile that it was a profound breach of the marriage contract. Divorce was available only on fault grounds, and only to the victim. The deserter or the adulterer could not get a divorce. The system decided who was at fault and then punished the guilty party. We will discuss the concept of fault in more detail in chapter 3.

Although the adversary system has not changed, modern divorce has. The role of fault is dramatically reduced. Modern no-fault divorce, now adopted in some form in nearly every state, eliminates the requirement that fault be offered or proven as a basis for divorce, and it allows nonvictims to get a divorce.

Some states retain traditional fault grounds in addition to no-fault. But very few divorces are settled on the premise of punishing the wicked and rewarding the victim.

However, the change in the way fault is defined in the courts does not correspond to the way people feel about fault and divorce. Few divorcing people really believe in no-fault as a concept, finding much greater comfort in the belief that their spouses are to blame for the divorce. Although the adversary system initially promises vindication, it disappoints in the end because there is no finding of fault and no emotional vindication.

The courts are too busy coping with a flood of litigation to pay much attention to marital fault. But other forms of conflict resolution such as mediation and arbitration have not yet taken hold in divorce. The organized bar does not widely support alternatives to litigation. The result is that litigation is the sole alternative for resolving most divorce cases even though it results in a fundamental contradiction. The adversary system, designed for *trials*, depends for its survival on *settlements*.

Although only about 3 percent or less of all cases go to trial, court calendars are jammed. Were this to increase only a few percent, the system would be unable to cope. A couple ready for trial, having endured years of waiting and expense, finally gets to court for this day of reckoning only to be disappointed and disillusioned when the judge and their lawyers compel them to settle before their case is heard. Lawyers call it "client control," and a lawyer who cannot persuade his client to settle may lose face with colleagues and judges. It is not unusual for a lawyer who handles a hundred cases a year to try only one or two.

Most settlements produced at the courtroom door tend to be bad settlements. The fighting spouses settle because they fear losing control to the court or because they are intimidated by the thought of trial. The settlement is not reached through mutual understanding or consideration of mutual needs. It is not surprising, then, that about half of all settlements break down, bringing the couple back to court for years following the divorce.

Although the adversary system is an outmoded, inefficient

way to get a divorce settlement, you cannot get a divorce without some contact with the system and its lawyers. At some point, one or both partners must hire lawyers. You will be better able to use and control your lawyer if you know something about how lawyers are taught to think and behave.

THE LEGAL CULTURE

Lawyers are trained to be advocates and adversaries. Good lawyers win for their clients. They are not trained to care particularly whether their client is guilty or innocent or whether their client breached the contract. A lawyer who gets his/her guilty client acquitted or who succeeds in helping his/her client successfully breach his contract is a winner and, hence, a good lawyer.

Under this system at its best, the lawyer's image is that of a crusader for justice, the lawyer who never rests until the innocent client or worthy victim has been vindicated. At its worst, the lawyer's image is that of a cynical shyster, out to beat the system on behalf of whoever can pay the most. But most lawyers are neither knights in shining armor nor crafty villains. They are just practitioners of their trade of advocacy.

Advocacy creates a sense of justice for lawyers that is different from a layperson's notion of justice. *Substantial* justice, the justice that prevails when the guilty are convicted, is the domain of judges and juries, not the lawyer-advocate. What concerns lawyers most is *procedural* justice.

The adversary system has an elaborate set of procedures to make sure that neither side takes unfair advantage of the other. Many constitutional protections, such as the Fifth Amendment, are designed to ensure fairness in criminal prosecutions. Rules of evidence, rules of discovery, rules of court are all procedural safeguards to insure fairness in the adversary system.

Lawyers are concerned with procedures often to the dismay

of their clients, for procedural requirements make for lengthy and expensive divorces. I have seen lawyers spend thousands of dollars of their clients' money on procedures intended to discover hidden assets that could not possibly be worth enough money to cover the cost. But the fear that the other side might get away with five dollars' worth of cheating is enough for some zealous lawyers to justify spending a hundred dollars to prevent it.

A second problem of the legal culture is that it tends to aggravate rather than reduce divorce-related conflicts. I have often found when mediating a divorce for a couple locked in litigation that the husband and wife are unaware that their positions are really quite close. They can be a few dollars apart but still be fighting in court. Most lawyers, trained as advocates, tend to emphasize the clients' *divergent* interests. They do not encourage or emphasize the common or *convergent* interests of the couple. Yet divorcing people have many things in common, the most important usually being children. These common interests that could provide a basis for cooperation are often ignored by lawyers, especially by those who revel in their identities as fighters.

Lawyers are trained to approach each case as if it is to be a fight to the finish—as if the case will go to trial. Their concerns for procedure and their postures as combatants compel them to prepare for trial even though they expect to settle out of court. This is truly a waste of money.

LAWYERS AND EMOTIONS

Divorce is an emotionally charged process. The feelings are intense, and the stress is extreme. Lawyers are trained to cope with legal events and procedures and to avoid emotion in favor of fact. Most lawyers have had little or no formal training in human development, child development, or human relations. What most lawyers do when faced with the emotional issues of divorce is to dig even deeper into procedure, rules, and adversary relations. Your lawyer is trained to argue your position—even when your position is wrong.

In the process, your lawyer feeds your anger, distrust, and disappointment. Your feelings of emotional betrayal may get converted into the conviction that your spouse can never be trusted. The "bad" husband/wife becomes the "bad" father/mother. Such distortions justify all sorts of protective court procedures. This built-in tendency for lawyers to stress differences, coupled with their ignorance of emotional processes, is one reason the fights get out of control.

I have had many experiences with clients who came in thinking they had to have a custody fight when all they needed was some reassurance that they would not lose their children if custody was with the other parent. I don't mean to imply that lawyers purposely cause such battles. But many lawyers are not trained or sensitive enough to emotional issues to successfully steer their clients away from custody fights.

YOUR INSTINCTS MAY BE COUNTERPRODUCTIVE

Divorce is painful no matter how you approach it. The choice you must make is whether you are going to give in to the understandable impulses that make it more painful for you or whether you are going to struggle with the system and yourself to make it work for you over the long term. Most couples can go either way. There is a time early in the divorce when you decide whether you will divorce decently or poorly. My argument with the legal system is that it pushes you in the wrong direction, encouraging and reinforcing your worst impulses rather than your best.

The critical human task for every divorcing couple is to take responsibility. Taking responsibility for the end of your marriage is the prerequisite for understanding your own behavior, your own contribution, and your own role in the process that led to the separation. Your active involvement in solving the problems sets you up to take responsibility for your future. I use the word *responsibility* here in the sense of *taking charge*. In divorce, taking responsibility is a practical imperative. The alternative, reinforced by the adversary system, is to shift the blame, and thus the responsibility, to the other spouse.

CASE STUDY: DONALD AND KAREN

Now, let's look at the case of Donald and Karen—a divorce that went bad.

Donald and Karen were married twelve years ago. Difficulties began to develop when their first child was born and Karen left her job. She found her new domestic life confining and often boring. Donald wasn't much help. He was quite pleased with Karen's playing a traditional role, "if only she didn't complain so much."

Karen's resentment of Donald's freedom and his insensitivity toward her needs began to grow, and she became increasingly cold and hostile. Both Karen and Donald had great difficulty confronting each other directly with their growing dissatisfactions and frustrations. Like most of us, they didn't like to fight. Even worse, they didn't know how to fight. So except for the occasional blow up, they withdrew emotionally from each other. Sex became infrequent and mechanical.

About a year before the separation, Donald began an affair with Susan, a co-worker. Time with her was interesting and exciting and made him feel alive and wanted. When he told Karen he wanted a divorce, she was shocked, then enraged. How could he betray her? A friend encouraged her to find the toughest lawyer in town "to make Donald pay." Karen found a young lawyer with a reputation for being tough and aggressive. The lawyer sympathized with her and, after collecting a sizable retainer, filed suit for divorce based on grounds of adultery and extreme cruelty.

(Commentary: Karen is beginning to act out a common role, that of the aggrieved victim. Two people rarely reach the decision to divorce at the same time. Invariably the one who first makes the decision becomes the one who, in effect, rejects the other spouse. The rejected spouse, in this case Karen, is at a disadvantage. She has not yet had time to decide that the marriage should be ended. Unlike Donald, she has not had the opportunity to think through her future or make plans. She has not been out in the world pursuing a career and has not had the advantage of a lover to bolster her low self-esteem. What she needs is time. Time to look hard and honestly at the marriage. Karen probably could use some professional help to sort out and accept the fact that for a long time she has been unhappy and unfulfilled in the marriage and that Donald was neither an understanding nor a compatible mate. She needs time to realize that she deserves better, that she can be more direct and ask for more in a relationship, and work to get it. Eventually, she may even feel less disturbed by Donald's affair and see it not as a judgment on her but as his adolescent way of coping with difficulties in his life. In short, she needs time to take responsibility. Then she can regard the divorce for what it is—a sign that she has to reevaluate her needs in a relationship and her own ways of fulfilling them.

When the rejected partner does not have time to take responsibility, it is easy for him or her to slide into the role of victim. Victims are, by definition, not only innocent (therefore blameless, without fault and without responsibility) but also passive. Victims have no control, and they need to be taken care of. Victims require villains—they go together. In this way, victims perpetuate their role as victims. Karen's lawyer and the adversary system are ready-made for her to shuck responsibility and to define Donald as the villain. Her lawyer does not tell her that in the end the case will probably be settled without a trial. Nor is Karen told that Donald's adultery will probably have negligible impact on the economic outcome. The lawyer helps freeze Karen in her victim role. Karen surrenders control of the divorce (and her future life) in exchange for a temporary illusion of justice and vindication.

Now a struggle for strategic advantage begins that further reduces the couple's chances of a reasonable transition to the next phase in their lives.)

THE BATTLE HEATS UP

Karen's lawyer, Ms. Graves, files a complaint for divorce alleging two grounds. First, the complaint alleges that Donald committed adultery with Susan and names Susan as the co-respondent. Second, the complaint charges Donald with extreme cruelty to Karen, citing in elaborate and lurid detail all the insensitive things Donald has ever done since they married. Karen is gratified to hear that the sheriff served the complaint on both Donald and Susan at their workplace. At least the bastard got some of his just deserts.

Donald is humiliated and enraged. He had tried to assure Karen that he wanted an amicable and fair settlement and would make every effort to be reasonable. Now all bets are off. Donald talks to his friends and is referred to Mr. White, a vigorous warrior in the courtroom. Mr. White files an answer to the complaint denying the allegations. He also files a counterclaim for extreme cruelty. His counterclaim goes into detail about Karen's sexual frigidity, her slovenly housekeeping, and her generally unpleasant demeanor. Karen now tastes humiliation and feels Donald has made these unfair accusations public. It confirms everything she now believes about him.

As the atmosphere in the house is now unbearable, Donald

asks his lawyer's advice about moving out. "Well," advises Mr. White, "if you move out, you concede the house. It will make it very difficult to get her to sell it and divide the equity. Besides, if you tough it out, it makes her more amenable to settling this thing just to end the pain." So Donald stays, living amid deadly silence and unrelenting hostility.

Karen, in the meantime, asks her lawyer about taking a job. She feels the sooner she gets back to work, the faster she can reestablish her career. But here her lawyer advises that her salary may well reduce her alimony award. Karen decides to stay home even though she doesn't want to.

(Commentary: What we have here is a reasonable use of tactics. Reasonable, that is, if this were a chess game or even a real war. But applied to this family, the results are disastrous. Donald stays in the house even though he and Karen are at dagger points and the children are continually exposed to their mutual hatred. Karen gives up an important opportunity to regain her sense of independence and competence. Donald is not encouraged to examine his role in the breakup and take responsibility for it. And the damage to the children is incalculable. The myth of winning has taken hold, and Donald and Karen allow their real needs to be dominated by the legal contest. They are now in limbo, unable to move on. In some states they could stay in this "holy deadlock" for up to three years before a trial either resolves the situation or, more likely, forces a settlement.

Something else is also happening. The adversarial system is training Donald and Karen to relate to each other in a new and destructive way in their soon-to-be relationship as ex-spouses. They are taught to speak to each other only through their lawyers. When Donald has a proposal to make to Karen, he calls Mr. White. Mr. White calls Ms. Graves who in turn calls Karen. Karen thinks about it for a day and calls Ms. Graves who calls Mr. White who calls Donald. With missed phone calls, "out to lunch," "away from his desk," and "he'll have to call you back," the exchange requires three weeks. Each lawyer charges each phone call a minimum of ten minutes per call. At an hourly rate of $150 per hour for each lawyer, the cost of this exchange comes to $200. It would have taken Donald and Karen ten minutes to complete the exchange themselves.

Donald and Karen are also learning that they cannot trust each other. Each cannot understand how the other could have let his/her lawyer publicize such terrible things in the complaint and counterclaim. Each one is sure that the other is out to take advantage. Donald thinks that Karen should get a job and that she is just waiting to take him for a big alimony award. Karen thinks Donald will do anything to get her and the kids out of the house.

The adversary system teaches you to defeat yourself. Over time it helps you act in ways contrary to your own interest and your own needs.)

THE CONFLICT ESCALATES

After three months Donald cannot tolerate living in the house any longer and is willing to take his risks to get out. He gets an apartment forty minutes away from the house. He assures the children that he will see them every other weekend.

After the third weekend spent with Donald, the children tell their mother they don't want to go to his apartment anymore because it's boring and there's nothing to do. Besides, Susan is there all weekend, and she's very bossy. Jennifer is particularly adamant about not liking Susan. Karen is furious that Donald would have "that woman" overnight with the children present. She calls her lawyer and insists that she do something right away.

Ever responsive and protective of the moral welfare of the children, Ms. Graves files a prejudgment motion seeking two forms of relief from the court. First she asks the court to enjoin Donald from having Susan overnight when the children are with him. Second, because the children do not like going to Donald's apartment, she asks the judge to reduce his visitation to one weekend a month. Donald's lawyer opposes the motion, and the matter is argued in court. The judge, a conservative man, finds Donald's conduct immoral and bad for the children. He grants the relief sought by Karen and her lawyer.

(Commentary: Karen has won another skirmish in court. But has she really won? Actually, both Karen and Donald, failing to understand their own interests, have defeated themselves.

Donald, understandably enough, wants to spend the weekends with the children, whom he dearly loves, and with Susan, whom he also loves. Moreover, as he hopes to marry Susan, he wants Susan and the children to become acquainted and to like each other. Now he feels deeply hurt that the children have rejected Susan. He blames Karen for poisoning them toward him and Susan both.

In fact, Donald has made two self-defeating moves. When he rented an apartment he moved out of the children's social orbit. The children, particularly Jennifer, like to spend the weekends with their friends. With their father's apartment so far away, they cannot see their friends when they stay with him, which is one of the reasons they are bored and unhappy. Donald's second mistake is introducing the children to Susan too soon. In the first year or so following the separation of their parents, most children nurse fantasies that their parents will be reconciled. It takes time for them to give up the hope their parents will reunite. It would not have mattered if Susan were a saint, the children still would have rejected her. In his eagerness to have the children like Susan, Donald achieved the opposite result. But because he does not understand, he blames Karen.

Karen also damaged herself with this victory. She desperately needs more time to herself. She needs Donald to take the children more often, not less often, so she can begin to rebuild her own social life and get some time off. To punish Donald, she has now reduced the little relief he was providing. Second, Karen has now, with the authority of the court, established a rule of behavior that will apply to both of them: If you have the children overnight, you cannot have a friend of the opposite sex in the house. When Karen finds a man she wants to be with, he will be able to stay over only one night a month.

Finally, the couple has lost the opportunity to establish a helpful relationship while building their new lives. The ability of each to develop new relationships requires the cooperation of the other. The children need help in accepting the new potential mates of each parent. It is actually in Karen's interest for the children to like Susan and to look forward to seeing their father. Karen has expressed her jealousy to the detriment not only of Donald but also most acutely of her children and herself. Donald's and Karen's legal fees for this motion totaled about $3,000. Karen's lawyer feels that she did her client a true service by winning for her in court and protecting the morals of the children. She has little or no understanding of families, child development, and the needs of remarried families. She has no sense of what is genuinely needed. She won, but her client lost.)

HOW IT TURNED OUT

Now, let us "fast forward" into the future to see what happened to Donald and Karen and their children. Donald and Karen have been divorced for a year, and neither is very happy. After a three-year separation and a two-year legal struggle, they negotiated a settlement the week before the trial.

Donald married Susan a week after the divorce. Now he and Susan are seeing a marriage counselor. Donald is estranged from his fifteen-year-old daughter Jennifer, but sees his son Tim, who is now ten, once or twice a month. He misses the close contact he once had with both his children.

Karen is also struggling. She returned to work and is trying hard to build a career in advertising. She wishes she had started sooner. Her salary plus child support and alimony barely cover her bills, with nothing left for recreation. She has problems with her daughter, who is rebellious and resentful, and her son is doing poorly in school. Karen wishes she could find a man, but between work and the kids, who has time? She wonders how it ever turned out so badly. (Donald cannot figure it out, either.)

Karen and Donald are like millions of others. They do not understand why things are so tough after their divorce. Somehow, what was supposed to be a transition to something better has not worked out. They have had a bad divorce, and they— as well as their children—are paying the price.

CONCLUSION

The legal system of divorce in the United States has no logical relationship to the needs of divorcing families. American divorce feeds the voracious economic appetite of the adversary system at the expense of its clients. If the primary objective is a negotiated settlement that meets the real needs of the family, we need a system designed for that purpose. The adversary system should be reserved for the few cases that cannot be settled otherwise. Your divorce needs to be negotiated with a minimum of contact with the adversary system.

Chapter Three

THE EMOTIONAL CRISES
OF DIVORCE

Adjusting to divorce is a process that may take from one to four years. Many factors influence how long it will take you to navigate this difficult transition successfully. But two are of special concern to us here: How well you manage the beginning of the divorce, and how well you negotiate your agreement. These steps are closely interrelated.

In this chapter we shall assess critical emotional choices you face early in the divorce that will determine how well you negotiate your agreement. If you control your passions and anger, you will negotiate well, but if you let those passions and anger control you, you will probably negotiate poorly. The purpose of this chapter is to help you maintain control by understanding the emotional crises that commonly distort and prevent successful negotiation.

UNDERSTANDING DIVORCE AS TRANSITION

There are many ways to describe the emotional process of divorce. It begins with a crisis. It ends with some kind of adaptation or maladaptation. In between is a process of transition that some describe as three stages, others see as four, five, six, or seven stages. At the end of this chapter is a list of books that will give you more detailed information about the emotional process of divorce.

For our purposes, there are two parts to the emotional process of divorce: upheaval and transition. Upheaval refers to all the turbulence immediately following the decision to divorce. It is a time of grief, anger, resentment, feelings of abandonment, and fear of the unknown. It is characterized by unleashed passion and intensity and unpredictable reactions of all family members to sudden change.

Not everyone moves through the divorce process at the same pace. Men tend to reorder their lives faster than women do. On the average, it takes women three to four years to reestablish fully an external sense of order, while it takes men, on average, one year or less. Some people get stuck and never fully adapt.[5]

EMOTIONAL CRISES

Although not all divorcing persons experience the same emotions and reactions, there are a number of emotional crises that are common to divorcing couples. In this chapter I will identify some of these crises and show you how *what you feel* during this time may affect *the way you negotiate*.

THE DECISION TO DIVORCE

The initial phase of divorce is the hardest for most people. Even though some experience a sense of relief, the decision to divorce invariably means the death of dreams and fantasies of what might have been. It brings profound disappointment and, for many, acute anger.

Some people experience the decision to divorce as a threat to survival itself. Divorce brings out all the fear that comes from taking apart the old and familiar, no matter how uncomfortable it may have been.

Unlike other life crises that send friends and family running to help, divorce causes emotional supports to fall away. Friends often stay away for fear of taking sides—or worse, they do take sides and fan the flames. There are no ritualized forms of mourning for the death of a marriage and no social customs for drawing comfort from others and reorganizing resources.

Your children are very needy and you and your spouse have diminished capabilities to meet their needs. Misunderstandings and missed signals are common. Gone is the assumption of good will that used to carry you through disagreements and bad moods. Now, any argument can turn into a screaming match. Each of you is prone to making mistakes and prone to interpret the other's mistakes as betrayals. You are simply at your worst at this time. Getting through the emotional upheaval of splitting up without getting into a war calls for you to exercise restraint when you least feel like it. But how each of you behaves in the beginning of your divorce sets the tone for everything that follows.

LACK OF MUTUALITY

In most cases, one spouse reaches the decision to divorce before the other. Generally, the one who initiates the divorce is in a stronger psychological position because he or she has a greater sense of control and predictability. How well you and your spouse resolve this problem is probably the strongest predictor of success in managing the divorce.

Marriages die slowly. If you are the initiator of the divorce, you have probably thought about it for a long time. As the relationship deteriorates, there may be a prolonged period of stress and conflict. At some point, you call a halt. "It's over," you tell yourself. But you don't tell your spouse right away. Perhaps you have one or several affairs, think about divorce, consult a lawyer, and begin—emotionally at least—to separate. You get used to the fact first. *Then* you tell your spouse.

When you finally break the news, you are surprised to find that your spouse is shocked. While you, as the initiator, have prepared, your spouse has not. He or she experiences your announcement as rejection and abandonment. As one client put it, "I felt that I had been dumped, without warning and without justification. I was simply stunned." Such feelings are common even in marriages that have been troubled for a long time.

Breaking the news can take many forms. One man simply leaves unannounced. A woman has an affair and arranges for her husband to find out. An argument escalates, and all of a sudden bags are being packed. There are gentle partings, and there are cruel partings. The more you do to make the marital ending graceful and humane, the easier it will be for both of you. Dramatic, angry endings leave you both frozen in rage. This makes it very difficult to create a constructive dialogue when it's time to negotiate.

TWO DANGERS OF NONMUTUAL DIVORCE

The most common problem that arises when one wants the divorce and the other does not is that the non-initiator may slip into the role of aggrieved victim. Victimization as a psychological posture results from the non-initiator's need to deny responsibility for the divorce and to punish the initiator for "destroying" the marriage. Those who play the victim tend to act out an entire constellation of destructive behaviors. They depict the initiator as a villain from whom they demand acts of contrition, admissions of guilt, and reparations. Often these demands are accompanied by an insistence that the initiator retract the decision to divorce and work on the marriage.

Some victims become obsessed with the fault of the initiator. "The divorce is his fault. I didn't tell him to fool around with that woman!" "Its her fault; don't ask me to suffer any more than I have. Let her take responsibility; let her pay!" The organizing principle for the victim is that only the initiator should shoulder responsibility and the dislocations that go with divorce. Because the victim is blameless there is no reason for him/her to do anything. Victims behave passively and helplessly invite others to rescue them from distress. And the rescuer is invariably a lawyer who offers, at least for a time, the illusion that the victim can be protected and vindicated in court.

If your spouse assumes a victim role, or if you yourself play the victim, your prognosis for a decent divorce is poor. Such divorces are characterized by intense litigation and unsatisfactory results. Sooner or later the initiator becomes enraged by the punitive message of the "victim" and begins to fight back. Fighting then rapidly escalates into a war. Every effort must be made to avoid this problem: The initiator should be aware of the danger and should involve the other spouse in the decision to divorce as early as possible. Keeping your decision a secret while you get ready may be more comfortable in the short run but destructive over time.

This raises a second danger—bad timing in the way the decision to divorce is communicated. Whether it is you or your spouse who "started" this divorce, you must stay sensitive to your spouse's readiness to divorce. If you are the initiator, you have already resolved many of the issues your spouse is wrestling with now. You must give him or her time to catch up. Frequently the non-initiating spouse can begin to work through the emotional ending of the relationship before hard decisions are made. The closer you can come to mutuality, the better your chances for negotiating a reasonable settlement later. A decision to divorce is mutual when both of you agree that the marriage should end. Then, you both "own" the divorce and can take responsibility for struggling with the problems created by it.

When one spouse refuses to accept the divorce, or genuinely believes the marriage ought to continue, the probability of protracted conflict increases. Thus, it pays to invest considerable time and patience, if necessary, in talking about the divorce and reaching a mutual decision to end the marriage. Both of you could probably benefit from family therapy to help you through this decision.

During this early stage of divorce the initiator should resist the impulse to seek a quick resolution of the issues involving it. The initiator often presses to work out the arrangements for the kids, how the money will be divided, and how much support will be paid in order to "have it over with." To induce your spouse to cooperate you may even offer a very generous settlement. But your good intentions may backfire if the timing is wrong, and your impatience may evoke panic in your spouse. It often happens this way.

CASE STUDY: MARIE AND NICK

Nick is initiating a divorce and wants to show that he is fair. He tries to reassure his wife, Marie, that he wants an amicable settlement without acrimony or bitterness. He urges her to join him in this endeavor and get things done quickly. Marie receives this news with alarm, not relief. She does not share his desire to resolve things quickly nor does she feel anything right now except bitterness and fear. All the changes Nick sees as necessary, Marie regards as terrible. He wants to sell the house to reduce expenses and free up equity. She interprets this as his determination to force her and the kids out. He wants her to get a job to help cover the deficit. She sees this as his indifference to the needs of the kids, whom she regards as too young to have a working mother.

Nick's sense of urgency is threatening to Marie. His reassurances of amicable intent ring hollow and reinforce her fear; at the same time, they dash her hopes of reconciliation. Because she is not ready to hear him, Marie interprets everything Nick says in the worst possible light. At best, she rejects his proposals, at worst, she hires a lawyer to "protect" her.

NONMUTUALITY: IMPLICATIONS FOR NEGOTIATIONS

The early period of divorce is a bad time for serious negotiation about long-term issues. Ideally, all you should do at first is maintain the economic status quo, avoid adversary legal processes, and work out a temporary arrangement that allows you both to survive this period with a minimum of legal conflict.

This may seem impossible: How can we act with restraint at the very time we are in angry crisis? How can I treat with respect someone who I feel betrayed me, or didn't love me, or abandoned me? But as a practical matter you have no choice. Premature negotiation produces either bad settlements or protracted litigation. If your spouse is not ready, one way she/he can slow you down is to begin legal proceedings. These hold off negotiations until the case comes to trial in two years. Do not push.

Negotiation of a settlement agreement when it is too early is unproductive because the initiator may feel intense guilt—which can lead to an overgenerous settlement he or she may later refuse to honor. And if you believe your spouse is at fault and should pay for his/her sins, you can be assured negotiations will break down, so negotiation of a permanent settlement is unlikely.

A second obstacle to negotiation early on is that you are too overwhelmed to do the work required. You do not yet have sufficient information. You have not yet had an opportunity to try out your new roles, to think through your needs, or to make long-term decisions. In the early stage of divorce, it's all you can do to cope with the bubbling cauldron of emotions you are

feeling. You are not yet ready to hear each other or to cooperate in the manner required for success.

BUT WHAT DO I DO WITH THE ANGER?

Divorce is the last act of the marriage, and entire families get
frozen in the last pose when the curtain comes down. If that
final image is only acrimony and disarray, it will dominate you
and your children for years. Disappointment, sadness, and
grief can be mourned, and, in time, they fade. But hatred, a
sense of injustice, or a feeling of betrayal only get stronger as
they are nursed, and they can paralyze you for years.

What do you do with the anger? You work with it; you
explore it with a good therapist. There is an important distinction between feeling anger and acting it out. Acknowledging
what you feel is healthy. It's the acting out that begins a
destructive cycle of tit for tat between you and your spouse.
Dealing with what you feel helps you to come to terms with the
ending of marriage and your contributions to its good and bad
parts.

It is important in the initial phase of divorce to mourn the
marriage and to let your spouse mourn as well. Even the end
of a chronically difficult relationship is a deep disappointment.
If you don't mourn, you don't finish with the marriage. It lives
on, in its worst form, interfering with all you do.

From every perspective, it is in your interest to bring the
marriage to an end with as much civility as possible. If you
have any doubt that this is in your own interest, have no doubt
that it is in the best interest of your children. The mental health
community is unanimous in its opinion that divorce should be
organized so as to minimize the impact on children. How you
behave now will determine what happens to the kids. The
greater the strife, the greater the disorganization, the worse it
is for them, the harder their adjustment, the greater their de-
pression, the greater their destructive behavior.

This is more than a moral imperative for parents. The

long-term impact on your children will reverberate toward you. Your children's pain and acting out will take up your time, money, and energy later on when you're trying to rebuild your life. Your children's maladjustment to the divorce will wreck your next marriage or relationship. To borrow a dictum, you can pay now, or you can pay later. Your restraint, emotional honesty, integrity, and simple courage are required now.

GOOD FAITH REQUIRED

There are some elementary rules that allow both of you to get through the early phase of the divorce process without touching off a war. Lawyers and legal proceedings are like any other weapon. If one side has it, the other side gets it, too. If one side uses it, the other side does, too. Often it is not your intention to gain the upper hand that touches off the war. Rather it is your fear that your spouse is attempting to get the advantage that prompts your preemptive strike.

You must do everything possible to avoid creating the impression that you are taking advantage. You need to be cautious before concluding that your spouse is up to some mischief. There are some absolute *Nos* you must observe:

1. No raids on the safe-deposit box
2. No changes in life insurance
3. No changes in title to assets
4. No secret bank accounts
5. No increase in debt without mutual agreement
6. No cutting off the credit cards
7. No abuse of credit cards
8. No cutting off support
9. No interference with access to the children
10. No sabotage of children's affection for the other parent
11. No threats of legal action

12. No insistence on premature negotiation
13. No provocation with paramours
14. No legal proceedings

WHAT INITIATORS NEED TO DO

- Inform your spouse of your decision to divorce appropriately, using professional help when necessary.
- Be clear in stating your resolve to divorce—do not hold out false hopes that you will change your mind.
- Allow time for discussion and for expression of feelings. The discussions about the divorce may require more than one session and may go on for weeks or even months.
- Acknowledge your spouse's feelings of sadness or anger as well as your own. Be prepared to talk about these things more than once. It may take more than one attempt for you to be heard.
- Reassure the non-initiator of your patience and goodwill.

WHAT INITIATORS NEED TO AVOID

- Don't lay blame to justify your decision. The marriage has died—your spouse didn't kill it.
- Avoid unilateral changes of circumstance: Don't cancel credit cards, raid the safe deposit bank or empty the savings account. These actions only create panic and guarantee hostility.
- Don't tell the children, your relatives, or your friends until you both are ready.
- Don't begin legal action. You want to negotiate your settlement first.

WHAT NON-INITIATORS NEED TO DO

- Seek maximum emotional support from friends and family. Use the services of a good psychotherapist if you feel it's necessary.
- Be honest with yourself about the marriage. Do you really believe that the marriage should continue? Do you really believe that the marriage could work?
- Take the time you need to think and if necessary to mourn the ending of the relationship.
- Stay responsible.

WHAT NON-INITIATORS NEED TO AVOID

- Don't give in to your impulse for revenge, vindication, and recrimination—it will only provide your spouse with justification to behave poorly.
- Don't surrender to uncontrolled anger. Despite your powerful feelings, you can *choose* how you act.
- Don't make yourself into a helpless victim.
- Don't precipitate legal action.

SEPARATING AND MOVING OUT

If you are going to divorce, you will have to separate. The sooner one of you moves out, and the smoother the move, the better off all of you will be.

Once again, consider the typical family profile in which there are minor children. Usually, the mother will stay with the kids, and the father will move out. The question is whether he moves out before or after a separation agreement is finalized.

Many men worry that if they move out their legal position will somehow be weakened. Unfortunately, many divorce lawyers routinely advise clients against such a move without considering the psychological damage that results. The advice not to move may be motivated by several misguided fears: The client or the lawyer worries that if negotiation is unsuccessful, the husband's move will be used to prove that he deserted his wife. The husband also worries that he'll forfeit his claim to ownership of the house or forfeit his right to move back in later. Let's look at each of these fears.

If you and your spouse agree in writing that you (or your spouse) are departing by mutual consent and that the move is neither abandonment or desertion, that issue is gone. You can also agree in writing that the one who moves out can reoccupy the house upon reasonable notice. Moving out does not mean you abandon your property rights, so that, too, is nothing to worry about.

Lawyers sometimes think that if you stay, the irritation and discomfort this gives your spouse will motivate her or him to make concessions in negotiation. If one of the issues to be resolved is whether or not to sell the house, the lawyer and you may worry that your moving out constitutes a concession on that point. The problem is that you, not your lawyer, has to live with it.

Living for any length of time with a dead marriage is terribly stressful for the entire family. It prevents both of you from adjusting to separation. Neither of you can get on with building a new life. Neither gets the peace and solitude needed to heal. The anger and rancor between you can only grow more intense as a result. The fact that you continue to live together confuses your children, who are hoping that you will reconcile. It confuses your relatives and friends and makes you both inaccessible to people who could provide relief. I have seen people live in this state of holy deadlock for years. It's like growing hate in a hothouse. There is absolutely no hypothetical tactical advantage that is worth the damage done by such folly.

Moving out is more often a problem when the wife is initiating the divorce and the husband is being asked to move. Sometimes men demand custody in an attempt to avoid moving out of the house. They join the kids and the house as a single entity, claiming that whoever gets the kids gets the house. It's even worse when the man convinces himself that he really is the better parent and ought to have sole custody in order to get the house. It's not that he wants the house. It's just that he is frightened of change and of being on his own. If this is you, you need help fast. If this is your spouse, you both need help fast. This is too destructive a development, and it assures you both a miserable divorce.

I believe that most custody fights start because the non-initiating male is trying to maintain the structure of his life by holding on to the house and the children. This is not to suggest that mothers should always get primary custody or that any man who struggles for custody is just holding on. But many custody fights fit this unfortunate pattern.

Often people decide that they can't afford a separation for financial reasons. My advice is to treat the situation as an emergency and to use savings, or even borrow, to make a separation possible. If you absolutely can't do this yet, then at least separate within the house. Use different bedrooms, even if the kids have to double up, or turn the family's den into another bedroom. There is nothing so confusing as negotiating a divorce settlement with someone with whom you are still sleeping. And if you are still having or expecting sex, then both of you are exceptionally confused.

PAINFUL ILLUSIONS: TEMPORARY SEPARATION AND RECONCILIATION

TEMPORARY SEPARATION

One of the most common tactical mistakes initiators make is to seek a *temporary separation* when what they truly want is a divorce. The common cliché used is "I need a little space." Behind this charade is the hope that the non-initiator's anger will be reduced if the fantasy of a future reconciliation is held out as a possibility. In truth, relationships are not improved by separation. When your partner realizes that you were just trying to ease your escape, he or she will be much more bitter and distrustful of whatever you say in the future. If it's over, say so—and then deal with the emotions that follow.

Conversely, if your spouse is the initiator and tells you he or she wants to try a temporary separation, be skeptical about the likelihood of reconciliation. A request for a trial separation should trigger a trip to a good family therapist for some intense soul-searching and realistic confrontation. Better to deal openly with the reality than with a covert agenda.

RECONCILIATION

Most divorcing couples make at least one attempt to reconcile. Usually, this fails. The impulse toward reconciliation is understandable. As the reality of the divorce sinks in, people get scared. Maybe it's better, you think, to stay with the known (marriage) than to face the unknown. Maybe the initiator is overcome by guilt and gives in to the entreaties of the other. Sometimes there is simply a persistent attachment that continues even though trust and affection are gone. Marriages are not given up easily.

Reconciliation without good marital therapy is doomed to fail. In the absence of a skilled therapist, you are certain to act out the original script of the marriage—the one that didn't work the first time. Moreover, reconciliation is attempted within a profoundly wounded relationship. Trust is limited, vigilance is heightened, and each of you is waiting for the other to stumble. Even with good therapy, the probability of successful reconciliation is low. But at least you both may learn something about your relationship and more easily accept that your marriage is over.

DIFFERENCES BETWEEN MEN AND WOMEN

Men and women have different experiences in divorce, partly due to their different emotional styles, and in part because of the different roles men and women play in both the intact family and the divorced family. Consequently, men and women face different dangers when coping with divorce.

SOME DANGERS FOR MEN

In 90 percent of divorces that involve children, it is the father who moves out of the home. Usually because finances are tight, his new dwelling is smaller than the marital home, and furnished with whatever can be scraped together. This often makes the husband feel as if he has come down in the world and he resents bearing the brunt of the divorce, especially if he is not the initiator.

In addition, the husband feels lonely because he has lost the daily structure previously provided by the wife and children. Men report feeling at loose ends when they come home to an empty apartment at the end of the workday. Some men, those whose social life was managed by their wives during the marriage, have difficulty taking charge, and on the weekends that they don't see their children, they feel lost. For some, the weekends that they do see the children are equally stressful because they never had extended time with the kids before without the wife's playing an important supporting role. Loneliness is worse for men because for most, their friendships with other men are based on mutual interests and activities rather than on intimate communication. Put simply, this means that many divorcing men have no one to talk to about their feelings.

Men face the emotional challenge of managing their feelings and sense of loss as they live through the transition. Men raised to keep a "stiff upper lip" will have a hard time. Their conditioned response to strong feelings is repression and denial. The result is that the feelings don't go away; they just get acted out in destructive ways. Men who are the non-initiators and who manage feelings with classical male denial are particularly at risk here.

A second risk for men is a premature "rebound" relationship with another woman. Because they don't spend sufficient time acknowledging their own feelings and the role they have played in the divorce, such men rush into new relationships that simply repeat the patterns of the marriage. The result is another troubled relationship that further complicates adjusting to the divorce. The average divorced male is remarried within one year following his divorce.[6] This is too soon for him and too soon for the children.

SOME DANGERS FOR WOMEN

Although women may be subject to loneliness after separation, they tend to have better resources for dealing with it because they're better able to acknowledge feelings and seek support either in intimate discussions with other women, or through psychotherapy and support groups. For those who stay in the marital home with the children (the majority of mothers), the divorce does not disrupt the daily structure of their lives as it does their husbands'. They have the daily companionship of the kids and the comfort of familiar surroundings.

However, divorcing women have other sources of acute stress. The sheer burden of adapting to many changes while attempting to function as a single parent can be overwhelming. Mothers who are attempting to return to employment just as the separation takes place have the most difficult time. Many feel deep conflict about spending less time with the kids, and if the woman initiates the divorce, she may feel guilty. If the husband is the initiator, her worry about the children makes her even angrier at her husband.

Job hunting by itself is anxiety provoking because it puts her in a position to be rejected. If her self-esteem is already shaky because of the divorce, she may feel very insecure.

Women also have a harder time with dating and meeting new male companions and potential mates. There are fewer available single men than available single women, partly due to demographics, and also because social conventions approve of liaisons between men and younger women but not the other way around. The result is that men have a much higher probability of remarriage than women.[7]

The dangers for women result more from feeling overwhelmed than from feeling isolated and lonely. The greatest danger, from their perspective, is the feeling that they need to be rescued. Drowning people look for a life raft, and for divorcing people, lawyers look like life rafts. Although the wife's lawyer can protect her from a husband who refuses to do his fair share, the lawyer can't protect her from the economic and psychological realities of divorce. The lawyer may help to create an illusion that legal action can solve her problems. But it can't, and as long as she clings to the illusion she can't move forward.

A second source of rescue is the children. The wife who is

living with the children may communicate her distress to them so intensely that they conclude it is their job to take care of her. One way they care for her is to become her representatives to her husband, one of the most destructive possibilities in divorce. The parental relationship between the mother and the children is distorted because she becomes the object, rather than the giver, of care. Then the children's relationship with their father becomes adversarial. The children wind up losing both parents, psychologically, at the very time that they most need parental support.

The distinctions made here between the emotional dangers for women and men are not absolute. There are some women who rush into new relationships and there are some men who seek rescuers. All the emotional pitfalls that endanger one gender endanger the other.

TRANSITION

Depending on how both of you handle the upheavals of the divorce process, a period of transition begins any time from a few months to a year after the decision to divorce is raised. While the first period is a time of crisis, confusion, and intense anger, the transitional period is a time when things have cooled off a bit and you have begun to reestablish some equilibrium. You have either separated or are anticipating permanent separation. Each of you is well on the way to accepting the reality of the divorce. You have recovered from the shock of the first weeks alone, but you may nevertheless be lonely. You have begun to look around and see what your life now is like, which old friends are still there, and which relatives are still close. You have begun to think about longer-range goals. You may have begun to date and to be more active socially. You begin to recover your self-esteem and your self-confidence. As in all these processes, there is no schedule; there is only recovery at your own speed.

This is the time to negotiate your agreement. Completion of

the settlement agreement becomes an emotional watershed in the process of divorce. Your ability to emerge from the marriage and to rebuild your life is limited until you work it out. The settlement will express your agreements on how you will raise your children, what your income flow will be, and what property will be yours and yours alone. Until these decisions are made, you will feel that you cannot really make long-term plans because you are still tied to your spouse.

EMOTIONAL PREREQUISITES FOR GOOD NEGOTIATION

Good negotiation requires that you understand your own interests and that you understand the interests of your spouse well enough to seek creative solutions to problems as they occur. Compromise is necessary, but it must be *intelligent* compromise.

Negotiation makes both intellectual and emotional demands on you. You must gather, assimilate, and use the information necessary to make decisions. You must learn about your assets, your finances, and your needs. Your first emotional requirement is to be settled enough to learn and to concentrate. Some of the topics—e.g., pension evaluation, equitable distribution—require you to pay attention. If you are still falling apart, you can't do the work.

You must also maintain civility toward your spouse. The less civility, the more you rely on intermediaries. Later, we'll talk about how to use professionals for this purpose. A good mediator can keep you on track despite an occasional outburst. But if the sight of your spouse sends you into a sputtering rage, you will need a lawyer to negotiate for you.

Ultimately, the greatest emotional requirement is responsibility for yourself. You must feel that you are in charge, and you must understand that the decisions you make shape your future. You should be able to measure the usefulness of a proposal by whether or not it serves your future objectives. To do this well, you will first have to let go of the past and give up your attempts to vindicate your anger and resentment from the past.

EMOTIONAL OBSTACLES TO NEGOTIATION

The breakdown of your own restraint and playing the victim role are the biggest obstacles to your ability to negotiate. It is time to put aside blame. Fault is no longer relevant. If your guilt is still so palpable that you are willing to be blamed, you are not ready to negotiate.

During this transitional period, relationships between spouses are still sensitive. Now is the time to learn new ways to relate to each other. Respect for each other's privacy and for each other's need to establish an independent life is necessary and must be reciprocal. It is not unusual for newly separated spouses to conduct voyeuristic interrogations of relatives, friends, and children. "What did Daddy do?" "What did she look like?" "Who is she?" etc. This is hard to avoid after having been intimate with someone for many years, but you must mind your own business.

CONCLUSION

Remember that negotiating the agreement is a process that could last three or four months, depending on how much time it takes to develop and master the financial information. How you behave toward each other while *not* at the negotiating table is going to influence the attitudes you bring to the negotiations. There are an unlimited number of ways you can sabotage your negotiation. But to what end?

The key to all this is to remember the distinction between acknowledging your strong feelings and acting them out. Acknowledging feelings is healthy and helps you to cope. Acting out is generally destructive and hurts your chances of successful negotiation. You cannot go through a divorce without feeling strong and hurtful feelings, but you can choose to desist from hurtful behavior. Your ability to avoid hurtful behavior will determine the quality of your negotiated settlement.

Surviving the Breakup. Judith Wallerstein and Joan Kelly, Basic Books, New York, 1980.

Second Chances. Judith Wallerstein and Sandra Blakeslee, Ticknor & Fields, New York, 1989.

Uncoupling. Diana Vaughn, Vintage Books, New York, 1986.

Chapter Four

THE ECONOMICS
OF DIVORCE

*M*ost of the conflict associated with divorce involves money. For most middle-class people, particularly those with children, divorce is difficult economically because there isn't enough money. Most couples consume between 95 percent and 105 percent of their net income. When they divorce and attempt to establish two households on the same income that previously supported one, they find themselves sorely stretched. Generally, the cost of the second household is at least 40 percent of the cost of the first. When one spouse moves out, expenses do not decrease significantly, because so many household costs are fixed. The result is that, when the wife adds up her budget and the husband adds up his budget, the total costs after separation typically exceed total income by about one-third.

I don't tell you this in the naive hope that it will bring you solace, but you need to know from the beginning that the economic crunch is a constant for most couples. Some handle the problem well. They trim their consumption or increase their income or do both. Other people handle the problem poorly and make a mess.

LIMITED FINANCIAL OPTIONS

Because deficits are a fact of divorce, there are limited options available. In this chapter we will look at what is involved strategically and emotionally in reducing expenses and increasing income. Overall, this chapter is designed to prepare you to negotiate support with a reasonable and realistic perspective.

First, and always preferred, is balancing the budgets. You reduce your combined spending to meet your current net income. Or, you do whatever you can to increase your income to meet your combined spending. When it is not possible to balance the budgets, the second strategic option is deficit spending: Use some of your savings (or other accumulated assets) or borrow money. Deficit spending is never preferred, but can be both a necessary and an intelligent resolution. We will look briefly at situations in which deficit spending makes sense, as well as those situations where it doesn't.

THE EMOTIONAL PITFALLS

Many people have difficulty adjusting to a shortage of money. Most angry, hard-fought divorces are caused by the inability of one or both partners to accept a fair distribution of the belt tightening and economic dislocation required by divorce.

Three emotional problems tend to drive conflict over money. The partner who doesn't want the divorce has no motivation to accept economic dislocation with grace, because he or she sees this as just another sign of victimization. Blaming the other spouse is how the victim justifies digging in his or her heels and refusing to cooperate. In a few cases this actually works, at least for a while. An initiator who feels very guilty may attempt to appease the non-initiator by agreeing to lopsided and unfair financial arrangements. Sooner or later, such guilt-induced agreements fall apart. In divorce, guilt has a short shelf life. The more common result of the "victim's" unrealistic economic demands is that they provide additional proof to the initiator that the divorce is justified and that the resisting spouse is unreasonable. Once the initiator becomes convinced that the spouse has no interest in fairness, he or she then feels justified in taking an unfair position in response. This is how divorce lawyers get rich.

The second problem is the emotional immaturity of the parties. Fair divorce is something only grownups can create. A childlike insistence on denying reality and avoiding financial responsibility produces economic demands that cannot be met without the financial destruction of the other spouse. People who feel entitled or vengeful simply ignore fairness or reasonableness and demand vindication. They rarely get it and eventually cause their partners to adopt similar unreasonable positions.

The third problem for many people is a confusion between their identities and their ability to consume. For such people, cutting back on economic consumption is experienced as a loss of self. When the prospect of frugality is experienced as such a loss, it may trigger panic and anxiety instead of responsible negotiation.

The most common consequence of the financial shortfall is that it provides a stage on which couples act out the emotional script of the marriage. Issues that were not successfully resolved during the marriage play out around the economic issues. Economic shortfalls tend to trigger the entire range of anger and frustration that characterizes the end of a marriage. Listen to a typical couple as they begin to come to grips with their economic reality.

CASE STUDY: HENRY AND SUSAN

Henry and Susan sit in my office upset and frustrated. During the past week, on my instructions, each has prepared a budget reflecting the costs of their two households. Henry recently moved out of the house into a one-bedroom apartment, leaving Susan and their two teenagers in the house they have owned for the past nine years. Henry, a biologist for a local pharmaceutical company, earns $65,000 a year. After taxes, he brings home $3,700 a month. Susan works part time in a flower shop and has take-home pay of $650 a month. It is obvious that each one has tried hard to calculate a reasonable budget. Susan's budget shows a need for $3,400 a month. Henry's budget requires $2,600 a month. With a combined net income of $4,350, they have combined proposed budgets of $6,000. They are short about $1,650 a month.

Susan speaks first. "There's nothing in this budget I can reduce. With two growing teenagers, I can't cut back on food. And both kids outgrow their sneakers and shoes every two months. Jimmy has two years of orthodontia to go, and Marie is supposed to start next month. What am I supposed to do?"

Irritated, Henry breaks in. "This divorce was your idea. Don't expect me to live in poverty because you want me out of your life. You asked me to leave. Why didn't you think of money then? I can't live on what's left over if you spend so much. There's nothing I can do to earn more money; I'm earning as much as I can. If you want more, you ought to get a real job. And if that's not enough, we'll have to sell the house."

Susan is obviously upset by Henry's remarks. "There's no way I can let two teenagers go unsupervised after school. I thought we had an understanding about that. And how can you even think of uprooting the kids? Both of them are upset as it is, and they just can't handle any more change right now. You're being unfair."

(Commentary: As Henry and Susan bicker, they reveal the problems most couples face at some point. The divorce is going to disrupt many of their long-held assumptions. It is now clear that many changes that neither wants will be necessary. Some of the most painful will involve changes that the children will not like. They may have to move to a smaller house or even an apartment. They may have to defer orthodontia or some other planned expense. If Susan has to go back to work full time to make ends meet, the kids may have less parental supervision. All of these are upsetting changes.)

REDUCING SPENDING

How hard you fight about money will be determined by how realistic you and your spouse are able to be about the necessity to cut spending, and the emotional meaning money has for you. Consider, for example, two other couples I worked with.

CASE STUDIES: RICHARD AND JOAN; LINDA AND VINCE

Richard is a realtor who earned a lot of money during the real estate boom of the 1980s. When he initiated the divorce, Joan resisted, insisting that the marriage continue for the sake of the children and because she believed that divorce is wrong. As the real estate business has slowed down, Richard's income has declined. From a high of $200,000 a year, it has fallen to less than $100,000 a year over the space of one year. Joan had prepared a budget with the help of her lawyer. The budget required $90,000 a year after taxes, about what she had been spending in prior years. She was adamant in her insistence that there was no fat in this budget and very little room for reduction. She told me that it would be devastating for her and the kids if they had to move into a smaller house. And it would be equally devastating for her if, after working so hard for all these years, she had to go backward instead of forward. It was clear that in her mind any cutting back on consumption was "going backward." Joan was used to good restaurants. She had always shopped in the best stores. The couple owned an expensive weekend house. She insisted that it would be unfair to deprive the children of the lifestyle they had always known.

I suggested to her that her budget exceeded Richard's total net income for the year and that at some point she was going to have to consider how to live on as much as 40 percent less. It appeared that a budget in the range of $4,500 a month would be realistic, considering the circumstances. That, she replied, would be tantamount to poverty, and there was no way she was going to live in poverty. The couple had been referred for mediation after a year of intense litigation with no settlement in sight. They could no longer pay their legal fees and were in acute distress.

In contrast, consider Linda and Vince. Vince was also a businessman whose business was in trouble. His retail clothes business had been getting worse for a year and a half. His income had fallen to less than $60,000 a year. Linda, employed as a bookkeeper, earned $24,000. Linda was the initiator of the divorce. She said that Vince was so overbearing and insensitive to her and the children that she regarded the divorce as a major improvement in her life. She wanted Vince to move out of the house, but he was resisting. He insisted that they couldn't afford it.

Linda prepared a budget that required $2,200 a month, a

figure that would require minimal child support from Vince. I reviewed her budget closely because I was concerned that in her eagerness to convince Vince to leave, she might be agreeing to something she would later regret. How, for example could she clothe herself and her two daughters on $100 a month? "Easy," she answered, "I've never spent more than that on clothes. I have always worn my clothes a long time and have made or altered clothes for the girls. The kids have had lots of hand-me-downs from cousins because it's a big family and we're always trading clothes for the kids. It's no big deal; we're always well dressed."

It was the same when we looked at the other figures in the budget. Linda had lots of friends. Vacation meant spending a long weekend at a friend's summer cabin or going camping. She had never owned a new car and didn't really care. "Don't worry," she assured me. "We can do fine on this budget. It's more than worth it to end this miserable marriage and get on with my life."

Why is it that Linda believes she will "do fine" on $2,200 a month while Joan is devastated at the thought that she may have to get by on more than twice that? Is one of them wrong? Has Linda left some critical expenses out of her budget? Has Joan put things in her budget she can do without?

DOWNWARD MOBILITY VERSUS BELT TIGHTENING

Linda is tightening her belt. Joan is experiencing downward mobility. Although both will have to do with less, for Joan its a matter of deprivation, while for Linda life is about to improve because she's getting out from under Vince's tyrannical ways. Neither is wrong, but it is evident that Linda, on half of Joan's resources, is going to be the better off of the two, because money is not the measure of her life. In contrast, Joan's sense of well-being is tightly linked to her consumption level. Joan is in trouble.

If you are in the middle class, divorce means you will face

the need to cut back. I do not suggest that doing with less is something to be happy about, but I do suggest that you have some choice about how you will let it affect your divorce. Joan has two problems that distinguish her from Linda. First, she draws a large measure of her identity from consumption. But second, and more important, Joan did not want the divorce. The economic consequences of divorce are further evidence to her that life is out of control and that "everything" is being taken away from her. There is nothing that she can do to stop the divorce, or to retain her old standard of living. There are, nevertheless, important choices open to her.

Joan can choose an orderly retrenchment that leaves her prepared to build a new life, or she can choose to let her life regress into a mess. She must cut back, but she can choose what items to keep and what to let go. She can retain a comfortable middle-class life—but only if she takes charge of the process and manages the change. Her efforts will be doomed to failure if she tries to maintain everything as it was before. Joan would be well advised to use a good psychotherapist to help her sort out her feelings and reassess her priorities, because she needs to make some hard choices for herself.

WHAT IS REASONABLE?

Let us return for a moment to Henry and Susan. As we review the budgets, each looks at the other's budget and begins to criticize. "Look at how much you've budgeted for restaurants," she says. "That's simply unreasonable." Henry quickly defends. "I don't know how to cook. What am I supposed to do? Why do you have to spend so much money on clothes?"

"I don't spend too much on clothes. What I spend is less than most women. You don't know what's reasonable."

The question "What is reasonable?" is the heart of the matter. Susan has budgeted $100 a month for clothing, hardly a lavish sum for a middle-class woman. Henry has budgeted $200 a month for restaurants, a sum that is easily spent if you eat out more than a few times a week. In fact, there is no single item on either's budget that I or anyone else can say is unreasonable.

There's just one problem. Unreasonable is measured by whether you can afford it. Reasonable expenses become unreasonable if you don't have enough money to pay for them. Expenditures are also unreasonable when they reflect distorted priorities. If your eating in expensive restaurants means that your kids don't get adequate clothes—that's unreasonable. And if your kid's fancy new skateboard means that you don't get the brakes in the car fixed—that's unreasonable.

So for Henry and Susan, the solution to the problem of reasonableness depends on their ability to reconcile needs and desires that cost more than they earn. As a couple, they face the challenge of getting past their anger to negotiate fair priorities for using the family resources on behalf of *all* family members.

ECONOMIC FAIRNESS

Earlier we looked at the persistence of fault as a psychological factor in divorce, despite the almost universal existence of legal no-fault divorce. Here, Henry, like Joan, did not want the divorce. For each of them, it is very tempting to say to the initiating spouse, "You want this; I don't. I shouldn't have to pay the price for your divorce—that's not fair." Translated, this means that Henry says that he should not have to reduce his standard of living. He thinks that because Susan is initiating the divorce, she should trim her needs more drastically than he so that she absorbs the necessary reduction in consumption. As a negotiating position, this is invariably unsuccessful.

It is easy, in the hot emotional climate of divorce, to be

confused about what we really need. The gratification of our desires becomes confused with the gratification of our needs. Two facts are inescapable: Divorcing people *must* make do with less, and most people *can* make do with less and still manage to live decently and with dignity. The danger is getting caught in a struggle to salvage a higher standard of consumption than the family can afford when the only place the additional money can come from is your spouse. You can both drive Toyotas or one of you can drive a Mercedes, and one can ride a bicycle. Your insistence on the Mercedes leaves your spouse with the alternative to ride a bike or to fight you. If Henry insists on the Mercedes, Susan must ride a bike. And Henry's suggestion that the imbalance is justified because Susan "caused" the divorce will not persuade Susan.

Placing blame is appealing because people believe that it will help them avoid responsibility for the inevitable economic consequences of divorce. The economic issues become the emotional battleground as partners try to convince each other that "It's your fault. *You* suffer." Rationalization and self-deception can feed this destructive process. Henry may decide that he needs the Mercedes because it's safer than a Toyota. Thus he deceives himself into believing that his fight is not about fairness but about safety. Susan may decide that yes, the Mercedes is safer, and she will have the kids most of the time, so she needs the Mercedes. How could Henry be so indifferent to the safety of the children? But for all the subterfuge, the issue remains the same. They can both have Toyotas or one can have a Mercedes and the other a bike.

Fairness means that relative deprivation and relative gratification are about the same in both households. But fairness is not presented here as a moral imperative. Fairness is a survival technique in divorce. Your goal is a divorce that allows you to get on with your lives with as little damage as possible. When you adopt an unfair position, you force your spouse to fight a battle in which you both can only lose. No one accepts blame graciously in the context of divorce. Even if you win, the result is an embittered ex-spouse and an emotional mess. People who emerge from a divorce feeling that they have been treated unfairly sooner or later get even.

WHAT ARE THE BUDGET OPTIONS?

The size of your deficit will determine how you balance the budget: If your deficit is 10 percent, a balanced budget can usually be achieved with minimal dislocation. But if your deficit is 40 percent, you must consider both reducing expenditures and increasing income. You will need to accept some significant changes in lifestyle.

INCREASING INCOME

In some divorcing families the most obvious source of increased income is for the wife to return to full-time employment. This can be a difficult and painful decision. Consider Susan once again. Her half-time employment in a flower shop was designed to supplement the family income while allowing her to be generally available to the two teenage children. Henry was always regarded as the principal breadwinner, while Susan assumed primary responsibility for the kids and for running the house. Susan's earning capacity was considered to be relatively unimportant. But this is no longer the case.

During her years as part-time manager of the flower shop, Susan acquired valuable experience and credentials. Her potential income as a full-time manager in a retail store is, in this case, more than double what she earns now. As a full-time manager of a retail store in her town, Susan can probably earn a gross salary of $25,000 a year, plus health insurance worth another $1,800 per year. Her take-home pay would be about $1,500 per month, an amount that would almost cover the entire marital deficit.

She must make a difficult choice. She must either devote

more time to earning money, which will reduce the time she has available for the children, or stay available to the children while making some painful cuts in her budget. It does not feel good to have to make such a choice. But divorce requires hard choices and a reexamination of the things that seem important. Many teenage children manage without direct after-school supervision. It may be that Susan's easy availability to the kids is no longer a feasible alternative. Or, it may be that Susan's children are wild and irresponsible and absolutely must be constantly supervised.

There are no automatic answers. What you must do, however, is reexamine all the premises that you took for granted before the decision to divorce. The more that you are prepared to reorganize, the more you will be able to adapt and the better off you will be. The more determined you are to maintain the status quo and deny the need for change, the bigger mess you will have later.

Although an increase in income by the unemployed wife is the most frequent choice, additional income may also be available to the husband. In the case of Henry and Susan this was not feasible because Henry was at his income ceiling. There was no place he could have moved to with a higher salary. Because he already worked long hours, there was no practical way he could consider a second job. But in other cases I have seen, husbands do manage to increase their own income. One example is a lawyer who had been struggling to build his own practice for several years. He liked being his own boss, but his entrepreneurial skills were minimal, and he was earning about half of what he would earn working for a firm. After much soul-searching, he decided that he would rather get a job at a higher income and sacrifice his autonomy than stay in his own practice living a very frugal life. In another instance, a college history teacher had always used his summer vacations for leisurely study and preparation of next year's lectures. He decided that now he would teach summer school to augment his income.

Whether similar alternatives are available to you will depend on your circumstances and on your willingness to assume responsibility for sometimes bold and sometimes disappointing changes in your life. In more cases than not, there are things you can do. Once again, you can choose to control the changes, or you can choose to run away and be controlled by them.

CUTTING EXPENSES

Ultimately even those of you who can increase your income will still have to cut expenses. You can resist and wait until a judge imposes this on you, you can make yourself and your spouse miserable, or you can get to work and get it done.

There doesn't seem to be any correlation between wealth and the ease with which people shoulder the responsibility of reducing expenses. It's all relative to what you're used to. I know a man who is so invested in status that he would be deeply embarrassed to be seen in anything but an expensive luxury car. I recall a woman who spent $100 a week having her hair done and her nails manicured. There is nothing wrong with such expenses as long as you can afford them. But in the context of divorce you usually can't afford these luxuries.

You *need* clean, decent, and comfortable shelter in a safe neighborhood. You *need* safe, reliable transportation. You *need* to be acceptably groomed, and you *need* some recreation to spice up your life. You may desire an expensive house in a prestigious neighborhood, a BMW, shopping sprees, trendy restaurants, and annual visits to the Caribbean. But you're fooling yourself if you really believe you *need* these things.

Most of you will have to carefully review every item in your budgets. You will have to decide which items are more necessary than others. Do I want to stay in this house and be cash poor, or would I be better off in less expensive housing but with more discretionary spending power? How important is it for me to save for the future? Am I willing to forgo a new car or a vacation in order to continue contributing to the company savings plan? Is it vital that my child be able to choose any college she wants, or am I going to tell her that she should think seriously about the state university? Am I willing to wear last year's fashions and have the house painted this year, or would I rather have the house peel another year than feel that I'm not well dressed? Am I willing to sell my boat to get out from under the monthly payments, or would I prefer to keep the boat and give up skiing in the winter? Can I manage without going to expensive restaurants and use that money to buy the computer my son says he needs for school? These choices and many more like them must be made to bring your expenses into line with your income. Avoid the ever attractive temptation to shuck the responsibility onto your mate. Although you can reasonably expect your spouse to be as responsible as you, it is *you* who must be in charge of your life.

When we get to our discussion on negotiating support, you will need to be ready to establish your priorities for cutting expenses. You will be in a much better position to demand economic responsibility from your spouse if you have already demonstrated your own willingness to make difficult choices. Generally, I encourage people to concentrate on their own budgets, their own income-generating capacities, and their own budget reductions rather than focusing on their spouse's. This promotes cooperation rather than bickering.

DEFICIT FINANCING

Most of us have been taught to safeguard our savings and minimize our debts. People in the midst of divorce have strong reactions about debt. Some who have long tolerated high levels of borrowing suddenly insist that the couple immediately pay off all outstanding debt. Others, who have not accumulated much debt, suddenly become heavy borrowers as a way of putting off the day of reckoning when budgets must be reduced and consumption curtailed.

The same kind of extremism also can apply to savings. For some people, savings in the bank are the ultimate symbol of security, so they refuse to spend savings in the face of genuine deprivation, while others have an irresistible impulse to spend everything. If you and your spouse have had disagreements about savings or debt during the marriage, you will certainly have them during the divorce.

Deficit spending, whether it uses up savings or whether it incurs debt, is sometimes responsible, sometimes irresponsible. If you achieve long-term solvency and balanced budgets, it is responsible; when you deny the need for reduced consumption and put off the reckoning to a later date, it is irresponsible.

For example, suppose Susan can complete the MBA she started years ago but would require one year of full-time graduate school. For that year she would earn nothing and pay tuition of $8,000. Consequently she would give up $20,000 in net earnings and spend another $8,000. Would it make sense for the couple to borrow to pay the expense? Inquiry into local hiring practices reveals that MBA graduates of the local university are getting jobs with annual starting salaries of $41,-000, a difference of $15,000 a year for Susan. From the perspective of a three-year plan, graduate school financed by a second mortgage on the house makes sense because increased income pays off the debt, leaving Susan with a significantly enhanced earning capacity. This is an example of responsible deficit financing.

On the other hand, Richard and Joan's daughter, their oldest child, is about to marry. They have always wanted to give her a big wedding, but in the face of the divorce they are hard pressed for money. They can borrow the $20,000 so they don't disappoint their daughter, or they can tell the daughter that they can't afford it and discuss more modest alternatives. Borrowing under these conditions doesn't seem to make much sense. Divorce is not a time to splurge, it's a time to conserve.

Deficit financing is appropriate only when it *strengthens*

your financial position. If spending savings will enhance your income, it makes sense. If you need to use some of your savings to set up a second household, that makes sense. The use of savings to achieve goals of economic autonomy and responsibility is often necessary and should not be avoided just to keep savings intact. But you should not use your savings just to delay balancing your budgets. Spending your savings should be linked to the achievement of clearly defined goals.

WHAT ABOUT SECURITY?

Economic security is the holy grail for most families. We all want to be secure from the threat of economic deprivation. We all want to know that we have reserves for troubled times. We all want to know that our children will have what they need to thrive. For many people, economic security becomes confused with emotional security or with their general sense of well-being, in which case, they can never have enough money to feel "secure." Feelings of insecurity, both emotional and financial, abound during divorce, so it's important that a divorcing couple try to keep the two issues separate.

For most people, real economic security means having enough money to meet basic needs. For most divorcing people, it is impossible to come out of the divorce with enough assets so that they can live off their savings for any extended period of time.

If you have been married a long time and have put away money for retirement, you may discover that there is not enough to support two households in the manner you had expected. If you have fantasized about early retirement you may now find it a remote possibility.

Most middle-class people I see have total assets that, at best, equal two to three times their annual income. This is comprised largely of equity accumulated in the marital home as a consequence of inflation, as well as some employment-related assets such as savings and pension plans. When these assets are divided, each partner is left with some equity but hardly enough to provide an independent income sufficient to maintain the pre-divorce standard of living.

Does this mean that you must come out of the divorce economically insecure? Clearly not. For many, the key to security, or at least as much security as is realistically possible, is your own talent. In all probability, the most valuable economic asset you have, the one that can produce the most income, is *you*. If you are capable of earning $40,000 a year, your skill is comparable to an investment of about $500,000 ($500,000 at 8 percent interest equals $40,000 annually). If there is something you can do that will increase your earning power by $10,000, you will, in effect, increase your "wealth" by about $125,000. Similarly, if you engage in a prolonged divorce mess and get yourself thoroughly depressed and disabled, you squander your most valuable asset. The faster you liberate your own creativity, the faster you can attend to the development of your own economic potential. If you need another credential to significantly enhance your earning power, go get it. If you need to make a job change or even a career change, do it. The couples who adjust most quickly and successfully are those who use their savings and other economic resources as part of a creative plan to enhance the individual earning capacity of each spouse.

It may seem unrealistic to talk about making such major changes at the very time that you feel so stressed by the divorce. The natural instinct is to try to maintain stability while you get your bearings and then, maybe later, consider other changes; but this is not particularly productive. Divorce is a crisis that challenges you to navigate a difficult transition. The sooner you land on your feet—and with your legs prepared to keep running—the better will be your adjustment to the divorce.

Chapter Five

WHAT YOU NEED
TO KNOW ABOUT
DIVORCE LAW

*P*eople approaching divorce are often surprised by the absence of clear rules. Clients ask their lawyers, "How much child support do I get?" or "How much alimony do I have to pay?" or "How long do I have to pay it?" or "How much of my pension does she get?" With few exceptions, the lawyers cannot give precise answers.

Either you and your spouse will negotiate a settlement between yourselves or a judge will decide the outcome for you. In most states there are now formal guidelines that the court must follow in awarding child support. But in most states—on most issues—judges are free to apply their own discretion after hearing the evidence, and this discretion extends even to child-support guidelines.

You take your chances when you go to trial. Most judges do their best to be fair and professional, but, like the rest of us, judges are vulnerable to their own prejudices and biases. If you don't like the judge's decisions you will either learn to live with them or you can appeal to a higher court—but few people appeal. Appeals are expensive and difficult to win because the burden is on the person making the appeal to prove to the higher court that the trial judge misinterpreted the law or abused the discretion permitted the judge by law. Even if you are one of the few who wins on appeal, all you get most of the time is a new trial. I have seen many cases in which a spouse concluded quite correctly that the judge was absolutely wrong but that it did not pay to appeal the decision. The only way to be sure that your divorce meets your needs is for you and your spouse to negotiate the resolution yourselves.

When you negotiate your agreement, you negotiate a contract voluntarily. You sign it voluntarily. You cannot decide that *neither* of you will support your children, and you cannot subject your children to danger or neglect. But within very broad limits you are free to decide—together—how you will resolve the issues.

Settlement agreements are negotiated "in the shadow of the law."[8] That is, you negotiate with an eye on what you think would happen if you were to go to trial and let the judge decide. Experienced lawyers often think they can predict what would happen at trial. Divorce lawyers tend to develop a consensus or sense of industry standards about the results of trials. They may agree that the judges "always give the wife half the house" or "a third of the husband's pension." They might agree that in a particular case $200 a week for child support would be unlikely, with $100 a week a more usual outcome. Lawyers who have appeared many times before the same judge may acquire useful generalizations: "Judge Jones is a woman's judge," or "Judge Smith doesn't like alimony." Much of this may indeed be true, but you can't depend on it. You may not get that judge, or you may get that judge on a bad day, or your lawyer may be wrong. Although most lawyers will freely predict the outcome in court, few will guarantee you that result. You need to treat such predictions with healthy skepticism.

Statutes and legal precedents are a general guide to which rules apply, but at best, the "law" provides a skeletal outline, and you must fill in the blanks. If you fail, the judge will decide, in a process notably lacking in precision, fairness, or efficiency. Judges know that you can do a much better job of it, which is why they don't interfere in a settlement agreement. Ultimately, the "law" governing your settlement agreement is what you together believe to be fair and in the best interests of your family.

WHAT IS A DIVORCE?

A divorce is a dissolution of a marriage. This act by the state, performed by a court, ends the legal status of marriage. It ends your rights as a spouse, such as your right to inherit part of your mate's estate or your right to be supported by your spouse. It also ends your obligations as a spouse. You no longer owe sexual fidelity to your spouse. It changes your relationship to the society. You now file your taxes as a "single" taxpayer. All the rights and obligations that constitute marriage are ended by the court's final judgment of divorce.

JURISDICTION

Each state has its own laws governing marriage and divorce, and each has its own requirements for jurisdiction (the authority of the court to decide—and enforce—the matter). In order to get a divorce, you must establish that the court has jurisdiction to grant the divorce. This is generally done by showing the court that you are a legal resident of the state. You get divorced in the state where you live, *not* in the state where you were married. A judgment of divorce from one state is valid in all states.

GROUNDS FOR DIVORCE: FAULT AND NO-FAULT

Most laypeople are confused about the difference between "grounds for divorce" and the issues of divorce. Grounds refer to the reasons for which you ask the state (the judge) to dissolve your marriage. There are "no-fault grounds" like incompatibility and "fault" grounds like adultery. We will discuss these in more detail shortly. The issues of divorce refer to the ways you will manage your children and money. There the issues are custody, visitation, child support, alimony, and property distribution. These will be discussed at length in the next chapter.

Until about twenty years ago, to get the court to dissolve a marriage one spouse had to prove that the other had breached the marriage contract in some grievous way and was "at fault" for the failure of the marriage. Certain behaviors such as adultery, desertion, or extreme cruelty were "grounds" for granting a divorce. Insanity, addiction, and deviant sexual practices were also valid grounds in some states.

As attitudes changed during this century, the concept of "fault" became less and less useful for divorce. Yet, because existing divorce laws required one party to be the victim of the other's breach of contract, people who didn't want to be together any longer were unable to get a divorce unless they lied, and one spouse could hold the other in the marriage against his or her will.

In the past twenty years most states have passed "no-fault" laws to address these contradictions.[9] No-fault laws may be either of two types. The first requires that either spouse simply prove that the marriage doesn't work, and the testimony of either spouse is generally accepted by the court. Some states such as Florida, Michigan, and California call this irretrievable breakdown of the marriage. Others such as Delaware and Nevada call it incompatibility. The result is the same—a divorce is granted upon proof that reasonable marital harmony is no longer possible. The second variation of no-fault divorce bases the divorce on a required period of separation. Thus, if you live apart for eighteen months in New Jersey, twelve months in New York, twelve months in Wisconsin, or six months in Minnesota, that separation will be accepted by the court as proof that the marriage is dead. Some states have adopted both types of no-fault statute.

STATES WITH "NO-FAULT" GROUNDS FOR DIVORCE

	INCOMPATIBILITY OR IRRECONCILABLE DIFFERENCES	PERIOD OF SEPARATION
Alabama	X	X (2 years)
Alaska	X	
Arizona	X	
Arkansas		X (3 years)
California	X	
Colorado	X	
Connecticut	X	X (18 months)
Delaware	X	
Florida	X	
Georgia	X	
Hawaii	X	X (2 years)
Idaho	X	X (5 years)
Illinois	X	X (2 years)
Indiana	X	
Iowa	X	
Kansas	X	
Kentucky	X	
Louisiana		X (6 months)
Maine	X	
Maryland		X (1 year)
Massachusetts	X	
Michigan	X	
Minnesota	X	X (6 months)
Mississippi	X	
Missouri	X	
Montana	X	X (6 months)
Nebraska	X	
Nevada	X	X (1 year)

STATES WITH "NO-FAULT" GROUNDS (Continued)

	INCOMPATIBILITY OR IRRECONCILABLE DIFFERENCES	PERIOD OF SEPARATION
New Hampshire	X	
New Jersey		X (18 months)
New Mexico	X	
New York		X (1 year)
North Carolina		X (1 year)
North Dakota	X	
Ohio		X (1 year)
Oklahoma	X	
Oregon	X	
Pennsylvania	X	X (2 years)
Rhode Island	X	X (3 years)
South Carolina		X (1 year)
South Dakota	X	
Tennessee	X	X (3 years)
Texas		X (3 years)
Utah	X	X (3 years)
Vermont		X (6 months)
Virginia		X (1 year)
Washington	X	

Source: *Family Law Quarterly*, Volume XXIV, No. 4, Winter 1991, pp. 328–329.

THE PRACTICAL SIGNIFICANCE OF GROUNDS

As a consequence of no-fault legislation, most marriages can now be ended without the need to prove that one spouse is at fault. Only South Dakota persists in requiring proof of fault in all divorces. In most states, no-fault divorce is available even if your spouse doesn't want the divorce. In a few states such as New York and North Carolina, no-fault is available only if the parties already have a separation agreement. For most people, proving marital fault is no longer a prerequisite for divorce.

Until the mid-1960s, there was a real economic reward for the winner of a fault-oriented divorce because alimony awards were often affected by the issue of marital fault. Today the legal doctrines of some states continue to place importance on fault while other states disregard it. In twenty-eight states, fault may not even be used by the court as a factor in awarding alimony. In fourteen states, fault may be used as a factor in awarding alimony.[10] In only eight states—mostly in the deep South—fault is a ban to alimony. Thus, if a woman has an affair in Mississippi and her husband proves it in court, she is disqualified from receiving alimony. States also vary on the use of fault as a criterion in distributing marital property. Seventeen states bar fault completely as a factor in distributing marital property. Twenty-three permit it to be considered and in the rest of the states the statutes are silent on the role of fault.

Although marital fault would seem to be important in shaping the way divorces are resolved, there are several reasons why fault is actually less important than it appears. Most judges rarely view fault as a one-sided matter and believe that in most cases both spouses have contributed to the failure of the marriage.

Judges are much more likely to pay attention to factors such as economic need, the capacity of each spouse to earn money, the length of the marriage, and the ages of the spouses. So even if the law in your state *permits* the judge to consider fault as a criterion for alimony or property distribution, it does not mean that it *will* be considered, or that the judge will accord it much weight.

The fact that so few cases go to trial also reduces the practi-

STATES IN WHICH
FAULT MAY BE CONSIDERED
IN ALIMONY

FAULT NOT A FACTOR	MAY BE CONSIDERED AS A FACTOR	FAULT BARS ALIMONY
Alaska	Connecticut	Alabama
Arizona	Florida	Georgia
Arkansas	Kentucky	Idaho
California	Michigan	Louisiana
Colorado	Missouri	North Carolina
Delaware	New Hampshire	South Carolina
Hawaii	North Dakota	Virginia
Illinois	Pennsylvania	West Virginia
Indiana	Rhode Island	
Iowa	South Dakota	
Kansas	Tennessee	
Maine	Wyoming	
Maryland		
Massachusetts		
Minnesota		
Mississippi		
Montana		
Nebraska		
New Jersey		
New Mexico		
New York		
Ohio		
Oklahoma		
Oregon		
Vermont		
Washington		
Wisconsin		

Source: *Family Law Quarterly,* Volume XXIV, No. 4, Winter 1991, pp. 355–356.

STATES IN WHICH
FAULT MAY BE CONSIDERED
IN PROPERTY DISTRIBUTION

FAULT NOT A FACTOR	STATUTES SILENT	MAY BE CONSIDERED
Alaska	Arkansas	Connecticut
Arizona	Nebraska	Florida
California	Nevada	Georgia
Colorado	New Hampshire	Hawaii
Delaware	New Mexico	Idaho
Illinois	Ohio	Kansas
Indiana	Oklahoma	Louisiana
Iowa	Utah	Michigan
Kentucky		Mississippi
Maine		Missouri
Massachusetts		Nevada
Minnesota		New Hampshire
Montana		New York
New Jersey		North Dakota
Oregon		Pennsylvania
South Dakota		Rhode Island
Washington		South Carolina
Wisconsin		Tennessee
		Texas
		Vermont
		Virginia
		West Virginia
		Wyoming

Source: *Family Law Quarterly,* Volume XXIV, No. 4, Winter 1991, pp. 343–345.

cal significance of fault. Remember, in those states that permit fault to be considered as a factor in the economic issues of divorce, it is the judge who makes the decision. In the 97 percent of cases that settle prior to trial, the judge never gets a chance to decide.

You have a choice. If you believe that fault is so one-sided and extreme in your divorce and that it *ought* to be a major consideration in the economic result, you still must decide whether to try to prove it. The likelihood that this strategy will get you more money is quite low, but, the probability that it will *cost* you more money is very high. Your decision to commit yourself to a fully litigated divorce will cost you and your spouse thousands of dollars in professional fees—not to mention the time, energy, and emotional costs. In the end, there probably will be less money to divide. As a practical matter, I advise you to forget about fault.

CONTESTED/UNCONTESTED V. FAULT/NO-FAULT

If you and your spouse agree on everything and put it in writing, you have an *uncontested* divorce; there literally is *no* contest. If there is any issue on which you disagree, you have a *contested* divorce. Technically, divorces can be contested on grounds as well as custody and economic issues. Cases are rarely tried on the question of grounds. Invariably, contested cases center around one of the five issues of divorce: property distribution, alimony, custody, visitation, and child support. These issues are discussed in detail in the next chapter.

Don't confuse *no-fault* with *uncontested*. In most states it is possible to have a bitterly contested *no-fault* divorce. The grounds are *no-fault,* but the couple disagrees about one or more issues. It is also possible to have an uncontested divorce on fault grounds. In that case, there is a signed separation agreement, and one of the spouses has filed for divorce on fault grounds—typically, extreme cruelty. We'll look at this later, but for now, the only thing you need to remember is that contested or uncontested divorces are not the same as fault or no-fault divorces.

DIVORCE PROCEDURE

Where conflict is intense, court proceedings may be very extensive, with many documents filed and many hearings. In an amicable divorce, there will be a minimal amount of documents and a very short hearing at the end. In fact, in an amicable divorce, there are usually no documents filed with the court until you have worked out your agreement. But you should be familiar with some of the major terms and events that are discussed below.

PLEADINGS

A divorce proceeding starts with a *Complaint or Petition for Divorce* or some other similarly worded document. The spouse who files the complaint for divorce is automatically the *plaintiff*. The complaint states that the plaintiff has *grounds* for divorce and describes the grounds. It establishes that the plaintiff or defendant or both are legal residents of the state, so that the court has jurisdiction. It tells the court about children, acquired assets, and other important facts about the marriage. The complaint ends with a *prayer* for relief. First it asks the court to dissolve the marriage. If there is already a settlement agreement, the court is asked to incorporate that agreement in the final judgment of divorce. When there is no agreement, the relief requested typically includes requests for custody of the children, child support, alimony, and distribution of property.

Generally, the complaint is filed in the court and then served on (delivered to) the defendant by an officer of the court. The *defendant* is the other spouse. The defendant files a responsive pleading called an *answer,* which can take several forms. If the divorce is already settled, the defendant may file an answer admitting the allegations of the complaint and joining the plaintiff in a request for dissolution. Some states allow the defendant just to file an *appearance,* which acknowledges receipt of the complaint but takes no further position. The defendant may choose to do nothing, in which case the plaintiff requests and gets a judgment by *default.*

In a contested matter, the defendant files an answer that denies all or some of the allegations in the complaint and asks the court to dismiss the complaint. The defendant might also choose to file a counterclaim, which is, in effect, the defendant's complaint for divorce. If this is done, the defendant is known as the *defendant-counterclaimant.*

DISCOVERY

Whether you have an amicable or a litigated divorce you each need to know all the relevant information about each other's finances. Lawyers generally refer to the process of obtaining this information as *discovery.* In an amicable divorce in which your negotiation precedes formal court action, each spouse voluntarily provides the other with all information requested. This may include appraisals on real estate or other property, tax information, copies of bank statements, and anything else that affects finances.

In litigated divorces, discovery is more formal and follows the filing of the complaint. For the most part, the lawyers focus on identifying and appraising the marital property, identifying sources of income and witnesses who will testify about relevant facts disputed by the parties. If custody is in dispute, discovery may also include psychological or psychiatric examinations of parents and children and investigation by social workers. Discovery includes two types of questioning by each side. *Interrogatories* are written questions submitted by each side to the other that must be answered in writing and certified (sworn) as to accuracy. The interrogatories may include *demands for production* of documents such as tax returns, stock certificates, or any other relevant items. In addition to interrogatories, each side may take *depositions*. A deposition is the sworn testimony of a witness or a party to the divorce. At a deposition, each attorney has an opportunity to ask questions of the witness while a court reporter records the testimony.

In all negotiated settlements, all relevant information should be provided upon request. Indeed, the refusal by one side to provide information often leads the divorce into litigation. Negotiation requires good-faith cooperation in making sure everybody is informed. You cannot negotiate well if you feel you are missing vital information or if that information is being hidden. It is in your interest to see to it that your spouse has all the important information.

MOTION PRACTICE

During the time a contested case is awaiting trial, disputes sometimes arise that the couple cannot resolve. Who will have child custody until the hearing? How much temporary support will be paid? Will business records be produced for examination? If a spouse feels that the intervention of the court is required, he or she files a *motion* asking the court to resolve the issue. The other spouse, through an attorney, then files a response, and a hearing is scheduled. At the hearing the judge may take testimony or simply listen to the arguments of the lawyers before issuing an *order* directing one or both of the litigants to do this or that. Motions can also be filed after the divorce is over. This is called *post-judgment litigation* and occurs when there are disputes about enforcing or changing the agreement or the final judgment of the court. Post-judgment motions might be filed to seek a change in custody or support or to compel payment of support.

Generally speaking, if you negotiate well from the beginning, you will not require motion practice.

TRIAL AND JUDGMENT

Almost all divorces culminate in a hearing before the judge. If the divorce is uncontested, the hearing is very short. Each spouse testifies for a few minutes that he or she understands the settlement agreement and regards it as fair (to prevent post-judgment litigation on the grounds of not understanding the agreement). One or both spouses will verify the grounds for divorce that were stated in the complaint.

Finally, the judge orders the marriage dissolved and the settlement agreement incorporated into the *Final Judgment of Divorce,* sometimes called the *Divorce Decree,* prepared by the lawyers for the judge's signature. When the agreement is incorporated, it becomes part of the court order. Once incorporated into the judgment, it has the additional power of a court order. When the final judgment is *entered* by the court, the divorce is over and the marriage legally ended.

Chapter Six

THE FIVE ISSUES
OF DIVORCE

Every settlement agreement must deal with alimony, property distribution, and, if there are children, custody, visitation, and child support. These five issues must be resolved by the divorcing couple in order to obtain an uncontested divorce. When a divorce is contested, it is usually because the couple has not been able to agree on one or more of these issues.

THE STATE'S INTEREST IN YOUR MARRIAGE

Marriage has been the principal vehicle for organizing the economic life of families. The nuclear family meets vital needs of society: it provides for the economic welfare of children, and it transmits society's values and norms from one generation to the next. Marriage, as a traditional means of organizing the economic relations of men and women, also organizes, in part, the ownership of property. There are rules that apply to the way husbands and wives own property together.

When a marriage breaks up, the state has several concerns that must be satisfied before a divorce is approved. It wants to know how the children will be supported, who will support them, and who will be in charge of them. The state is the *parent of last resort*. If children are abandoned, the state must provide for them. Because it wants this role minimized, the state, through its courts, requires that provisions be made for children at the time of divorce. Thus the court requires an agreement or a court order specifying the duties and rights of each parent with respect to raising and supporting the children. These are the issues of custody, visitation, and child support.

The issue of alimony, sometimes referred to as spousal support or maintenance, springs from a similar concern. The state does not want to support a divorced spouse. Until fairly recently, women in most middle-class families worked at home (as homemakers) rather than in the workplace. Although many women were employed out of the home in nineteenth- and early twentieth-century America, their employment was viewed as temporary and subordinate to their role as homemakers. As property was usually in the husband's name, the wife's economic dependency on the husband was virtually complete. When a marriage ended, a wife who had no economic resources outside the home could be left without funds and become a ward of the state. Alimony, the obligation of the husband to support his wife, was historically the answer to the problem. Today, at least in theory, that obligation is gender neutral, and, if circumstances warrant, the wife can be obliged to pay alimony to the husband.

The fifth concern of the state is clarity in title to property. Historically, the interest of the state has been to make sure that property could be freely transferred with *clear title*. When a marriage ends, the state needs to know who owned what property and needs to extinguish any claims each spouse had to the other's property. For example, married people have a right to receive part of the other's property if a spouse dies. Or a wife might have a dower right, the right to occupy the husband's house for her lifetime, if the husband dies. If these rights were not terminated upon divorce, strangers could not know for certain whether or not they were purchasing property free of the claims of a divorced spouse. The state insists, therefore, that upon divorce, property be clearly divided into two bundles: the husband's and the wife's.

Now, let's look more closely at these five issues of divorce. I will discuss their implications, the range of court involvement, and what choices you have as a couple in agreeing on these issues.

CUSTODY AND VISITATION

WHAT DOES CUSTODY MEAN?

Most people believe that custody refers to which parent gets the kids. In fact, custody refers to three parenting roles:

- The first is a question of *residence*. Where and with whom do the children live?
- The second is a question of *nurturance*. Who will take care of the children on a daily basis? Who will see that they are fed, clothed, and otherwise nurtured?
- The third question is one of *guardianship*. Who is in charge of the children? Who will make important decisions concerning their welfare?

Custody is, in other words, about parenting. Yet the term has come to arouse fear and anxiety and to signal the disenfranchisement of one parent.

The reason for this reaction is in the win/lose image of the adversary system. In the past, when divorce was fault-based and trials labeled the defendant as "guilty," a custody award to the winner gave that parent absolute power over the children. That power could be used to punish the other parent by cutting him or her off from the kids.

Most states today take a more humane view of the issue of custody. Even when custody is awarded to one parent, the law requires the judge to protect the parental role of the other parent with adequate rights of visitation. Over the past ten years, some states have changed their custody laws to eliminate the win/lose connotation of custody. Eleven states, including California, Connecticut, and Florida, have adopted laws expressing a clear preference for *joint custody,* an arrangement in which the full parental rights of both parents are preserved and enhanced. Some states have abolished *sole custody.* Others have made joint custody a legal presumption.

For now, the important thing to know is that as a couple you can negotiate *any* parenting arrangement you wish as long as the arrangement takes care of the children. How you label the arrangement is not important. You do not have to use the words "custody" and "visitation." The most important thing is that you negotiate a parenting agreement that realistically reflects your strengths and needs and the needs of your children. If you negotiate such an agreement and can live by it and be committed to it, the court will accept it with a sigh of relief. Judges do not like making decisions about your children and prefer that you make them.

Various custody arrangements will be spelled out in more detail in a subsequent chapter, but now you simply need to know the "legal" meaning of the basic concepts.

THREE CONCEPTS YOU SHOULD UNDERSTAND

SOLE CUSTODY

This refers to a custody arrangement in which one parent, the *sole custodian parent,* is essentially in charge of the child. Typically, the child lives with that parent full time, except when visiting the other parent. The sole custodial parent has the exclusive right to make important decisions about the child and is the only legal guardian of the child.

JOINT CUSTODY

This concept became popular in the 1970s, and most states now recognize it. Joint custody means that neither parent is the sole custodial parent; *custody is literally with both parents.* In a genuine joint custody, both parents share, more or less equally, parental rights and responsibilities. The children alternate their residence between father and mother according to a negotiated schedule, and both parents concur on important decisions.

Unfortunately, there is some confusion about the term "joint custody." It is often used euphemistically when the couple really wants one parent to be in charge but also wants to avoid the negative connotation of one of them being the "noncustodial" parent.

SHARED PARENTAL RESPONSIBILITY

This term is used by statute in some states to replace the term *custody.* The term is broad enough to include quite a variety of arrangements. Thus it can refer to any degree of shared parental responsibility—from equal responsibility for both parents to all responsibility for one parent. As a legislative concept it is a progressive reform. It expresses a desirable objective—that parenting should continue by both parents. You should be aware that shared parental responsibility also means that specifics must be spelled out as to who is responsible for what.

WHAT IS THE ROLE OF THE COURT?

The court serves as the parent of last resort. Generally the court never interferes when parents agree. However, if the parents cannot agree on basic custody and visitation arrangements, the court decides. The court retains this role until the child reaches adulthood.

Custody fights don't occur only prior to the divorce. Sometimes an existing custody agreement breaks down *after* the divorce, and one parent petitions the court for a change. The court can alter custody and visitation arrangements upon petition if the judge agrees that change would be in the "best interests of the child."

CAN A CHILD DECIDE WHICH PARENT SHOULD HAVE CUSTODY?

In most states a child does not have the absolute right to decide which parent to live with. As children become older, courts usually accord their wishes more importance. We can safely assume that the preference of a seventeen-year-old would be respected.

CHILD SUPPORT

The law states that it is the duty of both parents to support their children according to their ability. In most cases children live principally with one parent, and the other parent makes child-support payments to the "custodial" or primary residential parent. Let's look at some of the most frequently asked questions about child support.

HOW MUCH SUPPORT SHOULD BE PAID?

The amount of child support depends on the needs of the child, the lifestyle of the family, the number of children, and the income and expenses of the parents. A few years ago the federal government required all states to adopt guidelines to advise judges on child-support standards. As a result, your state now has such guidelines. In many cases the guidelines are applied only when total income falls below some particular threshold. But child-support guidelines do not necessarily resolve the question of child support. These formulas eliminate some conflict, but they may not reflect special needs of a particular child (tutoring costs, for example). Even with such formulas you must still negotiate an agreement, or, as with any other contested issue, the court decides. If your state guidelines apply to you, you should use them as a *minimum* standard. That is, you should not have less and you may decide that more is needed.

HOW LONG IS CHILD SUPPORT PAID?

Child support is paid until a child is "emancipated." *Emancipation*—or reaching majority—used to occur automatically at a predetermined age, such as eighteen, that coincided with reaching voting age or eighteen when graduating from high school. In theory, children are emancipated when they become self-supporting. This was simple enough in the days when most children went to work after graduating from high school.

Today many states and most separation agreements provide that a child is emancipated when the first of several events occurs: getting married, graduating high school, or entering military service. In many states, emancipation will be delayed to permit a child to complete college if the child is intellectually capable and the family can financially assist. You must review these details with your lawyer to find out how emancipation is treated in your state.

CAN THE AMOUNT OF CHILD SUPPORT BE CHANGED?

Child support can be changed by the court upon petition by a parent if the court finds that changed circumstances warrant it. Suppose a parent is disabled and cannot earn an income— or wins the lottery. Or suppose a child's needs substantially change. The law recognizes that some flexibility is required to meet changed circumstances. Like most other areas of divorce law, the judge has great discretion if the matter is tried to a conclusion. When negotiating your settlement agreement, you want to allow for changes as circumstances require.

ALIMONY: A CHANGING CONCEPT

Alimony, known also as *spousal support* or *maintenance,* is support paid by one spouse to another. Although the law is usually written to permit either husband or wife to receive alimony, it is so unusual for a woman to pay alimony to a man that in this book alimony will mean support paid by husbands to wives.

Of all the issues of divorce, alimony is the subject of the least consensus among lawyers and judges. Because there has been rapid change in the economic roles and expectations of women over the past thirty years, there has also been rapid change in the way alimony is viewed. When more women were full-time homemakers and economically dependent, the question of alimony was much clearer. A woman received alimony permanently or until remarriage provided another husband to support her. Moreover, a woman who was awarded alimony as the product of a fault-based divorce might expect a standard of living approximating that to which she was accustomed.

Today there is a growing expectation among lawyers and judges that women can and should support themselves. This has changed the way alimony is viewed both in terms of duration and amount. Alimony is likely to be for a shorter period of time than it once was, and often provides less than the standard of living during the marriage.

For women, these changing views of alimony have proved harsh. Middle-aged and older women who were raised with traditional values but came of age during the period of the women's movement have been caught unprepared and are often treated unfairly. The adverse impact of fifteen years as a homemaker on a career and salary level is profound. A forty-year-old woman just entering the job market is at a severe disadvantage.

For these reasons, alimony is often the most difficult issue to negotiate well. It directly addresses the lifestyles of both spouses, and when these are unequal, resentment invariably occurs.

ENTITLEMENT AND OBLIGATION

Statutes on alimony vary from state to state. Generally, *need, capacity to earn,* and the *duration of the marriage* are the most important factors affecting the amount of alimony awarded. Alimony addresses substantial inequality between the incomes of the two spouses. If the husband and wife have exactly the same income, there will be no alimony. Alimony entitlements grow as the disparity between his income and her income increases and as the duration of the marriage increases. A short marriage of three years will generally not create much of an alimony entitlement even though there is a great disparity in income. On the other hand, in a marriage of thirty years, where the husband has a much greater income than his wife, a substantial alimony entitlement is probable.

Alimony can be permanent or temporary. *Permanent* alimony is not really permanent, because any number of events can end it. If the husband dies before the wife dies, his obligation to pay alimony dies with him and does not pass to his estate. If the wife remarries, alimony generally ends. Many states permit the husband to petition the court to end alimony if the wife lives with another man in a relationship similar to marriage. So when we say "permanent," we really mean not limited to a specified number of years.

In lieu of permanent alimony, *temporary* or *rehabilitative* alimony has become more common. Temporary alimony is intended to support or supplement a woman's income for the period of time necessary for her to resume employment. In some cases, a wife wants to stay at home until children begin school full time. Or she may want to complete college or some other training program. The objective here is to help her become financially independent.

Both permanent and temporary alimony are subject to change if a significant change of circumstance alters the needs or capacities of either party. If a husband becomes disabled or unemployed and has a reduced ability to pay, most courts will reduce his obligation or suspend it entirely until he regains his income. A wife who becomes disabled might successfully petition the court to increase alimony. There are no precise rules and no precise tables to determine the amount of alimony or its length of time. Like most issues, it is completely negotiable.

THE ISSUE OF EQUALITY OF INCOMES

A difficult issue around alimony—not answered in the law—is whether the wife and husband should end up with equal incomes. In marriages of long duration, most judges and lawyers will seek some semblance of equality. But even in long marriages there is no assumption of automatic equality. The culture of lawyers continues to reflect the predominant male perspective that alimony is a "free ride" and unearned by the wife. The result usually feels unfair to the wife who sees her former spouse living better than she. In chapter 12 we will develop principles that will help you negotiate this issue fairly.

ALIMONY AND TAXES

Alimony, unlike child support, is tax deductible to the payor and taxable income to the recipient. (It's actually an adjustment to gross income rather than an itemized deduction.) Child support, on the other hand, is neither deductible to the payor nor taxable to the recipient.

DIVISION OF MARITAL PROPERTY

The distribution of the marital property is an area of law characterized by complex legal interpretation, precedent, and statutes. For most people the complexities do not apply because they do not have much property other than a house, perhaps a pension, two cars, and some household goods.

COMMUNITY PROPERTY OR EQUITABLE DISTRIBUTION

Until about twenty years ago, most states had one of two schemes for dividing marital property. The most common was called a *separate property* or *title* system. Simply put, it meant that the property belonged to whoever's name it was in. If a house was in the wife's name, she got it. If it was in her husband's name, he got it. If it was in both names, they split it. The second system, *community property,* was fairer and also simple. All marital property was equally divided between the two spouses. Both systems produced problems. The title system was frequently unfair because most if not all the property was in the husband's name. The community property system was considered equally arbitrary because it did not take into account the different contributions of the spouses and often gave property to a spouse who neither had earned it nor deserved it.

Today, only California, Idaho, Louisiana, New Mexico, Texas, Washington, and Wisconsin retain community property. All others have adopted *equitable distribution*. This reform gives the courts the power, within certain limits, to award the property to either spouse regardless of whose name the property is in. The court can take the property titled in the husband's name and give it to the wife, or do the reverse. Equitable distribution requires judges to distribute property so that the result is "fair and just." "But," you appropriately ask, "what is fair and just?" Legally, the answer is whatever the judge decides or whatever you negotiate. Equitable distribution simply subjects the distribution of marital assets to the same kind of discretion as the judge (and the negotiating couple) already has on other economic issues. There is no automatic assumption of a fifty-fifty division, and it is irrelevant whose name the property is in. You negotiate what is fair.

MARITAL AND EXEMPT PROPERTY

Some equitable distribution states permit all property to be divided. Others limit division to marital property—that which was acquired during the marriage. Some states distinguish between *marital property*, which is subject to distribution, and *exempt property*, which is not. Generally speaking, marital property is property acquired during the marriage. If you had no assets when you were married and you both saved from your salaries and bought a car, the car is marital property. But if you owned a car prior to the marriage and you still have it at the time of divorce, the car is exempt from distribution. Property is often exempt if it is inherited or received as a gift by one spouse. Thus, if your aunt died and left you her car, that car is not subject to equitable distribution if you live in a state that exempts inherited property. You should carefully review this with your lawyer if you inherited property or money during the marriage.[11]

PROPERTY DIVISION

A COMMUNITY PROPERTY STATES		B EQUITABLE DISTRIBUTION COMMON-LAW STATES		
1 Equal or Presumption of Equal	2 Equitable	1 All Property Considered	2 Only Marital Property Considered	3 Gifts—Inheritances Are Excluded
Alabama			X(1)	Yes (1)
Alaska		X		
Arizona	X			
Arkansas			X(2)	Yes
California	X(3)			
Colorado			X(4)	Yes (4)
Connecticut		X		No
Delaware			X	No
Florida		X		No
Georgia			X	No
Hawaii		X		No
Idaho	X			
Illinois			X	Yes

PROPERTY DIVISION *(Continued)*

	A COMMUNITY PROPERTY STATES		B EQUITABLE DISTRIBUTION COMMON-LAW STATES		
	1	2	1	2	3
Indiana			X(5)		No
Iowa			X		Yes
Kansas			X		No
Kentucky				X	Yes
Louisiana	X				
Maine				X	Yes
Maryland				X	Yes
Massachu- setts			X		
Michigan			X		No
Minnesota				X	Yes
Mississippi		X			
Missouri				X	Yes
Montana			X		No
Nebraska				X	No
Nevada		X			
New Hamp- shire			X		No
New Jersey				X	Yes
New Mexico	X				
New York				X	Yes
North Carolina				X	Yes
North Dakota			X		No
Ohio			X		No
Oklahoma				X	Yes

PROPERTY DIVISION *(Continued)*

	A COMMUNITY PROPERTY STATES		B EQUITABLE DISTRIBUTION COMMON-LAW STATES		
	1	2	1	2	3
Oregon			X		No
Pennsylvania				X	Yes
Rhode Island				X	Yes
South Carolina				X(4)	Yes
South Dakota			X		Unclear
Tennessee				X(4)	Yes
Texas	X(6)				
Utah			X		
Vermont			X		
Virginia				X	Yes
Washington	X				
West Virginia				X	Yes
Wisconsin	X				Yes
Wyoming			X		

Source: *Family Law Quarterly*, Volume XXIV, No. 4, Winter 1991, pp. 335–336.

Where property is clearly identified as exempt or marital, there is no problem in deciding what assets are or are not subject to distribution. But the matter becomes more complex when there is no clear distinction. Consider, for example, the car you owned before the marriage. You bought the car for

$10,000, put $2,000 down, and took a loan for the rest. The loan was paid off during the marriage using the earnings from income. The income that was used to pay off the car was marital property. The car is now *comingled* property because it is no longer possible to see exactly which part was acquired after the marriage began. Comingled property is subject to equitable distribution.

Over the course of a long marriage, *most* property tends to become comingled unless there is a concerted effort to keep it separate. If you owned your car free and clear before the marriage and after the marriage sell it for $2,000 and buy a horse, the horse is still exempt. But if you add $2,000 of marital savings to buy a horse, that horse is comingled property. Comingled property can become the subject of considerable disagreement.

THE SCOPE OF MARITAL PROPERTY

Marital property includes anything of value now or in the future that was acquired during the marriage from other than exempt sources. This includes *tangible* property such as cars, jewelry, and real estate and *intangible* property such as pension rights, patent rights, or even, in some states, professional degrees, such as law and medical degrees.

The concept of marital property deviates from the way we usually define private property. Generally, we would regard property as that which can be bought or sold. Professional licenses to practice law or medicine cannot be sold, but in some states they may be considered marital property subject to equitable distribution. Similarly a law practice may not be sold but is often valued as an asset for purposes of property distribution in divorce. To understand how this comes about we need to look further at the logic behind the law.

The equitable distribution system was intended to create a fairer distribution of marital assets. The statutes interpret marriage as an *economic partnership*. Domestic contributions of the homemaker wife are seen as an *economic* contribution that helps the husband to perform outside the home as an economic producer. If the wife stays home and cares for the household while the husband practices law, her contribution at home is converted to a share of the value of his law practice. This does not mean that she gets half or any other particular fraction. It means that a monetary value is to be put on the practice and taken into consideration in distributing the other assets. Although law practices, as a rule, cannot be sold, to ignore the value of the practice in the distribution of assets would be unfair. Some states include educational degrees earned during the marriage under the same logical assumption. You must ask your lawyer how *your* particular state treats these assets.

CONCLUSION

Whether you and your spouse can negotiate an agreement beforehand or you resort to fighting it out in court, the five issues of divorce must be resolved in order for you to get a divorce. Either way, you will need a lawyer. The next chapter will help you find the lawyer who will best serve your needs.

Chapter Seven

LAWYERS, MEDIATORS, AND OTHER PROFESSIONALS

*D*ivorces *can range* from hostile litigation on one hand to amicable settlement on the other, and the lawyer's role can range from dominant to supporting. Before you choose a lawyer, you need to think about what kind of divorce you think you will have and what role you want your lawyer(s) to play. Obviously, the more you move toward the litigation extreme, the more dominant a role your lawyer plays.

THREE ROUTES TO SETTLEMENT

Basically, there are three ways divorce settlements are reached:

- litigation by lawyers
- negotiation by lawyers
- negotiation by the divorcing couple with the advice of lawyers and a mediator.

TYPE 1: THE LITIGATED SETTLEMENT

The litigated settlement is the classic case that settles at the courtroom door. In this scenario, serious negotiation does not occur until the case is scheduled for trial. Negotiations may begin a few weeks before with a *four-way conference,* a meeting of the lawyers and their clients, to explore settlement. If both sides are unusually hostile, no meeting occurs until they get to court and the judge calls the two lawyers into his chambers to see if the case can be settled without a trial.

The atmosphere is highly charged with anxiety and strong emotions. Both sides are ready for trial. Extensive discovery has been conducted; witnesses have been subpoenaed and are awaiting instructions; and both husband and wife have been prepared for trial. Each lawyer has adopted a posture that she or he is ready to try the case and is indifferent to whether or not it settles. But in reality, both lawyers would probably prefer to settle and get back to their offices. The judge wants the case settled because he does not want to sit through a two-day trial, and his calendar is jammed. So, at the last minute, an agreement is hammered out.

The negotiation technique used here is usually straight horse-trading—you give in on this; I'll give in on that. You pay three hundred dollars a week child support; I'll agree to pay half the college costs. The lawyers go back and forth between their clients. Finally, with the judge demanding that the case either be settled or tried that minute, the agreement comes together. Lawyers and clients go into the courtroom; the judge takes the bench; and the agreement is put on the record. In ten minutes the whole procedure is over, and the couple is divorced.

TYPE 2: THE AMICABLE LAWYER-NEGOTIATED SETTLEMENT

In this type of settlement, the attorneys negotiate the settlement for their clients prior to any action being filed in the court. Here, the settlement is the primary focus, and both sides assume that the matter will indeed be settled, although litigation is always available as an alternative. Discovery occurs in a relatively cooperative manner. All financial information requested is produced. If appraisals are needed, the two lawyers may choose a neutral appraiser. Once the information is gathered, one or two four-way meetings occur in which the issues are resolved. After the agreement is prepared and signed by the parties, a complaint for divorce is filed by one lawyer, and the matter is "put through" the courts.

I recently conducted my own survey to see how many divorces in my home state of New Jersey fit the type 1 and type 2 models. According to the lawyers I questioned, about 5 percent of divorces are settled before any action is filed in court. About 94 percent are litigated with a settlement negotiated prior to trial. No more than 1 percent actually go to trial. This suggests that there are many thousands of cases being litigated that could be settled much faster and easier.

TYPE 3: CLIENT-NEGOTIATED
SETTLEMENT AND MEDIATED DIVORCE

Type 3 is not as common as types 1 and 2 because it is relatively new. Here the couple controls the process. It is the couple, not the attorneys, who do the work. They identify the issues, direct the discovery process, choose the experts (if any are needed), and master the information. Then they negotiate the settlement. In an ideal world, all divorces would be resolved this way. But in most cases, the relationship between both spouses is too strained for them to negotiate without help. The solution is to use a trained mediator.

A mediator helps create a safe atmosphere for negotiations. An experienced mediator has been through many divorces and has a good sense of the structure needed to settle the case. The mediator helps you and your spouse set an orderly agenda, helps you identify problems, and provides information useful for solving them. The mediator will encourage you to express your feelings directly rather than act them out. She or he helps you avoid misunderstandings and helps you clarify what you really mean.

Using a mediator does not mean you do not use a lawyer. In fact, you always need a lawyer for a divorce. There are two approaches to the role of lawyers in mediation. In the first, one lawyer represents both husband and wife after the mediator brings them to agreement. In the second, each partner has his or her own lawyer for advice during negotiation who also represents him or her after the agreement is negotiated. Although it is slightly more expensive, I recommend the two-lawyer approach because in the long run it gives each client the best security that no major errors were made.

In mediation, the lawyer is an adviser who answers questions, advises the client, and reviews documents for the client. The lawyer's role is to facilitate and assist the client's negotiation.

Type 3 cases end in the same manner as type 2 cases. A settlement agreement is drafted by the lawyers expressing the agreement of the couple and the contract is signed. The matter is then put through the courts.

WHICH TYPE OF SETTLEMENT IS BEST FOR YOU?

My preference for most couples is mediated divorce. Type 1, the heavily litigated divorce, should be avoided whenever possible. From the perspective of a couple seeking a nondestructive divorce, the choice is between type 2 and type 3: a lawyer-negotiated settlement followed by a simple uncontested divorce or a mediated divorce. Both types start with a premise of good-faith negotiation leading to settlement prior to the initiation of court proceedings. The difference lies in the advantages and disadvantages of a lawyer-driven process versus mediated negotiation.

LAWYER AS NEGOTIATOR: BENEFITS

Having your lawyers do it for you has the advantage of relieving you of the responsibility. You may feel uncomfortable dealing with each other. You may feel too angry or resentful to believe that you can work effectively together. One of you may feel at a disadvantage because you believe that your spouse is a better negotiator or more intimidating. You may feel that it is easier just to let the lawyers do it. This also means you do not have to learn much about the legal ramifications or the technical side of the contract. Initially, at least, it is far easier to put your divorce in the hands of an attorney and rely on him or her.

Ideally, you and your spouse will choose knowledgeable matrimonial attorneys. Each attorney will have the time to devote to your case, the time to meet with you and explain your choices, and the time to return your calls promptly. Each attorney will be a competent negotiator with a nonbelligerent style and will not provoke hostility in the other side. If you choose carefully and if you are lucky, the chemistry between the two attorneys will be good. They will have professional respect for each other and treat each other courteously. If all these factors work for you, it should turn out well. The settlement agreement will reflect your mutual needs and you will be committed to it.

LAWYER AS NEGOTIATOR: DRAWBACKS

The risk of the lawyer-negotiated divorce is that one or more of these qualifications may not be present. Good attorneys are very busy. You may find that the matter seems to drag on because the lawyers cannot devote enough time quickly enough. You may find that your attorney has neither the time nor inclination to explain everything to you to your satisfaction. Finally, there is no way to predict how the attorneys will interact with each other. If they do not get along, it will cost you a great deal of money.

Even under the best conditions, the lawyer-negotiated divorce tends to be expensive because you are paying two expensive professionals to negotiate. Each time one calls or corresponds with the other, or with you, it costs you money. Budget-conscious people are often reluctant to call their attorneys because they don't want to run up their bills. Such reticence can lead to communication gaps and bad agreements. If you use a lawyer to negotiate for you, don't try to save money by not communicating as much as necessary. It's a false economy.

MEDIATION: ADVANTAGES

In the conventional divorce, your attorney is in charge and you advise. Mediation reverses the process and puts you in charge. This means that *you* set the pace, *you* do the work, and *you* produce the agreement. When you need legal advice, you talk to your attorney. During the course of your negotiation, you will need several conferences and a greater number of phone calls. You will have your attorney review the financial records to verify their accuracy and sufficiency. At each stage, *you* will be in charge—and therein lies the strength of this process.

Generally, mediators are much more attuned to the psychological process of divorce than are attorneys. Many mediators are therapists who have been trained as divorce mediators. There are also attorney mediators who have received training that emphasizes the emotional processes of divorce. Attorneys who practice mediation generally are more interested in the emotional side of divorce than are litigators.

MEDIATION: DISADVANTAGES

The disadvantages of mediation are those associated with being responsible for the outcome. Both spouses must put in the time, acquire the information, and negotiate until the problems are solved. If one of you does not do his or her part, the process fails. Mediation requires negotiation between equals. If one of you is much more dominant than the other or if one is intimidated by the other, mediation can break down. Mediation should generally be much faster than law-yer-negotiated divorce, but foot-dragging and procrastination can slow it down. When appropriate, and when it works, mediation is, in my opinion, superior. But it certainly is not for everyone. If you believe that the relationship between you and your spouse is so poisoned, or so unequal, that the quality of negotiation will be poor, then you will be better off trying to find two compatible lawyers and have them take the lead in negotiations.

MY EXPERIENCE

Over the past ten years I have handled several hundred divorces in a conventional manner and have also mediated several hundred divorces. It seems to me that the couples who mediate come out of the divorce in better shape. The inci-dence of post-judgment litigation (going back to court after the divorce is over) appears to be dramatically lower among the group that mediates.

When children are involved, mediation forces the parents to

talk to each other and to learn new ways to talk about issues as divorced parents. In my mind, the greatest shortcoming of the lawyer-negotiated divorce is that divorcing couples are able to avoid talking to each other. If you have no children, this may not be a problem. But if you have children, you are going to have to talk about things, no matter how uncomfortable you are in doing so. Mediation helps you learn to do it.

Mediation also seems to produce greater commitment to the agreement. If you negotiate it, you own it. If someone else does so, and you are passive, it becomes easier to make believe that it was "imposed" on you. Mediation breeds responsibility. It is ideally suited to resolution of conflict where families are involved.

CHOOSING A LAWYER

Before you choose a lawyer you should decide which route you will take to settlement. Note that if you choose mediation, you will need to find attorneys who are sympathetic and supportive of mediation. Although this number is growing, the majority of matrimonial lawyers see mediation as a threat and do not like it. You can determine this by a phone call.

Interview several attorneys. Some attorneys offer free initial consultation; others charge for it. The initial consultation being free, however, should not be what makes up your mind. You would not expect other professionals to see you for free, and there is no reason to expect successful attorneys to give away their time.

References from people you know are a good starting point. But listen carefully. If a friend is recommending her lawyer, find out how long it took to settle her divorce. How available was the attorney? How quickly were phone calls returned? How satisfied was she with the result?

References from other lawyers are also useful. In many communities the divorce lawyers know one another. Find out which are respected among their peers and why. Take time doing your research and then interview several lawyers.

When you have your meeting with the attorney, go prepared with questions. Find out how willing she or he is to explain things to you. Ask how property distribution works in your state. Ask about child support, alimony, and any other issues you may think of. Note how well the attorney answers your questions and whether or not you learned anything. Explore your role in the divorce negotiations with the attorney and find out if he or she will support the level of involvement you want to have. Some lawyers take a paternal posture and want their clients as passive and compliant as possible. Others encourage their clients to play an active role. How does the attorney seem to regard your spouse? Does the attorney feed your anger or seek to quiet it? Does the attorney see the divorce as a war or as a more cooperative endeavor? How much reliance does the attorney place on court proceedings? On negotiations?

If you keep your ears open and ask the proper questions, you should be able to get a good sense of the attorney's approach to divorce in an hour-long interview. Just remember that there are no magic formulas. Be wary of slick answers, and be just as wary of lawyers who tell you they will solve all your problems.

GUIDELINES FOR FINDING A LAWYER

What you are looking for in an attorney is competence, compatibility, and availability. The so-called "killer" lawyer (a lawyer with a reputation for being very aggressive) should be avoided at all costs. Lawyers who are well known are very busy and very expensive. The bigger the reputation, the bigger the fee. Lawyers have just so many hours of their time to sell. The more people who want that time, the more the lawyer will charge per hour. Here are some of the issues you should think about.

GENERALIST OR SPECIALIST?

Whether or not you need a specialist depends on the complexity of your finances. A lawyer who does a lot of divorce work as part of a general practice can usually do a fine job in a typical middle-class divorce. But the key issue is experience. Whether the lawyer specializes or not, you want someone who has extensive experience with divorce and who stays current on changes in the law. If your finances are complex and/or if you are wealthy, you will definitely want someone who specializes in divorce. But do not buy more lawyer than you need; it is just a waste of money.

LARGE OR SMALL FIRM?

Most divorce lawyers practice in small firms. Divorce, unlike corporate litigation, does not require a large supporting cast. Many large firms have added a matrimonial department, but most divorcing people are represented by firms having ten lawyers or less. Most of the top guns in this field practice in small firms of just two or three lawyers. This is one area of law where there is no advantage to the large firm. Large corporate firms are likely to be very expensive and will use junior associates and paralegals to do much of the routine work. Thus, size of the firm should not be regarded as an important factor.

MALE OR FEMALE?

Many clients want to know if male lawyers are more sympathetic to men while women lawyers are more sympathetic to women. There are certainly some chauvinistic lawyers on the scene who have no understanding of family life. The insensitive lawyer should be avoided by both men and women. I have not found that the sex of the lawyer makes an identifiable difference in the outcome. I have heard women bitterly complain about their female lawyers as often as I have heard men complain about their male lawyers. You want a lawyer with the experience, skill, and sensitivity to meet your needs. When you find that lawyer, hire him or her.

WHAT TO DO WHEN YOU ARE UNHAPPY WITH YOUR LAWYER

Dissatisfaction with divorce lawyers is a common complaint of clients. In many cases it is caused by poor communication. Divorcing people want to be able to reach their attorneys, but busy lawyers may take a day or more to return your call. When you hire your lawyer, you should ask how long it takes to get your call returned. If a lawyer is in the middle of a trial, it is simply impossible for him or her to return your call promptly. However, your lawyer may also be overworked and unable to give you enough time. A second communication problem arises when the lawyer is too impatient to fully explain concepts and problems. "Just trust me—I know what I'm doing," is not the answer you want to hear. This is *your* divorce and you need to understand all issues thoroughly.

Not all client unhappiness with lawyers is the fault of the lawyer. You may have unrealistic expectations of your attorney. An anxious client who needs daily reassurance can be a genuine tribulation to a lawyer. Competent lawyers are busy and cannot always get back to you within an hour. Some clients regard every call as urgent, even when the answer can wait. Be reasonable in your expectations, but insist that your reasonable expectations are met.

Sometimes attorneys and clients have personality conflicts. It's unfortunate, but it happens. Do not stay silent if you are chronically unhappy with your lawyer. A good working relationship is too important. Overcome your embarrassment and tell the attorney exactly how you feel, as soon as possible. In some cases the problem may just be a misunderstanding and easily resolved. But in other cases, a change should be made.

In fact, if you are unhappy, chances are good that your attorney is also unhappy with the relationship. If you cannot repair a damaged attorney-client relationship, end it. Your attorney will be just as relieved as you are. If there is an outstanding balance due your attorney, you will be expected to pay it. If part of your retainer is unused, it should be returned to you promptly. Your file should be handed over to you in good shape, ready for another attorney to take it over and continue.

CHOOSING A MEDIATOR

Finding a good mediator may be more difficult than finding a good lawyer because mediation is relatively new. Some states have state organizations (e.g., New York, New Jersey, California, Minnesota, and Michigan). Other states have court-connected mediation programs, although in many of these the mediator is limited to custody issues. Because the divorce-mediation movement is only about fifteen years old, it is not yet fully established. Only a few states require mediators to be licensed.

There are several places you can look. First, ask among those you know. Mental-health agencies and family therapists are a likely source of referrals. In many areas, divorce-mediation services are listed in the yellow pages. The American Arbitration Association maintains a list of divorce mediators, as does the Academy of Family Mediators.[12] If there is an association of mediators in your state, it will be listed in the phone book. Using all these sources, you should be able to come up with a list of mediators to interview.

The most important consideration is experience. Because mediation is relatively new, it has many new practitioners. In your initial phone call ask how long the professional has been mediating and how many divorces he or she has mediated to a conclusion. Ask for the names of lawyers who have advised clients mediated by this person—and check the references. Ask what training this person has had. Find out who trained the mediator and who supervised him or her. Check out the sources. For the most part, this can be done over the phone.

Most mediators are either therapists or lawyers. Generally the therapists have superior skills dealing with the emotional obstacles to settlement, whereas lawyers have superior technical knowledge. If the divorce involves a complex mix of assets, use a lawyer-mediator. If the asset and income structures are simple, a well-trained therapist-mediator is probably better. But these are generalizations, and you may find a good mediator who does not fit this pattern. Some mediators work in co-mediation teams of lawyer-therapist. This is a rather expensive alternative and in my opinion creates too complex a set of relationships.

Ultimately, competence is everything. Mediation is a demanding craft. There are plenty of good mediators out there. Stay with it and you'll find one.

WHAT TO DO WHEN YOU ARE UNHAPPY WITH YOUR MEDIATOR

If you have begun mediation and are unhappy with the mediator, you should deal promptly with the problem. Sometimes it is a simple problem of "chemistry" between you and the mediator, in which case change to another mediator is in order. You should discuss this with your spouse, as such a change requires cooperation. Your unhappiness with the mediator can also reflect an unhappiness with mediation. You may want to discuss this openly with the mediator. You may have expectations of mediation or of the mediator that are just unrealistic. If this is true and cannot be worked out, terminate mediation and have your lawyers negotiate for you.

FEES AND RETAINERS

Divorce lawyers usually charge by the hour for their services. Depending on where you live, you can expect to pay anywhere from $75 per hour in the rural Midwest to $250 per hour in the Northeast and California. Very few lawyers will offer a fixed fee for your divorce. If there is a simple agreement to draft and all the lawyers need do is put an uncontested matter through the court, a nominal fee may be agreed upon. Most lawyers ask for a *retainer* in the beginning. The retainer is a prepayment against which the attorney will bill at the agreed-upon hourly rate. Like fees, retainers vary greatly. One lawyer may ask for $500, another for $10,000. It depends on the lawyer you choose and where she or he practices. When the retainer has been used up, most lawyers will bill on a monthly basis and expect payment to be kept current. Divorce clients are notorious for not paying fees. If you anticipate problems staying current, you should discuss this early on and not wait until the retainer runs out. If you expect that your spouse will pay your fees, let your lawyer know early on, as this may not be acceptable to the lawyer. Misunderstandings about fees can sour an otherwise good relationship between lawyer and client, and care should be taken to insure mutual expectations.

All the expenses you will be expected to pay should be identified in a written retainer agreement. You should find out in advance whether your attorney charges you for the time of his secretary and paralegal or whether he absorbs that as part of his overhead. Typically, you will be expected to pay for all the lawyer's time, including travel time, waiting time, phone calls, and correspondence. You will pay all costs of depositions, postage, and copying. Any experts hired will be paid for by you. Most lawyers expect these costs to be paid currently and promptly. Be sure to find out whether the unused part of your retainer is refundable if you decide to change lawyers. Some lawyers treat the retainer as nonrefundable. Find out before you sign the retainer agreement.

In general, the more the lawyer has to do, the larger the fee. If the matter is to be litigated, there really is no limit. A complex, contested divorce can represent more than 100 hours of a lawyer's time. At $200 per hour the fee can easily exceed $20,000 on *each side*. Contingency fees are generally not used in divorce cases.

The antidote to runaway legal fees is for you to keep control of the process and minimize the role of your attorneys. If you are a typical middle class couple and have a non-litigated, lawyer-negotiated divorce, your lawyers will probably spend between 15 and 30 hours each on your case, including time spent with you, correspondence, phone calls, document preparation and court time for a final hearing. If you have a mediated divorce, that time should be reduced by one-half to two-thirds.

Mediators' fees generally range between $75 and $250 an hour depending on where you are and on whether the mediator is a lawyer or a therapist. Lawyers generally charge more per hour than do therapists. The hourly rate in mediation should not decide who you use. That decision should be based on the qualifications, experience, and reputation of the mediator. On average, mediation of the typical middle-class divorce should require between six and twelve hours. So even if you use a mediator who bills $250 an hour, total costs for mediation services should be less than $3,000.

OTHER EXPENSES AND OTHER PROFESSIONALS

Depending on the size of the marital estate, a number of other professionals may be involved. When custody and visitation are at issue, or if the children are having problems that you disagree about, mental-health professionals—psychologists, psychiatrists, and/or social workers—may be involved. Accountants may be required to audit a business or professional practice. Pensions, real estate, businesses, and assets such as artwork and jewelry will have to be appraised.

All these experts are relevant to the discovery process—but be careful. In a full-fledged adversary divorce, the costs of discovery can soar. Some lawyers use exaggerated discovery to wear down the other side. For each different type of asset, two experts, one for each side, are often retained. Sometimes after hearing the two opposing experts contradict each other, a judge may appoint yet a third expert to testify as a neutral. If you get into his, hers, and theirs experts in an adversary divorce, you are in for astounding legal fees. Just how much discovery is needed is always a judgment call, but there certainly are lawyers out there who use discovery to build up their fees. You should discuss this very carefully with your attorney.

In the amicable negotiated divorce you can control discovery costs by carefully choosing neutral experts. Experts tend to get swept up in the adversary process. For example, an appraiser can vary the method, thus varying the result. Consequently, if the husband has a professional practice, one might expect the appraiser hired by the husband's lawyer to give the practice a much lower value than would the wife's appraiser. In litigated divorces, a frustrated judge will often, upon hearing two radically different expert opinions of value, appoint a third appraiser to function on behalf of the court. When this happens, it is very costly.

My preference is to choose *one* neutral expert. The appraiser or accountant is instructed to call the value or result as it truly is and not to tilt in either direction. If you choose competent professionals, the results will be much less exaggerated and will prove much less costly. This is something to discuss with your lawyer upon the initial interview. It is a *very important* detail.

CONCLUSION

The decisions you make about your role in the divorce and about who will help you negotiate are the foundation for your divorce. The rest of the divorce process and the final settlement agreement will depend on how wisely you choose.

There is no substitute for the work *you* must do to manage your divorce. You must gather information, interview attorneys and mediators, and make decisions. Making sure that your key advisers will support your choice of divorce style, will explain what you need to know, and will be reasonably available is vital to making sure that your divorce is what *you* want it to be.

Part Two

NEGOTIATING YOUR AGREEMENT

Chapter Eight

NEGOTIATING WITH YOUR SPOUSE

CASE HISTORY: TOM AND LINDA

Tom and Linda have been trying to negotiate part of their settlement, but they keep getting into a fight. The bone of contention is Tom's insistence that Linda agree to sell their house, something Linda finds unthinkable.

"How can you be so callous about the children? Don't you care about their feelings at all? It's bad enough that you've destroyed the family. Now you want to take away their home, too!"

Tom has heard this before, but it infuriates him just the same. "You know damn well there was no point in staying married anymore. I'm sick of your always blaming me for everything! The only equity we have is in the house. If we don't sell it, I'll never be able to have a decent place to live, and I'm not going to live in some crummy apartment just because you're so damn stupid!"

Tom and Linda despair of ever reaching agreement. Although they are capable of doing so, the way they are going about it is working against them. However, a few simple negotiating techniques can help them overcome the human tendency to express their anger in a manner that defeats them instead of helping.

FOUR STEPS TO SUCCESSFUL NEGOTIATING

First, they must stop attacking each other. Each time one attacks, they get further away from agreement and further away from their goals. Instead of attacking each other, Tom and Linda must jointly attack the problems they face.

Second, they must define their problem by identifying their interests. Linda wants to stay in the house until the children have finished high school. She doesn't want to move because she finds moving too upsetting and because she fears it will be too stressful for the kids. It is in her interest to stay in the house for now. It is also in her interest to get Tom to agree.

Tom wants a nice place to live. Otherwise, he fears that the kids won't want to spend time with him. Besides, he's always owned a house and wants to own another.

After identifying their individual interests, Linda and Tom are able to restate their problem: How can they provide housing for all family members in a way that avoids disruption and satisfies each parent's need to live in a house?

Third, they need to identify all the options that might solve their problem. Until now, they have been struggling over just one option—selling the house. Are there any others?

- Is there anyone in Linda's family who might buy all or part of Tom's interest in the house?
- Can they afford to refinance the house to free up enough capital so that Tom can buy a house?
- Does Tom really need to buy a house to have what he wants?
- Are there any houses Tom could rent that would meet his housing needs?
- How many years does Linda really need before she moves?

If the house were sold in three years, would that be enough time for everyone to adjust to the change?

- Could Tom accept living in an apartment for three years if he knew that he could buy a house at the end of that time?

Having identified their options, Tom and Linda can now investigate each one and gather the facts. They can't find a relative to buy out Tom's interest in the house. But they calculate their budgets and decide that they could afford to borrow against the equity in the house so that Tom can buy a small house of his own. Linda agrees to do that if Tom wishes. However, in the course of investigating all the options, Tom discovers a nice house for rent in the neighborhood he wants and concludes that it would actually cost him less to rent it than to buy it.

Tom can get a three-year lease, so he proposes to rent the house for three years. The couple agree that in six years, when their youngest child graduates high school, they will sell the family home. They also agree to discuss the matter three years from now to see if it makes sense to sell the house earlier, when their older child graduates. Tom and Linda have finally settled their previously unsolvable problem by using the fourth negotiating technique: finding a mutually satisfying solution to their problem. This part of their divorce is now settled.

THE FOUR STEPS TO SUCCESSFUL NEGOTIATIONS

1. Attack problems, not people.
2. Define the problem by identifying interests.
3. Identify all the options.
4. Find mutually satisfying solutions to problems.

(Suggestion: There are numerous books on the market that teach you how to negotiate. In my opinion, the easiest and quickest to read is *Getting to Yes* by Roger Fisher and William Ury of the Harvard Negotiation Project, Penguin Books, 1981. This now classic guide can be read in a single evening and may change how you negotiate not only this agreement but all other agreements as well.)

THE PARADOX OF DIVORCE NEGOTIATIONS

Negotiating well with your spouse requires that you behave in a way that contradicts how you feel. You feel angry, distrustful, resentful, and bitter. These feelings prompt personal attacks, blaming, ridiculing, and recriminating—behavior that drives your spouse away from the negotiation and reduces your chance for a satisfactory settlement. So the challenge is to create a setting that acknowledges how you both feel but also makes it possible for you to engage in creative problem solving.

There is an important difference between an *agreement* and a *contract*. Negotiating a contract is not enough. We know this because half of all couples with divorce contracts are back in court within two years. If you have to go to court to enforce your contract, it means you did not negotiate successfully. What you seek is *agreement,* and it is the quality of the agreement that will measure whether you succeeded. At best, a contract is a written reflection of what you agreed. If you are in genuine agreement it means that both of you will abide by the terms voluntarily because you regard the agreement as honorable and fair. Remember, people, not contracts, perform. There are innumerable ways to sabotage contracts. When you are done negotiating, you want to rely on each other to perform as promised. You do not want to rely on the courts.

Concentrating on agreement helps you distinguish between behavior that promotes it and behavior that retards it. Many popular notions about hard-nosed aggressive bargaining are based on the idea of beating an opponent into submission. But submission is not your objective. Agreement means that you and the other person share the same viewpoint on what is to be done, that you are both committed to that viewpoint, and, for our purposes, that you both regard it as *fair*. You cannot negotiate your spouse into submission and expect the agreement to survive.

But how can you cooperate with this person toward whom you don't feel cooperative? And how do you trust this person you no longer regard as trustworthy?

The answer is to concentrate on behavior rather than feelings or attitudes. You have little control over what you feel. However, you are capable of controlling your behavior in the right setting. So our task is to identify which behaviors help and which hurt, and then to create the setting that fosters useful negotiations.

SELF-DEFEATING BEHAVIOR

There are five kinds of behavior that are always self-defeating in divorce negotiation, because they aim at submission rather than agreement.

- Threatening and intimidating
  "If you don't agree to this, I'm going to hire the most vicious lawyer I can find and take you for everything you have."
- Trying to shame or blame
  "If you weren't such a dishonest person, you wouldn't have lied to me about that affair. You can't be trusted about anything."
- Acting helpless and passive
  "This divorce is not my idea. If you want it, you figure out how to afford it."
- Cutting off communication

"I can't stand talking to you anymore—from now on, let the lawyers do it."
- Personal attacks
  "You've always been self-centered and selfish, and that's why you're so uncooperative now."

All of these statements reflect feelings that, when translated into words, make it harder to agree. They are to be avoided. On the other hand, you can't ignore how you feel. It is difficult to sit on all those hot feelings in the presence of your spouse.

BEHAVIOR THAT PROMOTES GOOD NEGOTIATION

- Planning for your negotiation. You can't "wing it" in negotiation. Good negotiation requires preparation and planning. Planning consists of several components.
- First is gathering information. You will be working from a planned agenda, and each agenda item requires its own information. Support issues require budgeting. Property issues require appraisal and documentation of assets. So, part of your preparation for each negotiation session means having on hand the facts necessary for discussion and resolution. If you are going to negotiate about the house, you should have current mortgage statements, a current appraisal, heating and maintenance bills for the past year or two, and current tax statements.

You and your spouse must reduce the possible scope of things to argue about. The less you have to speculate about how much is owed or how much something costs, the less you will have to resolve. So do your homework and get the facts. If your spouse was supposed to get something and forgot or is dragging and you are in a position to obtain the information, go ahead and get it. What matters is the information, not who gets it.

- The second aspect of planning is anticipating the possible ways you can resolve the issues. Those become apparent when you need to analyze your needs and your spouse's needs.
- Listen and be heard.

The hardest part of negotiating your divorce agreement is being heard by your spouse. When marriages break down, the ability to communicate is among the first casualties. Getting the sympathetic ear of your spouse is not easy. In fact, each of you is poised to try to overpower the other whenever you start to hear something you don't like. This strategy works no better in the divorce than it did in the marriage. Thus we have another paradox: The only way to be heard is to listen.

Think about it. What makes it hard for you to listen to your spouse probably is your own frustration at not being heard yourself. While she or he is talking, you are either fuming or thinking about what you want to say next. What you are *not* doing is listening. When you finally get your chance to talk you can't respond to what your spouse just said because you're too angry—and because you never heard it in the first place. Your spouse is doing the same thing, so both of you are equally frustrated.

The only person's behavior you can control is your own. Therefore, your *only* chance to break the communication deadlock is to do the part that you can do without your spouse's cooperation. You can listen.

Listening doesn't just mean staying silent while the other talks. Listening is active. Listening is straining to hear everything that is said and to *understand* the meaning of it. Thus, as Linda tells Tom that the cost of moving is higher than the cost of staying in the house, he needs to hear both the economic information she is imparting and the emotional content behind it. Tom needs to hear her fear of moving and her fear of economic shortfall. To hear Linda's problem does not mean Tom has to agree, nor does it mean he has to fix it. It only means that he has heard it, and Linda won't have to keep telling him the same thing. Once she knows he has really heard and understood, she can move on. Or if Tom is talking about his inability to pay more support, Linda must listen to his worry that he won't have enough, that his bonus may not come through, or that he could lose his job. None of these things mean he shouldn't pay more support, but they reflect real risks that both Tom and Linda must understand.

Listening can be communicated. One way to let your spouse know that you heard is to repeat or briefly summarize what he or she said: "If I understand what you said, you feel that if you pay more alimony you won't be able to afford a two-bedroom apartment. Is that right?" You can also provide what might be called supportive murmurings—uh-huh, etc. Maintain eye contact, nod your head to show that you are listening, and visibly demonstrate that you are paying attention. Don't interrupt and don't contradict. Don't argue, just listen. If you do this long enough, even the toughest negotiating partner must eventually finish talking. I have had negotiations in which I have sat back and listened while my counterpart talked nonstop for over an hour. But eventually, even these verbal marathoners wear out. If you have listened, it will now be your turn to talk and be heard.

What I am suggesting here is the opposite of what you are used to doing. You should listen to your spouse because you need to hear what she or he is saying and because you need your spouse to listen to what you have to say.

Support Conciliatory Gestures

Few things are more discouraging in divorce negotiation than to concede something your spouse seeks but get no acknowledgement for it. You feel that no matter what you give, the only thing you get back is anger. It may seem ironic, but just because you are getting divorced doesn't mean that you don't continue to seek affirmation from each other. It is in your interest to provide encouraging reinforcement when your spouse agrees with you because it makes him or her more likely to agree again on another item.

If you behave as if you have just achieved a victory, you also communicate that your spouse has just been defeated. If you behave as if you were entitled all along, you communicate that he or she only agreed to what was already obligatory. In either case, you lose an opportunity to gain more cooperation. Remember, how you feel is not how you have to behave. You may feel entitled to what was just agreed, but you should behave graciously. "I'm really encouraged by what we just agreed. I think you're being very fair," costs you nothing and gets you more.

Attack Problems, Not Each Other

All the issues of your divorce can be stated in two ways: as problems to be solved or as battles to be won. In battle you defeat the other person. If one wins, the other loses. On the other hand, when you solve problems, you both benefit. Tom and Linda solved their problem by using family resources efficiently to finance two households. The agreement you seek must be voluntary if it is to last. It cannot consist of victories in battle; it can only be a set of solutions to problems. There are no divorce issues that cannot be restated as problems.

TOM: "You wanted the divorce, why should I pay alimony? I don't want to have to pay you anything!

LINDA: "I understand that the thought of alimony makes you feel bad. But the problem is that I need enough to live decently, and my salary alone isn't enough."

TOM: "Well, you should have thought of that before you decided to leave me!"

LINDA: "I did think a lot before I decided on the divorce, and it was a difficult decision. But now the problem is to work out a fair settlement. Do you have any thoughts about how we should do that?

TOM: "It's not my problem. It's your problem because it's your fault!"

LINDA: "But isn't it our problem if we can't negotiate a resolution ourselves and have to fight in court? How do we solve the problem of negotiating a settlement if the problem doesn't belong to both of us?"

TOM: "I don't want to fight, either, but I'm not happy about this alimony thing."

LINDA: "I know you're not. Should we review our budgets now?"

What is happening here is that Linda continues to bring Tom back to the problem, even though he tries to distract her by repeating the same accusations and attempting to evade responsibility. She could just as easily respond by attacking back. ("If you hadn't been so insensitive and uncommunicative, I wouldn't have had to leave you.")

She might feel better, but she would have taken them further from their goal.

Even in the face of provocation she *chooses* to restate each issue as a problem. When he continues to evade, she offers as a problem the task of reaching an amicable settlement instead of fighting it out in court. By choosing this path she repeatedly brings him back to the task. In most cases, sooner or later he will drop the attack and join her in the task.

Of course, negotiation moves much faster when both of you approach it as a no-fault, problem-solving task. But even then there will be moments when each of you backslides. When that happens, the other must restate the issue as a problem and keep the discussion moving.

Don't Take the Bait

It is unrealistic to expect divorcing spouses to go through an entire negotiation process without some outbursts of anger and resentment. These are inevitably experienced as attacks. Sometimes, it's a comment on the other's character. ("You're a liar! You know that's a lie!" "You're so selfish I can't stand talking to you!") Or the attack recites some historical fact about the marriage. ("You were never willing to do your share. I always had to do everything myself.") Sometimes your spouse will attack, and sometimes you will attack. Invariably what you hear is something you have heard many times before. There is something almost perversely comforting about the predictability with which divorcing couples thrust and parry with the same exchange of tired accusations.

When attacked, don't respond in kind. Only you can break the cycle. Don't rise like a fish to the bait. Pass it by and keep negotiating. When it becomes clear that you can't be hooked, your spouse will eventually return to work.

Attacking your spouse is something you do to distract you when you get uncomfortable. It not only helps you let off steam, it also changes the subject. But you have an agenda, and you should stick to it. Each time you decide not to take the bait, you reiterate your determination to negotiate in good faith and finish your agreement. This has a powerful impact on your spouse and will keep him or her at the table.

Explore Alternatives

Inevitably there will be disagreements. You need a method for resolving disagreements without getting stuck at an impasse. To avoid impasse, generate more alternatives until you both find one you can accept. By definition, an impasse exists when the two of you have only two alternatives. You are each committed to your own, reject the other's and are, therefore, stuck.

LINDA: "I have to have the children with me every Thanksgiving. It's a tradition in my family and I won't give it up!"

TOM: "I'm willing to alternate, but I'm not willing to let you have them every Thanksgiving. It's not fair."

Are there any alternatives here? Would it be acceptable if she had them every Thanksgiving and he had them every Christmas? Would it be acceptable if they agreed that she have them the first two Thanksgivings and he have them the third? Is it possible that her family might celebrate Thanksgiving the night before on alternate years? On every third year? Somewhere in here is a solution they can both accept.

Such alternatives exist for nearly every issue. Sometimes to find alternatives you have to look at other issues. Usually there is more than one issue on which you are stuck. Is there any way to pair or combine outcomes on several issues to create a package you can both accept? The important point is that you don't accept being stuck. Just keep generating options.

Acknowledge Convergent Interests

I often see couples who have been locked in litigation for a long time and who feel hopelessly stuck. They come into mediation because they can't afford to continue the battle but can't come to agreement. The most surprising discovery they often make is that they are 95 percent in agreement and only 5 percent in disagreement—but didn't know it. Once they see the larger picture, they are often able to let go and settle the dispute. The reason they were unaware of this before has to do with our tendency to focus on our divergent interests rather than our convergent interests. We concentrate on our disagreements, even when they are less important, and they overshadow our agreements.

When you and your spouse feel stuck on a point of disagreement, review the things on which you do agree. I recently worked with a couple who were in almost violent disagreement over dividing the household furniture. Both of them presented this as an acute issue because the husband was in the process of moving out of the house and didn't know what to take with him. They both defined themselves as completely deadlocked and worried. I reviewed their other assets with them. Had they discussed them yet? I asked. "No, we haven't been able to get past this one, so there is no point in talking about the others."

It turned out that they had almost a million dollars in marital assets. It also turned out, after half an hour of discussion, that they were essentially in agreement on how to divide all the other assets. The value of what was in dispute was about twenty thousand dollars, less than 3 percent of the marital estate. Redefining the dispute—from a great deadlock to one that was relatively minor, compared to the assets as a whole—made it much easier to agree.

The husband suggested that the wife keep the furniture that was most important to her, and where there was a great disparity in value between what each would keep, that she pay him some money as compensation. Once they realized how close to an overall agreement they really were, they were able to finalize it quickly.

Identify Your Interests

Identifying your interests is not simply deciding what you want. It means understanding your real needs *over time*. For example, your needs as a parent must be understood in the context of the life you will lead as a single parent. How much free time do you really need? How often do you need your spouse to take the kids so you can get other things done? What are your real needs for housing? Do you feel you must stay in the house or are you hanging on because you're afraid of change and disruption?

Chances are good that what you first thought were your interests had a lot to do with your desire to maintain the status quo. If you are not the initiator of the divorce, this is particularly likely. Once you accept that change is necessary and that you need to shape that change, your sense of your interests may change dramatically.

Identify Your Spouse's Interests

You can safely assume that your spouse has similar problems identifying his or her own interests. It is useful to try and understand what he or she really needs out of the negotiation. This discipline will help you develop creative options when you disagree. I recall a wife who was trying to get her husband to negotiate in good faith. The husband, who was strongly against the divorce, was unable to negotiate about the marital property because he defined everything that his wife would get as a loss for himself.

The case was resolved only after the wife made a list in which she identified his priorities from both an emotional and economic perspective. As a fireman with long service, he had a large pension that was the most important asset to him—and the one he was the most emotional about. There were also some lesser assets—such as his boat—that had little economic value but great emotional value. The wife crafted a proposal that divided the assets with an eye toward giving him every emotional "win" she could without creating an agreement unfair to her. This proposal broke the impasse and led to an excellent and rapid settlement.

Think Future, Not Past

Divorcing couples have a natural tendency to justify their demands by referring to their past history. ("I took care of the children all those years, I deserve more." "I slaved in the office all those years, I deserve more!") Such exchanges rarely produce agreement because they tap the same well of disagreement that produced the divorce.

Instead of looking to the past to support your arguments, look to the future. First, your future is uncontaminated by your marriage. You do not have to reconcile two fatally different versions of history. Second, your needs exist in the future, not in the past. What is it that will happen in the future that will change your needs? What benchmarks in your children's lives will make your life easier, harder, simpler, or more complicated? How will your choices change when your child starts school full time, no longer needs a babysitter after school, graduates high school, graduates college? How will these events change your need for income or housing or free time? Do any of these events signal the end of a particular problem for you or your spouse? Do any of the problems you are wrestling with have time limits, or do they go on forever?

Many couples lose this time perspective. They are so anxious about the present that they lose the ability to solve some readily solvable problems. Many of the problems you must solve last only a few years. Solutions can be crafted that take time into account. It is easier to solve small problems than big ones.

A careful consideration of the future creates a much better environment for problem solving.

CREATING THE SETTING FOR NEGOTIATION

The emotional trauma of divorce at times can overwhelm the most enlightened and best-intentioned people. Understanding what behaviors promote negotiation provides a partial solution to reaching agreement. The remainder of the solution comes with creating a negotiating setting in which you feel safe and which doesn't make unreasonable demands on two people with short fuses. You must select a place that makes sense, a time that works, and an agenda that you can handle. All of these things are realistic adaptations to the emotional realities of divorce.

CHOOSING A PLACE TO MEET

You should choose a neutral location for your negotiation sessions that is comfortable and free of distractions. A mutual friend may have a conference room in an office that you can use, or your mediator may provide the setting. Do not try to negotiate at home with the kids upstairs. If you are both still living in the same house, you might try to negotiate there when no one else is home, but it would be preferable to use a conference room elsewhere.

Choosing a neutral ground begins the process of equalizing your negotiation. Having a place to go imparts a businesslike atmosphere and underscores the purpose of your meeting. You want to create a little formality in order to screen out some of the distractions that arise from your intimate, but damaged, relationship.

CHOOSING THE TIME TO MEET

A comprehensive divorce agreement usually cannot be negotiated in one or two sessions. It will probably take not less than six sessions and as many as twenty to resolve all the issues of your agreement. Part of each session will be spent planning the next session, and part will be spent handling the mechanics of information exchange.

In mediation I find that the average divorce requires from six to twelve sessions, depending on the complexity of the issues and the style of the couple. Most people negotiate their agreement over a two- to six-month period. If you are in a hurry, slow down. Hurrying creates pressure, which creates resistance, which begets litigation. If you can craft a fair and workable agreement in four or five months, you will have gone *very fast.*

Realistic time expectations are important so that you don't unwittingly sabotage a successful negotiation process. Each of you needs time between sessions to reflect and decide. Rushing the other is invariably perceived as pressure and intimidation, and it slows progress. Each of you is also engaged in a learning process, and learning new information, particularly emotionally difficult information, takes time. In the course of the negotiation both of you will change your viewpoint on numerous issues, and that takes time as well. So drop your insistence on resolution in two or three weeks. It doesn't happen that way.

All negotiation sessions should have an agreed time for beginning and an agreed time to end. In special circumstances you may mutually decide to extend or to end a session early, but in principle, time should be specified. Your early sessions should be scheduled for a maximum of an hour and a half. After the first few sessions, you may plan for two-hour meetings if you have found the need for more time and can use the time fruitfully.

There are several reasons to limit the sessions. First, divorce negotiation is tiring and wearing. The topics are difficult and evoke painful feelings. It is not helpful to keep going to the point of exhaustion. I know that some negotiators believe people are more prone to make concessions when they are tired. That may be okay for union negotiations, but it's a bad idea for divorce negotiations. Remember, we are seeking affirmative agreements, not begrudging concessions. Agreements reached in a desperate attempt to have it over with tend to fall apart after a little rest and reflection.

The second reason to limit sessions is that each session will have only one or two topics on the agenda. Remember, you are going to do this in pieces. You do not need three-hour sessions, and you will have difficulty using lengthy ones constructively.

Finally, open-ended sessions invariably end only when you get stuck or discouraged. We want to try ending sessions on a positive note and to avoid unpleasant endings.

Plan your sessions about a week apart. If you are waiting for important information that won't be ready for two weeks, adjust the schedule accordingly. I suggest that you schedule at least two sessions ahead. That way, if you have a bad session, you don't have to struggle about deciding when the next one will be.

DEVELOPING THE AGENDA

Each meeting should have an agreed agenda. At the end of each meeting you should plan the agenda for the next one. With the exception of emergencies, the only topics discussed should be those you agreed last time would be on the present agenda. This is important. Most of the topics—parenting, support issues and property issues—require considerable reflection and, in many cases, preparation and research.

You should not attempt to solve a problem until each of you is ready. If you raise an issue on which your spouse is unprepared, not only do you distract from the scheduled agenda, you also create an unnecessary threat to your spouse. Agreeing on an agenda and *sticking to it* is part of your effort to create a safe atmosphere for negotiation.

. . .

The recommended order for the issues of divorce is:

1. Parenting: Custody and visitation agreements including agreement on decision making and on a precise schedule of time you will each spend with the children.
2. Child Support: Agreement on monthly child support, usually based on budgets you each have prepared.
3. Spousal support: (alimony or maintenance) If alimony is an issue in your divorce.
4. Division of the marital property.

Each issue will produce its own agenda. Each will require you to gather and exchange information, and this fact-gathering process must be integrated into an agenda for each meeting. The last ten minutes of each meeting should be reserved for planning the agenda of the next meeting. Only emergencies should be permitted to distract you from the day's agenda.

There is no formula for determining how much time you need for each topic. It depends on your particular pattern of agreement and disagreement. Some people can resolve parenting issues in one or two meetings. Others will need four or five to accomplish the same thing. No matter how long it takes you, be assured that you will get it done much faster this way than you will in court.

USING PROFESSIONAL HELP

It is unrealistic to expect most divorcing couples to do all their negotiating without help. There are too many opportunities for distraction, too many strong emotions, and too many complexities to do it all by yourselves. But use only as much help as you need. The more others play a role, the less it becomes your agreement. Settlements hammered out by surrogates have a much higher failure rate than agreements reached by the principals. You should aim to get just enough help and not a bit more.

Essentially, you need three kinds of help.

INFORMATION

You need information that helps you define your interests and your problems with greater precision.

First, you need to know what your assets are worth. If you don't or if you don't agree, choose neutral appraisers. Each type of asset will require its own appraisers. Real estate appraisers, art appraisers, and business valuation experts should be consulted when indicated.

Second, you need information on the financial consequences of various alternatives. Accountants can be of great help in minimizing the tax consequences of certain decisions. Financial planners can be useful in exploring investment strategies you could follow with your share of the assets. There is also nonfinancial information that you may need such as psychological advice on the impact of your parenting arrangements on your children.

ADVICE AND STRATEGY

Each of you may need assistance in formulating your negotiating positions and strategies. This is when your lawyers can be most helpful. Lawyers can provide information about "industry standards" in your local area. They can help you understand what might happen if you fail to reach agreement and have to submit the issue to a court. Although these prognostications are not always accurate, they can help you get a sense of what is a reasonable position. Lawyers can provide you with information about child-support guidelines and how they are interpreted in your state. They can also explain the law to you as it applies to distribution of marital property and what property is subject to distribution. If appraisals are necessary, your lawyer can advise you on the selection of appraisers. The lawyer may also be helpful in suggesting compromises to break impasses.

NEGOTIATION ASSISTANCE

Private face-to-face negotiation between you and your spouse, although preferred, may be too difficult. You may find that the strong feelings you each have interfere with your task and distract you from it. You may have problems controlling your anger, staying on the subject without digression, or being able to listen to each other. When this occurs, you need third-party assistance to keep the negotiation moving. This can be provided either by your lawyers or by a mediator. A mediator is a less intrusive form of assistance than your two lawyers and should probably be regarded as the preferred form of assistance. Mediation keeps the focus on both of you and keeps *you* as the negotiators. Using the lawyers may lead to a loss of control. The other disadvantage of using the lawyers as negotiators is that it is almost impossible to schedule one meeting a week for five or six weeks for negotiating. Lawyers want to finish in one or two sessions and will bring great pressure to bear on both of you to wrap it up, even if you are not quite ready.

BREAKING IMPASSES

Sometimes negotiators get stuck and just can't agree. When this happens, it takes extra effort to keep the negotiation from breaking down altogether. There are a number of things you can do to break an impasse:

Table the issue and move on to another topic. Unless you are at the end of the negotiation, there are probably other unsettled issues on which you can work. If you find yourselves going in circles on some particular issue, set it aside for a while. Decide to come back to it next week and move to the next thing on the agenda. This accomplishes several things:

First, it gets you back into constructive discussion on things on which you can agree and helps restore the optimism that gets lost as soon as you feel you are at an impasse. Second, as you accumulate agreements on other issues, it may reduce the relative significance of the issue on which you are stuck. Finally, progress on other issues may jar loose whatever was keeping you stuck. For example, if you are at an impasse on support, resolution of the property issues may change the premise of the support discussions, or alternatives that were not apparent before may become apparent now. The important thing is to continue negotiating. If you stop, you stay stuck.

Let time work for you. Frequently, when couples get stuck, it is because one spouse has not had enough time to reflect on an issue. I recall a case in which the couple was stuck on the matter of sharing the husband's pension. The husband, a policeman, had worked for twenty years to accumulate what was a very substantial pension entitlement. When his wife initiated the divorce, he was taken by surprise. He was also incensed to learn that under New Jersey law his wife had a right to a share of the pension. He was so angry that he could not agree to share it at all. It took on-again off-again sessions over a six-month period for him to accept both the reality of the divorce and the reality that he had to negotiate about the pension. Once he reached that acceptance they were able to negotiate a relatively quick resolution.

What is an impasse today may not be an impasse tomorrow. You should be very reluctant to walk away from negotiation just because you're stuck on one issue. Analyze why you are stuck and ask whether time will help you or your spouse shift your positions and resolve the matter.

SUMMARY

All successful negotiations follow four basic steps:

- Attack problems, not people.
- Define the problem by identifying the interests of all parties involved.
- Identify *all* the options.
- Find solutions to the defined problems that satisfy all parties.

You and your spouse can increase your chances of success by adopting behavior that promotes good negotiation:

- Plan and prepare for your negotiation sessions.
- Work at listening to your spouse and at being heard in turn.
- Support conciliatory gestures.
- Attack problems, not each other.
- When attacked, do not respond in kind.
- Explore alternatives.
- Look for areas of mutual agreement instead of concentrating on areas of disagreement.
- Identify your own interests.
- Identify your spouse's interests.
- Look to the future, not to the past.

Your negotiation sessions should be planned. The location, the meeting times, and the agenda should all be prearranged. This formality reinforces the importance of what you are doing and will help you observe the "rules" you have established. It will help you through the process of negotiation, when feelings can run high. When you need experts, use them. Most people need help somewhere along the way.

Finally, do not despair if you reach an impasse. You may skip a difficult topic and come back to it later, when you have resolved other issues. You also have the option of waiting and letting time change the importance of the issue or, perhaps, your view of it. In any case, an impasse does not mean you have failed. It simply means you have not yet finished.

Chapter Nine

NEGOTIATING YOUR PARENTING AGREEMENT

The issues of custody and parenting are difficult to negotiate because the things that determine whether your children thrive after the divorce cannot be written into a contract. If a parent does not pay the agreed-upon child support, a judge can enforce the order with jail for the nonpaying parent, if necessary. But no judge can make you cooperate as parents. No court will stop you from the subtle acts of sabotage that ruin each other's relationship with the children or that recruit the children as your spear-carriers against each other. If a court cannot enforce it, there is no point in putting it in a contract.

For this reason, the discussion in this chapter will differ from those in chapters 11, 12, and 13, which discuss the negotiation of financial issues. In the pages of the present chapter, we shall deal with several topics that should be discussed and negotiated but that will not become part of your separation agreement. These topics relate to your ability to learn new roles as divorced parents. Before you separated you did not have to think very much about the parenting roles played by each of you. These were, for the most part, taken for granted. You did what you did, your spouse did whatever he/she did, and somehow you got by. But now that you are separating you no longer can assume that your spouse's parental role will complement yours. Neither can you assume that your children's need for parenting will be met. Your children are very vulnerable when you separate and need everything that they can get from you. Consequently, both of you need to reshape at least part of your parenting patterns to accommodate your new situation.

You have two sets of interrelated needs here. First is coping with your own life, and second is helping the other spouse be a successful parent. Your own work life and parental life, in large measure, will depend on how well the other parent copes. If he or she copes well and is a good parent, your job will be easier. On the other hand, if your spouse is overwhelmed, you will pay the price. How well you resolve the issues we examine next will largely shape how well you adapt in your new life.

CUSTODY VERSUS PARENTING

Custody is a legal concept that does not fit the tasks that have been assigned to it. As a legal concept, custody promotes a narrow view of legal rights to the children at the expense of a comprehensive view of family needs. For example, part of a custody agreement describes the visitation rights of the *noncustodial* parent. It may provide that the father has the right to have the child every other weekend. The enforceability of the contract lies with the court's ability to punish the mother if she interferes with the father's right of visitation.

But note carefully what this right does not include. It does not include any obligation of the father to exercise his right to alternate weekends with the child. If he chooses not to take the child for the weekend, neither the mother nor the child can successfully go to court to make the father do it. No court will order a parent to visit with the child against the parent's will. Nor would any parent or child want to drag an unwilling parent into contact with the child. On the other hand, we know that the psychological loss of a parent will cause the child to suffer. Can we somehow insure that the father stays engaged with his child?

The answer is yes, but not in your written contract. The answer to this and a hundred other questions that ultimately determine the quality of your child's life will be found only in your unwritten understanding and agreements. What you do to insure your legal rights to the child may fall within the scope of *custody,* but what you do to insure the welfare of that child falls within the concept of *parenting.* It is very easy, in the heat of divorce, to lose the distinction. Few lawyers are of much help to you here, and the legal system is not designed for the task. You will have to do it yourselves.

CASE STUDY: LAURA AND JOHN

Laura and John, divorcing after a twelve-year marriage, are struggling over decisions about their children. John initiated the divorce four months ago, after years of discord, but has not yet left the house. Like many divorcing fathers, John fears that if he leaves, he will be ceding control to Laura and will lose his children.

They have two children: a ten-year-old daughter and a seven-year-old son. Laura has just passed the bar exam and wants to get a job with a law firm as soon as things are settled. She worked as a paralegal when they first married, then took six years off to have the kids and be home while they were small. When their son began nursery school, she entered law school, and graduated a year ago. John, a stockbroker, commutes to work, leaving at 7 A.M. and getting home about 7 P.M.

John has told Laura that he wants joint custody and wants to have the children half the time. She refused to even consider the proposal. She raised the children and deferred her career while John pursued his. She feels she is entitled to the children. "I am their primary parent," she tells him. "You have always been secondary. How many times were you home with them when they were sick?" she challenges. "How many times did you take them to the doctor or to a piano lesson after school? You have never even been a half-time parent. What makes you think you can do it now?"

"The kids need two parents," retorts John. "I'm not going to be one of those fathers who only sees his kids a couple of times a month. I'm not going to let you shut me out of their lives! If you can't agree to what's fair, I'll fight you for custody if it takes the next two years."

One month later, after many conferences with their lawyers, they still can't agree. John wants fifty-fifty joint custody. Laura is willing to let John have the children on alternate weekends. He can pick them up Friday and bring them home Sunday night. He can even have them overnight one night during the week if he wants, but she insists that the children must live with her. She wants to be the sole custodial parent and doesn't believe joint custody will work. They are both adamant and tell their lawyers, "No more concessions."

THREE POSSIBILITIES

John and Laura, like you and your spouse, have three possible outcomes:

FIRST POSSIBILITY: COOPERATIVE PARENTING

With proper guidance, Laura and John can negotiate an arrangement that keeps them both fully engaged in the lives of their children. John is a motivated father. He has a lot to learn, because in the past Laura did everything for the kids. But he can learn new parenting skills, and given a little time, opportunity, and coaching, he can play a vital part in his children's lives.

Laura needs to rethink her position. She is about to start her legal career, and it will demand a lot of time and energy. To achieve professional success she will need John's cooperation and help with the kids. Right now she feels angry and possessive so she ridicules his assertion of parental involvement. It would be better for her, and for everyone else in the family, if she could express her anger at John in some way other than dismissing and ridiculing his desire to parent the kids.

Cooperative parenting for them would mean that they share parental responsibility according to their needs and capacities. It would mean that her need to develop a living pattern realistically related to her career would be respected as would John's need and ability to expand his role as a parent. It would be an arrangement designed to help them grow in new roles while meeting the needs of their children.

SECOND POSSIBILITY: A CUSTODY FIGHT

Laura and John are also capable of getting into a full-fledged custody fight. John's insistence on clinging to the house increases the bitterness between them day by day. Each angry exchange locks them deeper in conflict. John begins to feel that his only alternatives are to be shut out or to fight for custody in court. He recalls all the things Laura has done over the years that would prove she really isn't such a great mother after all. He consults with his lawyer, who tells him he has a 30 percent chance of winning a custody fight. During one of their disagreements John threatens Laura with a custody fight if she doesn't give in. Panicked, she calls her lawyer and tells him to stop negotiating and get tough.

If Laura and John go through a custody fight, they will so poison their relationship that anything resembling cooperation in the future will be very unlikely.

THIRD POSSIBILITY: CONCESSION

The third alternative is that they have neither a custody fight nor a cooperative parenting relationship. Instead, they reach a grudging compromise in which they avoid an all-out fight but accomplish little more. In the end, John gives up on the custody issue because he can't afford it or doesn't have the stomach for the fight. He surrenders on the joint custody issue because Laura is adamant. Over time he will accept the notion that his life with the kids can't be what he wants. Although he maintains a visitation schedule with the kids, his time with them is often tense and uncomfortable. He tries to make special plans, but the kids often seem bored and listless. He drives a hard bargain economically, and Laura ends up feeling financially strapped. Her long hours at work, coupled with her parenting obligations, make her feel strung out most of the time. She has exclusive custody and control of the kids, but she feels tired and unhappy.

RETHINKING CUSTODY

When most people think of custody issues in divorce they think of custody fights. But custody fights are atypical. Even those divorces that begin as custody fights eventually are settled. Only 3 percent of all divorces go to trial at all, and most of those do not involve custody fights.

Most of the pain and damage suffered by children in divorce does not result from custody fights. It results from inadequate cooperation and understanding between parents who are in essential agreement about the legal aspects of custody. Therefore, if you have minor children living at home, your parenting agreement should be the subject of full exploration and negotiation.

All too often, opportunities for effective parenting are lost to fear, ignorance, and indifference. Too often, also, the contact between children and their fathers diminishes rapidly in the years following separation, thus realizing the worst fears of the children. The lack of cooperation between parents established at the time of the separation becomes a permanent fixture of the family and sabotages everyone's ability to adjust to new lives. The biggest problem is not custody fights; it is inadequate cooperation between parents.

THE TWO ELEMENTS OF CUSTODY

There are two elements to custody as a legal concept: a guardianship function and a caretaking function. The essential role of a child's guardian—traditionally a parent—is to be in charge of the child, to make decisions for the child, and to control the child's behavior. Guardianship is essentially an issue of *control.*

The second element of custody is the *residential* or caretaking role. Someone has to take care of the child and to provide the nurturing the child requires to thrive. In the intact family this role is divided between the parents as a result of many implicit agreements. But in the divorced family, the allocation of this caretaking function has to be made explicit. Traditionally, the caretaking function has been fused with control by awarding one parent "custody" and the other parent visitation rights. This right of visitation usually applies to specific hours and days set forth in an agreement or court order.

Joint custody has evolved as an attempt to avoid the harsh definition of one parent, typically the father, as the *noncustodial,* and therefore disenfranchised, parent. Let's return to John and Laura to see how these legal concepts get confused with the real issues.

For Laura, as for most mothers, her identity as a mother is important. Given her understanding of custody, she believes that one parent has to be in charge of the children and that she should be that parent. Ever since the children were born, she has been the caretaker. She took them to the doctor, dentist, music teacher, and haircutter. She arranged for a tutor, planned sleep-overs, bought their clothes, went to school conferences, organized their birthday parties, and generally supervised their lives. She was in charge of the children before the separation and feels it is only natural that she should be in control after the separation. What she is proposing to John (put in nonthreatening terms) is that her role as the nurturing parent should continue. But that is not how John experiences the proposal.

John has always been a good father. Despite his heavy workload, he has tried to spend time with the kids. He frequently put them to bed and read to them when they were small. On weekends he often took them to the park or played games with them. He enjoyed their company and was proud of their accomplishments. John recognizes that Laura was more involved than he but also feels that his hard work made it possible for Laura to stay home with the kids. What he fears now is that if Laura gets exclusive control of them she will deprive him of their affection and companionship. Because he does not trust Laura right now, he assumes the worst—that she will use sole custody to take the kids away from him. Thus, for John, joint custody becomes an antidote for loss of control. John believes that joint custody will force Laura to give him an equal say, keep him involved in the discussions about the children, and not shut him out.

RECONSIDER THE CONTROL ISSUE

Let's look more closely at this issue of control—making decisions about the children. I don't mean to minimize the importance of a parent's judgment, but in the context of divorce, the issue of control is often dramatized and blown out of proportion. Major decisions are few and far between. The likelihood of having to make a life-or-death decision for a child is relatively low, and for most of us it happens infrequently.

The decisions most often made by parents are small ones, important cumulatively, but rarely of profound importance individually. Yes, you can go to the movies; no, you can't leave your algebra homework for tomorrow; yes, you can get new sneakers, etc., are the typical parental decisions you make on a daily basis. This is the bread and butter of parental control, and, truthfully, it is not usually worth fighting over. For most parents, most of the time, the decisions to be made on a daily and weekly basis are important only in that a parent makes them.

Yes, there are some parents who are abusive, who have poor judgment, and who do things that have terrible results for their children. But these are extreme cases and are a small minority. The probability is strong that you are not married to such a person and that your spouse is as adequate as parent as anyone else. If your spouse is a dangerous parent, of course you should fight for control. Then the adversary system, with its inherent police powers, is the appropriate forum.

For Laura and John, the control issue has nothing to do with the needs of the children. It is simply a fear of being denied as a parent and somehow losing something to the other. But there is no real loss to be feared. They have the capacity to consult and even cooperate on the rare occasion when a really important decision has to be made.

However, control is a non-issue over which John and Laura may go to war. In this instance, the professional competence of a lawyer really makes a difference. If either or both have lawyers who stoke the fear, there will be a battle. But if a lawyer, a mediator, or a therapist directs Laura and John away from what is little more than a symbolic issue, they have a chance to work out a cooperative relationship.

Laura, like so many parents I've seen, says, "I don't mind

how much my kids visit with their father, I want them to live with me!" John says, "I don't want to just be a visitor. Why can't they live with both of us?" John prepares to get an apartment nearby so that when the kids are with him, they can play with the same friends. "They should live half the time with each of us," he insists. But Laura is adamant.

"Living with me" versus "Living with both of us" is another one of those issues that get Laura and John into trouble. She has told him she would agree to "liberal visitation." As she stated earlier, the children would spend every other weekend with John plus one night during the week. John has rejected this out of hand. But if he took a second look, he might be surprised. Because the actual difference between Laura's proposal and his fifty-fifty proposal is trivial.

In a two-week period, we count four weekend days and ten weekdays. John works a full workweek. Laura is about to begin a full-time job. The children go to school weekdays, leaving home at 8 A.M. and getting back home at 3:30 P.M. John leaves for work at 8 A.M. and returns home at 6:30 P.M. Laura, as a lawyer, can expect similar hours at best.

Laura has proposed that the children spend half their weekend time with their father by spending alternate weekends with him. He would pick them up every other Friday evening and return them Sunday night. They would also spend every Wednesday night with him and he would see them off to school on Thursday morning. Under the terms of this proposal, the children would spend all or part of the day with John seven days out of every fourteen. In any two-week period, they would be with him two Wednesday evenings, two Thursday mornings, one Friday evening, one Saturday all day, and one Sunday until 8 P.M. They would sleep at John's apartment four out of fourteen nights, but would see him seven out of fourteen days. Let's see how close this comes to John's fifty-fifty proposal.

On weekdays the only hours available with the kids are 7

LAURA'S PROPOSAL

	HOURS	LAURA	JOHN
Monday	7:00 A.M.– 8:00 A.M.	4.0	—
	6:30 P.M.– 9:30 P.M.		
Tuesday	7:00 A.M.– 8:00 A.M.	4.0	—
	6:30 P.M.– 9:30 P.M.		
Wednesday	7:00 A.M.– 8:00 A.M.	1.0	
	6:30 P.M.– 9:30 P.M.		3.0
Thursday	7:00 A.M.– 8:00 A.M.		1.0
	6:30 P.M.– 9:30 P.M.	3.0	
Friday	7:00 A.M.– 8:00 A.M.	5.0	—
	6:30 P.M.–10:30 P.M.		
Saturday	7:00 A.M.–10:30 P.M.	15.5	—
Sunday	7:00 A.M.– 9:30 P.M.	15.5	—
Monday	7:00 A.M.– 8:00 A.M.	4.0	—
	6:30 P.M.– 9:30 P.M.		
Tuesday	7:00 A.M.– 8:00 A.M.	4.0	—
	6:30 P.M.– 9:30 P.M.		
Wednesday	7:00 A.M.– 8:00 A.M.	1.0	
	6:30 P.M.– 9:30 P.M.		3.0
Thursday	7:00 A.M.– 8:00 A.M.		1.0
	6:30 P.M.– 9:30 P.M.	3.0	
Friday	7:00 A.M.– 8:00 A.M.	1.0	
	6:30 P.M.–10:30 P.M.		4.0
Saturday	7:00 A.M.–10:30 P.M.	—	15.5
Sunday	7:00 A.M.– 8:00 P.M.		14.0
	8:00 P.M.– 9:30 P.M.	1.5	
		62.5	41.5

A.M. to 8 A.M. and 6:30 P.M. to 9:30 P.M., when they go to bed.
Now, let's actually count the number of waking hours the
children would spend with John under each proposal.

According to our calculation there are 104 available waking
hours with the children. If John had his way—fifty-fifty—those
waking hours would be divided equally with each parent getting 52 over a two-week period. Laura's proposal gives her
62.5 and John 41.5 over that two weeks, a difference for each
of them of 9.5 hours over two weeks, or, 4.75 hours in one
week.

The actual difference in time between John's proposal and
Laura's proposal is not enough to make a difference in their
parental relationship with the children. When the children
spend the weekend with John, are they living with him or living
with Laura? In the context of daily life and practical matters,
the question is meaningless. But John and Laura experience it
as the issue of control. So they get into a battle over whether
to call their arrangement joint or sole custody.

IT DOES NOT MATTER WHAT YOU CALL IT

Here is the truth about custody and visitation. *It doesn't
matter what you call your parenting arrangement.*

Available research shows that, when imposed by the court,
joint custody does not work any better than sole custody.[13]
The sad truth is that courts have neither the capacity nor the
willingness to enforce joint custody arrangements. How can a
court order two adults to think and act like adults? In the
absence of the true cooperation that is the prerequisite of joint
custody, all that court-ordered joint custody means is mutual
stalemate.

I have seen many parenting arrangements that were labeled
"sole custody" provide successful mutual parenting of the
children. I have also seen arrangements called "joint custody"
that were abysmal failures. The only thing that really matters

is whether both parents stay fully engaged with the children, whether they develop the necessary minimum of cooperation, and whether they respect each other's need to develop new lives. If these elements are there, the system works. If they are not, it fails.

I do not believe that courts should ever order joint custody unless both parents request it. The concept, by definition, requires voluntary and mutual cooperation to succeed. When parents come to court with a joint custody arrangement they have already negotiated as part of their agreement, courts can, and always do, ratify and approve.

A relatively new development is joint custody negotiated because each parent wants less, not more, contact and responsibility. In such cases the two parents are very involved in demanding careers. Because each one wants more time to devote to career development, including more nights devoted to the job, we are seeing more mothers demand that the father accept joint custody and shoulder an equal part of the responsibility for the child. Joint custody arrangements accepted reluctantly by an ambivalent father are as problematic in outcome as the more conventional case in which the father is struggling for more, not less, access to the child.

NEGOTIATING THE PARENTING CONTRACT

First we will discuss what you negotiate and include in your formal agreement. Then we will discuss some issues that do not go into the agreement but which are as important as those that do.

DECISION MAKING

What you call decision making in your agreement depends on where you live. Some states make the designation of joint custody presumptive. That is, it is assumed, in the absence of compelling reasons to the contrary, that the parents will have joint custody insofar as decision making is concerned. In other states you can choose between a traditional designation of sole custody or two variations of joint custody. Joint custody generally suggests that the caretaking responsibility is more or less equally shared. The term joint "legal" custody has come to mean an agreement to make major decisions jointly, but an arrangement in which the caretaking is principally the responsibility of one parent. Florida, on the other hand, has abolished the term "custody" altogether and uses the term "joint parenting" for all cases.

Some form of joint decision making should be adopted as the norm. Clearly this does not apply to the day-to-day routine living decisions that must be made by whichever parent is on duty that day. However, major decisions concerning health or education of a child should be made only after some joint discussion. If it is your intention to make such decisions for your child without even consulting the other parent, you are headed for trouble.

It is in your interest to keep your spouse engaged with the kids. If you disenfranchise the other parent with respect to decision making, you also create the justification for that parent to shirk all other parental responsibilities. At a minimum, you need to show him or her the courtesy of a consultation.

Most parents find the designation as *noncustodial* parent deeply humiliating and hurtful. My preference is to see some form of joint custodial designation to avoid that humiliation, even if the children will be cared for primarily by one parent.

There are some small but important details of joint decision-making. You should arrange for notices from school concerning your child's academic performance or announcements about school events to be sent to both households. Most schools will cooperate in such requests. Medical reports or other documents related to your child should be copied and sent to the other parent as soon as received. You should not have to ask your spouse for a copy; it should be sent as a matter of routine.

PARENTAL ACCESS RATHER THAN VISITATION

The very concept that a parent *visit* with a child or that a child visit with the parent is fraught with trouble. Visiting is too diminished a concept to describe what should be happening when a child is with a parent. Like the designation of *noncustodial, visiting parent* is equally humiliating. It is preferable, in my opinion, to have a contractual provision that describes the time each parent will spend with the child.

"The children shall spend alternate weekends plus every Wednesday night with the father" is quite sufficient to provide an adequate description of the schedule. Calling this "visitation" adds nothing. What you need to negotiate and describe is a comprehensive schedule of time you will each spend with the children. This parenting schedule will give concrete expression to your mutual intentions about the nurturance of your children.

SCHEDULES AND ROUTINES

Many parents object to restrictions on their access to their children. Many fathers say that they don't want to be limited to fixed hours when they can see their children. They want a schedule of access that is similar to what they had before the divorce—namely, anytime they want. I have also heard mothers and fathers insist that they have free telephone access to the kids whenever they want.

There is no substitute for fixed schedules. Everyone, particularly the children, needs to know what is going to happen and when. The parent who demands unlimited access is either unrealistic or has a hidden agenda. In some cases, the refusal to agree to specific times hides a refusal to make a commit-

ment to the children. If that is your case, it is better to be
honest about your intentions than to engage in the deceit.
Young children need to know when they are going to see you
because they have a poor sense of time: What is a short time
for older people can be an eternity for a toddler. Older children also need to know so they can make their own plans.

Your agreement should specify when the children will be
with each of you. This is also vital to your own planning. Each
of you needs to know when you have time off so *you* can make
plans. Schedules and times should be adhered to rigorously.
You should not express your anger by being late when picking
up or delivering the children. It injures *them*. Similarly, late
cancellation of plans should be avoided whenever possible. If
you disappoint your child enough times, he will protect himself next time by making other plans. Late arrivals and late
cancellations quickly sour any co-parenting arrangement.

This does not mean that your arrangements should not be
flexible. There will be times when one of you has the flu, when
some emergency, or a long-planned vacation require a change.
You and your former spouse will need to adopt a reciprocal
posture of cooperation to accommodate each other. As in all
forms of accommodation, it works best if not overused.

When a change is necessary, follow a protocol. If you are
seeking a change, first discuss it with the other parent. If the
other parent agrees, then inform the child. If a child will be
disappointed by your change, it is your responsibility to tell
him or her and to make whatever reassurances and alternate
arrangements are necessary. I have heard too many angry
mothers complain that when the father canceled his time with
the child at the last minute, it was the mother who had to deal
with the child's disappointment. It is unfair and, in the long
run, destructive.

HOLIDAYS, VACATIONS, AND SICK DAYS

Your parenting schedule should include some agreement about how holidays and vacations are to be spent. There are two parts to this issue. First, there are some holidays when it is important to you that you spend the day with your children. Family-oriented holidays like Thanksgiving and Christmas, other religious holidays, and some patriotic holidays like Labor Day and Memorial Day may be examples. On such holidays, when each parent is eager for as much access as possible, the most common arrangement is to alternate each year. This year you have Thanksgiving; next year your spouse has it. This generally works well. Many people who celebrate Christmas find it useful to divide Christmas into two parts: Christmas Eve and Christmas Day. One takes Christmas Eve while the other takes Christmas Day. The next year they switch.

You should spend a little time designating which holidays are important to you and which are not. When parents are from different religious backgrounds, there may be some holidays unimportant to you but important to your spouse. Whenever possible the schedule should be adapted accordingly. Each of you may want to schedule vacations away with the children each year. The schedule should provide for these periods when the routine will be altered.

The second part of the issue is providing coverage on days the kids have no school. Holidays and vacations are not always a blessing for working parents and can be a problem when both parents are employed—a situation that applies to most divorced parents. Children in most states go to school about 180 days a year. There are 260 weekdays in the year. This means that a child is not in school 80 weekdays, or the equivalent of 16 working weeks each year. A working parent who gets two weeks vacation plus the standard 12 holidays a year off, is off from work only 22 weekdays a year. Consequently there are many weekdays that schoolchildren do not go to school, but that parents must work. The responsibility for providing coverage for the kids must be shared in some equitable manner.

Another problem occurs when your child is sick and must stay home from school. In most intact families there is an implicit assumption that the mother will stay home with the child. In a divorce context this assumption no longer works. Most divorced wives work full time in order to carry their weight financially. A mother who is expected to develop a career has as much of a problem taking the day off as does a father. Staying home with a sick child is a task that should be shared by both parents.

Similarly, you should talk about the plans for the kids during summer vacation. You may find that you can no longer afford the activities that occupied the kids in the past. Summer camp, for example, may now be out of reach. If that is the case, it must become a joint problem for solution, not just left to one parent to resolve.

SCHEDULE FOR COMPREHENSIVE PARENTING

Divorce negotiations often begin before people have fully understood the implications of separate households. One resulting problem warrants some special discussion here. Divorce often requires that a father learn new skills, skills that formerly were provided exclusively by the mother. If this is a problem for you, it needs to be acknowledged and explicitly discussed.

In the classic visitation pattern, fathers spend time with the children on alternate weekends, vacations, and one or two weekday evenings a week. This arrangement easily promotes what many have called the "zoo daddy" syndrome. The major symptom is the assumption by the father, and soon by the children, that time with Father is time when they will be entertained. Each weekend is to be marked by some special event in which the father valiantly strives for "quality time" with his children. Time with Daddy quickly takes on an artificial air.

Scheduled access to the children should provide an opportunity for them to share the lives of both parents. Special occasions and treats should occur with about the same regularity as in married families. Children should not come to expect special entertainment every time they see their father. They should have an opportunity to "hang out" with the father, share quiet time, make lunch, do the laundry, go grocery shopping, or even do nothing together for an afternoon.

If it is the father's day to be with the child and the child is sick, the child should not stay home with the mother unless she or he is literally too sick to travel to the father's home. Fathers are capable of entertaining sick children, reading to them, and cleaning up after them. In other words, the key to maintaining a full parenting role is to assume a full parenting role. Both parents are capable of the full range of nurturing behavior, including those dull, repetitive, and often unpleasant tasks that go with the territory.

These are the considerations that go into negotiating the written contract. Now let's look briefly at some of the agreements that you need to make that do not get written down.

LET YOUR SPOUSE BE COMPETENT

The requirement that fathers master a broader repertoire of parenting skills imposes on the mother a reciprocal obligation to promote such mastery. For many men, the full range of tasks that come with being a single parent is something new. Even though the majority of mothers are employed, most studies suggest that working mothers perform the same domestic chores performed by nonworking mothers. In other words, women tend to run the household and to be more responsible than men for supervising the daily affairs of the children. There are, of course, families in which these tasks are evenly shared, and when these families divorce, there is less adjustment to make. There are also a few families in which the father plays the domestic role, but these families are unusual.

Fathers who seek to fully parent their children after separation and divorce need to learn how to do most of the things they previously left to their wives. These may include cooking, cleaning, laundry, and other such tasks. It also means planning and arranging for the kids, being emotionally available, comforting them, taking care of them when they're sick, and otherwise nurturing as necessary. While they learn, they need others to support, not belittle, their efforts or shaky first steps. Whether your spouse is the child's mother or father, it is in your interest that he or she succeeds as a parent.

RESOLVE YOUR DIFFERENCES PRIVATELY

Differences between you and your spouse should be addressed directly and in private. Your children should not be allowed or invited to participate overtly or covertly. If you disapprove of something your spouse has done, tell him or her, but do it privately. Seek comfort from your friends, your relatives, your clergy, or your therapist, but *not* from your children.

The most challenging and most important aspect of any co-parenting relationship is your ability to help your child maintain a full and satisfying relationship with the other parent. It is absolutely essential to the well-being of the child that she (or he) be able to believe that she has two good parents who love her and will take care of her.

Although you may be very angry at your spouse and regard him or her at times as a terrible person, you must not transmit that message to your child. This can be very difficult, particularly when you feel that you are the victim in the divorce.

Victims frequently seek solace from their children and subtly subvert the children into playing a parental role for them. It is a terribly destructive thing to do. Children have a right to be children and to be taken care of by their parents.

The sense of betrayal that one parent may feel is easily transmitted to the children. A mother who is left by her husband casually refers to the fact that "Daddy left us" or "Daddy doesn't love us anymore." Or the mother short on cash tells the children that "Daddy's too selfish to give us enough money." Or the father undermines his wife's authority by telling the kids, "If you're unhappy with your mother, come live with me." These and other comments that express your resentment weaken the bond between your children and their other parent. They also teach the child early in the divorce that he can divide and conquer by manipulating his parents and playing them against each other. Children are not oblivious to power and influence. Your running down the other parent can create a competitive scheme in which the child is allied alternately with you and then your spouse, depending on which one accedes to the child's wishes.

In the end, when you undermine the relationship between the child and the other parent you pay a heavy price. You have a troubled child who becomes your sole responsibility. Despite negative feelings for your former mate, you destroy your own resources when you sabotage that relationship. You legitimize attempts to do the same to you, and you increase the chance of problems with the child.

MIND YOUR BUSINESS WHEN THE CHILD IS WITH THE OTHER PARENT

When the child is with the other parent, your position must be one of noninterference. Before you jump on your "ex" for feeding the children food you disapprove of, for letting them stay up too late, etc., ask yourself if it is really worth it. Your inability to mind your business when your child is with your ex-spouse will probably be far more damaging in the long run than all the candy bars in the world. Do not direct, do not criticize, and do not rescue. Let the children and their mother/father deal with one another. Let them work out their relationship.

It is undoubtedly troubling when the other parent takes a radically different approach to nutrition, bedtime, or discipline. But children adapt to different rules in two households. It is easier when you are in agreement on these things, as consistency may be easier on the kids. But differences must be respected, or the conflict over these assumes disproportionate importance. If the other parent is too permissive, let him or her cope with the consequences. (If you must disapprove, do it privately, away from the child.)

On the other hand, it does help when you can accommodate a strongly felt preference of the other parent. Some parents have very strong feelings about nutrition, for example. You may not agree. But is it sufficiently important that you cannot accommodate it? There will be many honest differences you will both have to live with, but where you can meet your ex-mate's strongly felt principles without major sacrifices, why not? It may get you what you want next time in another area.

The point here is that your ability to lead your life reasonably well depends in large measure on how well your children do when they are with the other parent. That requires a competent parent at the other end, and your cooperation or sabotage (as you choose) can make the difference.

COOPERATE AROUND NEW MATES

About 80 percent of divorced people remarry. Assuming that many of those who do not remarry nevertheless develop serious relationships, the probability is very high that within a few years you will have at least one new relationship with a "boyfriend" or a "girlfriend" (for want of better terms). The new relationship, after all, is central to the second chance for which people divorce. In the best of circumstances, building a new relationship when you have children by a prior marriage is tricky. If your new friend also has children by a prior marriage, the situation is even more complex. That is why the divorce rate for second marriages is higher than for first-time marriages. The entire step-family issue has sunk many a new relationship.

Most family therapists will tell you that your children can do a lot of damage to your new relationship. They will also tell you that your former spouse can make a great difference, depending on what attitude she or he takes toward your new prospective partner and how she or he imparts that attitude to the children.

As difficult as it may be, the more you are able to help your children accept your former spouse's new relationship, the better it will be for them and for you. I understand how difficult this can be when you have been left for someone else. Even when you were not left for a competitor, if your former mate finds a new relationship before you do, intense jealousy is normal. If you share these feelings with your children, you will give them a message that they betray you if they like this new person. It puts them in a bind because no matter how nicely that person treats them, they cannot accept him or her out of a protective feeling for you. This, in turn, puts them on a collision course with their other parent, and everyone suffers. It also sets the stage for the situation to be reversed when *you* begin a relationship.

CONCLUSION

A central theme of this book is that most of the things you do by reflex are wrong. Nowhere is this principle more apparent than in the way divorcing couples negotiate about their children. This is where your impulse to punish your spouse damages you the most. Similarly, it is where your ability to look into the future and negotiate accordingly does you the most good.

Chapter Ten

PREPARING YOUR BUDGETS AND ASSESSING YOUR NEEDS

DOING THE BUDGETS

*B*udgets *are necessary* to negotiate child support and alimony. You need a systematic way to list your needs and establish your priorities. That is the purpose of budgeting. You begin with two budgets: his and hers. Then you separate your own from the kids' so that you end up with three budgets: his, hers, and the children's. On the following pages you will find a standard budget form. You will each need several copies of the blank budgets. Preparing a budget is more of a process than a single event. Invariably, you will have to do the budget more than once because the first few times you will probably prepare budgets that exceed your income. As you compare your needs to your income, you will make many changes. So be prepared for some rigorous homework.

HOW TO BEGIN

Working out your budget requires that you know what things cost and how much you usually spend. You may already have a good deal of this information, or you may have very little. If your spouse handled the money for the family, you may not know how much it costs to heat your house or to buy food each week for the family. You may not know how much you spend each year on telephone bills, auto insurance, or appliance repairs. But the time has come to learn. It's a matter of simple arithmetic, and you have no choice but to learn how to do it now.

You and your spouse should cooperate in sharing information, but you should each do your own budgets. You both need access to the family checkbooks so you can calculate expenses. You need copies of past tax returns, insurance premium statements, bank statements, old bills, and any other records that can help you understand past spending patterns. Use the phone liberally to call for information on car payments, future tax payments, advice on insurance costs, medical insurance, and anything else for which you may need data or advice. The more precise your research, the better your planning and negotiations.

THE FIRST BUDGET

Your first budget should cover the following:

1. The budget for the first year of separation, assuming two separate households.

If you have not yet separated, the one who is moving out first should research the local housing market and determine the range of prices for housing. Even if you own a house and think you are going to sell it, it is likely that selling will take some time and that one of you will stay in the house until it is sold. Build your initial budgets around that scenario. You can, and probably will have to, develop alternative budgets as you go. Therefore, don't assume that just because you write it down, the budget can't be changed. Even if selling the house is a hot issue between you, start your budgets on the assumption that one of you will stay and the other will move. Of course, if you have already agreed that the house must be sold, do both budgets on the assumption that both of you are moving.

2. The living arrangements of the children.

If the children are going to reside primarily with their mother, her budget should reflect the cost of housing, feeding and clothing them. The father's budget, then, should reflect whatever costs he will incur for the children when they are with him. For example, if the children are to spend weekends with their father, he should include the cost of feeding them for the time they are with him. If he is arranging for housing to provide them with their own bedroom in his dwelling, that cost must be included in his budget.

If you are not yet separated, you may have to guess at some figures. You won't know exactly what the housing and utilities will be for the second household if the separation has not yet occurred but you will be close, if you've done your homework.

3. A conservative estimate of your present standard of living.

Although chances are not strong that you will be able to continue without change, this is a good starting place. You should not include expenditures that you have not made in the past. This is not the time to decide that you are entitled to three vacations a year if one a year has been your pattern. If you have been driving a modestly priced car, now is not the time to budget for a luxury car. Common sense is your best guide. It is also not a good idea to inflate your budget in order to improve your bargaining position with your spouse. The budgets are your working documents. They are the practical basis for solving a host of practical problems. If you fool around with them, if you play bad-faith games, you seriously reduce your capacity for cooperative negotiations.

SOME PRACTICAL CONSIDERATIONS

You will note that the budget is divided into three sections: shelter, transportation, and personal. Each one requires some special thought. But first, a few reminders.

1. Monthly figures. The budget provides for monthly expenditures. If you know what something costs per week, multiply it by 4.3 because there are 4.3 weeks in an average month. For example, if you spend $100 per week on groceries, your monthly cost is $430 ($100 × 4.3). If you know the annual cost, divide by 12 to get the monthly cost. Thus, if your auto insurance is $800 a year, your monthly cost is $66.66 ($800 divided by 12 = $66.66).

Even though some things are paid for seasonally (heat, lawn care, summer camp), be sure to convert the annual cost to a monthly cost so that you can approach your cash flow systematically.

2. Be realistic. Just because something is on the budget form that follows does not mean that you have to put in a number. For example, some children take lessons, others don't. If your child doesn't, don't budget for the possibility.

3. What are your costs? Include in your budget all the expenses for your household whether you are currently paying those bills or not. For example, if you are already separated, and the husband is not living in the house, but making the mortgage payments directly to the bank, the mortgage payment should appear in the wife's budget. The budget is a statement of your household *costs*. That is a different issue from who pays.

USING THE BUDGET FORM

The budget form has three sections: Shelter (Schedule A), Transportation (Schedule B), and Personal (Schedule C).

BUDGET FORM
MONTHLY EXPENSES

SCHEDULE A:
SHELTER   1   2

Tenant
rent   _____ _____
heat   _____ _____
utilities   _____ _____
tenant insurance   _____ _____
other   _____ _____

Homeowner
mortgage   _____ _____
real estate taxes   _____ _____
homeowners insurance   _____ _____
heat   _____ _____
utilities   _____ _____
other   _____ _____

Tenant or Homeowner
telephone   _____ _____
cable TV   _____ _____
other   _____ _____

Total Shelter Costs   ═════════════ ═════════════

SCHEDULE B:
TRANSPORTATION

auto payment or depreciation _____ _____
auto insurance   _____ _____
maintenance   _____ _____

BUDGET FORM
MONTHLY EXPENSES *(Continued)*

SCHEDULE B:
TRANSPORTATION   1   2

fuel   _____ _____
commuting expenses   _____ _____

Total Transportation Expense   ========= =========

SCHEDULE C:
PERSONAL EXPENSES

1. food at home and
   household supplies   _____ _____
2. restaurants   _____ _____
3. nonprescription drugs,
   cosmetics, etc.   _____ _____
4. clothing   _____ _____
5. dry cleaning   _____ _____
6. hair care   _____ _____
7. entertainment, sports, and
   hobbies   _____ _____
8. gifts and contributions   _____ _____
9. newspapers and periodicals   _____ _____
10. life insurance   _____ _____
11. medical insurance   _____ _____
12. unreimbursed medical   _____ _____
13. unreimbursed dental   _____ _____
14. orthodontics   _____ _____
15. psychotherapy/
    counseling   _____ _____
16. prescription drugs   _____ _____
17. payments to non-child
    dependents   _____ _____

BUDGET FORM
MONTHLY EXPENSES *(Continued)*

SCHEDULE C:
PERSONAL EXPENSES   **1**   **2**

18. prior alimony/child support   _____   _____
19. monthly debt service   _____   _____
20. domestic help   _____   _____
21. children's private school
    costs   _____   _____
22. day care expense   _____   _____
23. children's lessons   _____   _____
24. children's tutoring   _____   _____
25. summer camp   _____   _____
26. babysitting   _____   _____
27. other   _____   _____

Total Personal Expenses   ================   ================

Total Budget {Schedules
    A + B + C = }   ================   ================

Schedule A is where you list all the expenses associated with
your housing. Schedule B is where you list all the expenses of
transportation including your auto and commutation expenses. And Schedule C is where you list all your other expenses. You will also note that there are two columns in each
schedule. The first column is used to calculate the total expenses of your household—that is, your expenses including
whatever you spend on the children when they are with you.
The second column is used later to list separately the expenses
of the children.

SHELTER: SCHEDULE A

The one who is staying in the house should show all the costs for the house in his/her budget, even though both may continue to own the house. This includes mortgage, taxes, second mortgage or home equity loan, maintenance, and repairs. When in doubt about costs, look at what you spent last year or the past two years to estimate your costs for repairs or utilities. Distinguish between routine expenses and extraordinary expenses. A wood-sided house needs painting every five or six years. If you know that it costs $3,000 to have your house painted, you can divide $3,000 by 60 months (five years) to get $50 a month as a routine cost for painting. On the other hand, if your boiler is in good condition, or if your roof is only four years old, do not attempt to budget a monthly expense for these long-term contingent replacements. Again, common sense must be your guide. You don't want to understate expenses, but you don't want to overstate them, either.

If you are the one who is moving out, your budget should reflect what you expect your housing cost to be over the next few years. This most frequently involves a rental. If you are certain that you will purchase a residence, use the figures for the purchase. If you are not sure, prepare alternate budgets for shelter and look at the issue both ways. If you have taken temporary housing, a room in a boardinghouse, or a room in your sister's house that is not where you are going to live permanently, that should not be the basis of your budget. Find out what it will cost for housing that meets your needs, and budget based on that.

TRANSPORTATION: SCHEDULE B

Most of us are dependent on cars and we worry if our car is unreliable. But cars can also be a source of ego gratification unrelated to their function. Your initial budget should reflect your experience over the past few years. However, if you have been sharing two cars and one of you used the "good" car while the other used the "clunker" to commute to the train station, that pattern will not work in the reorganized family. The old car will probably have to be replaced. But budget realistically. A new car can be bought for $7,000 or for $40,000. What has been your historical pattern, and what do you really need?

On the budget form you will see a space for auto payment or depreciation. Whether you borrow and pay off a car or whether you pay cash for your car, the budget should reflect a monthly cost. Even though you own your car without an auto loan, you use up part of the car's value each month. You need to incorporate in your budget an amount of money that, if set aside, will provide a replacement when this car wears out. I suggest that you begin by finding out what your present car costs new and divide that by 72 months, on the assumption that, with average use, your car should last six years. Thus, if you are driving a Buick Regal that would cost $14,000 to buy new, your depreciation expense will be $194 per month ($14,-000 divided by 72 = $194).

Also remember that if you and your spouse have two cars on the same auto insurance policy, you must change that when you have two households, and the cost per car may change. Check with your insurance agent.

PERSONAL EXPENSES: SCHEDULE C

If an expense is not for shelter or for transportation, it falls into this category. Some of these items are obvious, but others, I have found, can be troublesome. To help you, I will go through the items consecutively, commenting on those that may cause complications.

1. *Food and Household Supplies:* This is essentially what you spend at the supermarket each week, multiplied by 4.3 to get

a monthly figure. If you have not done the shopping or if you don't know what it costs, now is the time to learn. Make a list of all the food you will need for an average week, go to the market, and find out what it costs.

2. *Restaurants:* This may be troublesome because restaurants can drain your discretionary income. If you have not done the cooking and if you don't know how, this is a danger zone. You can learn to cook, or you can spend a small fortune to eat all your meals out. This can be a real problem for traditional males who don't want the divorce. Because they are not motivated to adapt, they tend toward large estimates of their restaurant expense. Be realistic.

3. *Nonprescription Drugs, Cosmetics:* These are items that you may purchase in drug stores or in supermarkets. If they are part of your routine supermarket expenses, don't repeat them here.

4. *Clothing:* Clothing can be a difficult category because the line between functional necessity and ego gratification is very fuzzy. Begin with your historical pattern but note that if you have *historically* shopped as entertainment or if you have always dressed in "style," this item may need some dramatic trimming next time around.

5. *Dry Cleaning:* No comment necessary.

6. *Hair Care:* No comment necessary.

7. *Entertainment, Sports, and Hobbies:* This category may be hard to estimate because it is a discretionary expense in which your spending pattern is casual and for which you may have no records. What is your recreational pattern? Do you go to the movies often? How much does that cost? Do you go bowling or skiing or fishing routinely? How much do you spend on these in a year? Try to figure this out with as much precision as you can.

8. *Gifts and Contributions:* This includes what you routinely spend on birthday or Christmas presents as well as annual contributions to your church or civic organizations. Begin

with your historical estimate, but note that much of this is discretionary spending.

9. *Newspapers and Periodicals:* No comment necessary.

10. *Life Insurance:* This category can be tricky and we will discuss it more later on. Put down what you pay now for any policies on YOUR life and note that it needs more work.

11. *Medical Insurance:* If you are now covered by your spouse's employment-related medical insurance, that will cease once you are divorced. Find out if you are covered or can acquire coverage through your own employer. You may also be able to convert your coverage under your spouse's policy to an individual policy—find out. For this first budget, show the cost for the children's insurance on the budget of the spouse that provides it. If it is provided free by an employer, it costs nothing. If there is a deduction from your paycheck, show that here.

12. *Unreimbursed Medical:* Most medical insurance plans have some deductible or co-payment requirement. Find out what it is. Also look at what you spent in the past. Be sure to deduct what you get back from the insurance company. The unreimbursed medical expenses for the kids should be reflected in the budget of the spouse with whom they will principally reside.

13. *Unreimbursed Dental:* This is the same as medical, except that most people have little or no dental insurance. Look at the last five years to establish your pattern. Some people can go years without substantial dental work. Other people have bad teeth and frequently spend substantial sums. Do not include the children's orthodontia here.

14. *Orthodontics:* This is separated from routine dentistry because if your child needs it, he or she needs it only once, and it costs a lot of money. If your child is currently being treated, you already know the cost. Spread the total cost over the years of treatment and establish a monthly cost. If you have a child who has not started treatment but who the *dentist* says will

probably need it, find out when it will begin, when it will end, and approximately what it will cost. Take the total cost and divide by the number of months between *now* and when treatment is over to establish a monthly estimated cost. Be sure to subtract from the cost whatever payment will be made by insurance.

15. *Psychotherapy:* This is another expense for which medical insurance usually covers only part, if any. If you are in therapy, discuss with your therapist how long you may expect to continue. Few therapists will give you a precise answer, but you should be able to get some estimate. Some kinds of therapy, such as psychoanalysis, usually are long-term. Other types are short-term—less than one year. Be sure that you understand and agree with your therapist on your therapeutic goals. If you are there for short-term supportive therapy through the process of divorce, that should be a limited time. Make sure that your therapist qualifies for third-party payment if you are insured. Not all therapists have the required credentials.

16. *Prescription Drugs:* Make sure that you account for insurance coverage. Otherwise, no comment necessary.

17. *Payments to Non-child Dependents:* Usually this refers to your parents or perhaps a sick or indigent relative. Payments for alimony or child support from a prior marriage generally are taken into account in determining your financial obligations to this marriage because such payments are the product of a contract that has been incorporated into a court order. However, that does not apply to the contribution you make to support your father or brother. Your spouse has no obligation to your relatives. If you regularly make such contributions, put them in, but be aware you will have to negotiate gently and carefully.

18. *Prior Alimony or Child Support:* No comment necessary.

19. *Monthly Debt Service:* This does not include your car loan or your home equity loan, both of which have already

been included. This is for your current credit card debt or other short-term installment debt. Generally it is better to try to find some liquid assets to pay off such debt, but if you cannot, remember that this is a time-limited expense. Once you pay these off, they should not remain in your budget.

20. *Domestic Help:* This is another tricky topic. If you have such help now, put it in your budget. If not, this is not the time to add such expenditures. The one exception may be when a residential parent is about to return to full-time employment and domestic help is part of a larger child-care system. However, be aware that this item becomes a target of your spouse when you start looking for ways to save money.

21. *Children's Private School Expense:* This discretionary item can be the topic of considerable controversy. If a child is currently in private school, put it in the budget. If the child is not in such a school, and you and your spouse are not in agreement about its necessity, it is best not to include it at this time. If applicable, the item should be included in the budget of the residential parent.

22. *Day Care Expense:* If your child is already in day care, you know what it costs. If the child is at home but you are contemplating a return to work, you must provide for child care. You must also provide for after-school care. In most states, kids go to school between 170 and 190 days a year, leaving a total of 70 to 90 *weekdays* when they are not in school. Careful research is needed here because the cost and quality of child care vary widely.

23. *Children's Lessons:* Piano, ballet, etc.

24. *Children's Tutoring:* If necessary, this is usually short-term. But for children with learning disabilities, this can be a long-term, substantial expense.

25. *Summer Camp:* What has been the historical pattern? This may be a necessity rather than a luxury if both parents work full time.

26. *Babysitting:* This is the babysitting when you go out for

the evening. Routine after-school care for working parents should be included in day care expense above.

27. *Other:* List all other long-term routine expenses not provided for on the form.

SEPARATING THE COSTS OF THE CHILDREN

After you have completed the budget for your household using the first column, the next step is to separate the costs for the children. The budget form in this chapter has two columns. The second column is for figuring out the cost of the kids. The second column will show what part of the expense listed in the first column is for the children. Complete the budget item by item. When you get to Schedule C, you will need some patience. Items like clothing can be researched if you have not kept careful records in the past. Some items such as dry cleaning may not apply to the children at all. Others, such as hair care, are easily figured out. Still others like food, entertainment, and gifts may take some pondering. You will not get each item exactly right, but by working on each separate one you will obtain a pretty good estimate of the cost of your children. You should do this whether the children live primarily with you or with your spouse.

Even if the children live most of the time with your spouse, you will probably incur costs when they are with you. If you have them overnight frequently, you may provide a bedroom just for them. The cost of that room should be included in your total calculations. Similarly, if you have babysitting expenses when they are with you, those should be included. Do not overstate the expenses. You want a comprehensive and realistic view of the costs of the kids.

Some child-related expenses are easier to identify than others. For example, all babysitting expenses are designated as child expense. But what about your automobile or your house or the utilities? It would be unrealistic simply to allocate a fixed proportion to the kids. If there are two kids, and only one of you, why not just allocate two-thirds of each item's cost to the kids? The reason is that there are some expenses you would have regardless of the children. If you had no children living with you, you would still need a car, auto insurance, and maintenance. Most of your transportation expense would be the same. The portion of your auto expense allocated to the kids should be only the extra driving you do on their behalf. In most cases, it would be inappropriate to allocate more than 10 or 15 percent of this expense to the children. The same applies to housing and utilities. If you have to provide two bedrooms for the children, what is the difference in your community between the cost of a one-bedroom and a three-bedroom rental apartment? That is probably a good approximation of the real economic cost of housing for the kids, even if you own a house. It is best if you do not try to use a simple formula to do this task. To do it well requires some homework and research. Your reward is that your budget will have credibility if it is well supported, and you will have a good basis for planning and negotiation.

SOME PRELIMINARY CALCULATIONS

When you have completed the task of separating the costs for the children, total each column in schedules A, B, and C of the budget form. What you now have is the total budget for the household in column 1 and the total cost of the children in column 2. Note that the costs of the children are part of the costs you have listed for the entire household; they are not in addition to the household costs. The next step is to subtract the cost of the children from the total household costs. The result is the budget that you require for yourself, independent of the children.

CASE STUDY: ALAN AND JOAN

It will be easier to understand this sometimes vexing task if we follow a couple through the process. Alan and Joan have already separated. Alan has moved out of the house into a nearby apartment, leaving Joan in the house with their two daughters ages seven and three.

Alan is a quality control supervisor for a local company. His annual salary is $54,000. Joan teaches in the local high school where she earns $28,000 a year. The budget for each is as follows:

JOAN'S BUDGET
MONTHLY EXPENSES

SCHEDULE A: SHELTER	HOUSEHOLD 1	CHILDREN 2
Tenant		
rent		
heat		
utilities		
tenant insurance		
other		
Homeowner		
mortgage	850	
real estate taxes	200	
homeowners insurance	40	
heat	80	
utilities	30	
other		

JOAN'S BUDGET
MONTHLY EXPENSES *(Continued)*

SCHEDULE A: SHELTER	HOUSEHOLD 1	CHILDREN 2
Tenant or Homeowner		
telephone	35	
cable TV	15	
other	40	
Total Shelter Costs	1,290	330

SCHEDULE B: TRANSPORTATION		
auto payment	210	
auto insurance	80	
maintenance	50	
fuel	60	
commuting expenses	100	
Total Transportation Expense	500	30

SCHEDULE C: PERSONAL EXPENSES		
food at home and household supplies	450	250
restaurants	80	30
nonprescription drugs, cosmetics, etc.	25	15
clothing	250	150
dry cleaning	15	
hair care	30	15
entertainment, sports, and hobbies	150	100

JOAN'S BUDGET
MONTHLY EXPENSES (Continued)

SCHEDULE C:
PERSONAL EXPENSES

	1	2
gifts and contributions	50	40
newspapers and periodicals	10	
life insurance	15	
medical insurance		
unreimbursed medical	80	40
unreimbursed dental	60	20
psychotherapy/ counseling		
prescription drugs	40	25
payments to non-child dependents		
prior family child support		
monthly debt service		
domestic help		
orthodontics		
children's private school costs		
day care expense	600	600
children's lessons	60	60
children's tutoring		
summer camp	45	45
babysitting	50	50
other		
Total Personal Expenses	2,010	1,440
Total Budget {Schedules A+B+C=} for Joan and the Children	3,800	1,800

ALAN'S BUDGET
MONTHLY EXPENSES

SCHEDULE A: SHELTER	1	2
Tenant		
rent	900	
heat		
utilities	40	
tenant insurance	20	
other		
Homeowner		
mortgage		
real estate taxes		
homeowners insurance		
heat		
utilities		
other		
Tenant or Homeowner		
telephone	50	
cable TV	15	
other		
Total Shelter Costs	1025	300

SCHEDULE B:
TRANSPORTATION

	1	2
auto payment	340	
auto insurance	90	
maintenance	30	

ALAN'S BUDGET
MONTHLY EXPENSES (Continued)

SCHEDULE B:
TRANSPORTATION

	1	2
fuel	80	
commuting expenses	80	
Total Transportation Expense	620	

SCHEDULE C:
PERSONAL
EXPENSES

	1	2
food at home and household supplies	360	120
restaurants	260	60
nonprescription drugs, cosmetics, etc.	15	
clothing	150	
dry cleaning	40	
hair care	30	
entertainment, sports, and hobbies	200	60
gifts and contributions	100	
newspapers and periodicals	15	
life insurance	40	
medical insurance		
unreimbursed medical	10	
unreimbursed dental	20	
psychotherapy/ counseling		
prescription drugs	15	
payments to non-child dependents		

ALAN'S BUDGET
MONTHLY EXPENSES *(Continued)*

SCHEDULE C:
PERSONAL

EXPENSES	1	2
prior alimony/child support		
monthly debt service	130	
domestic help		
orthodontics		
children's private school costs		
day care expense		
children's lessons		
children's tutoring		
summer camp		
babysitting	60	60
other	110	
Total Personal Expenses	1555	300
Total Budget {Schedules A+B+C=} For Alan with the Children Part Time	3200	600

To calculate each parent's budget you subtract the total in column 2 from the total in column 1. In our example, Joan's total budget is $3,800 per month. She calculates the cost of the children at $1,800 per month. When the children's budget of $1,800 per month is subtracted from the total household budget of $3,800 per month, the difference is the budget for Joan without the children. Her budget of $2,000 plus the children's budget of $1,800 is $3,800.

Alan has also calculated his household budget and the allocation for the children. His total household budget in column 1 is $3,200. Because the children reside primarily with Joan, the allocation for the children is smaller in Alan's budget and is shown in column 2 as $600. Thus, we see that Alan's budget for himself is $2,600 (column 1 [$3,200] minus column 2 [$600]).

After Alan and Joan have completed these calculations, they are able to review their collective financial needs.

	HOUSEHOLD BUDGET (PER MONTH)		CHILDREN'S BUDGET		SPOUSE'S BUDGET
Joan	$3,800	—	$1,800	=	$2,000
Alan	$3,200	—	$600	=	$2,600

Total Required = $7,000
Total cost of children = $2,400

LOOKING AT INCOME

Calculating initial budgets is the first step when preparing for support negotiations. The second step is to analyze how the budgets relate to your family income and how that income is distributed between you and your spouse. To do that realistically you have to consider the difference between pretax and after-tax income.

Pretax income is your gross salary. In our example, Alan earns $54,000 per year and has a monthly gross salary of $4,500 ($54,000 divided by 12). Joan earns $28,000 a year and has a monthly gross salary of $2,500 ($28,000 divided by

12). However, most of their expenses in the budgets will be paid with after-tax dollars. This is what is left after you subtract social security, federal withholding tax, state and/or city income taxes withheld (if applicable) and any other deductions. For Alan and Joan the figures are as follows:

	MONTHLY GROSS	SOCIAL SECURITY	FEDERAL TAX WITHHOLDING	STATE TAX WITHHOLDING	NET MONTHLY PAY
Alan	$4,500	$342	$743	$114	$3,301
Joan	2,500	190	281	56	1,973
					$5,274

In this case Alan has take-home pay of $3,301 per month and Joan has take-home pay of $1,973. These figures will change slightly because when they are divorced they will pay income taxes as single taxpayers, rather than as married filing a joint return. They will use different tax tables, and the tax on each one's income will be different.

Depending on how you and your spouse have arranged tax exemptions and depending on what you do with the marital home, your own net after-tax income may increase or decrease by as much as 10 percent. As you reach the point where you want to fine-tune your calculations, it is helpful to consult with an accountant who can project your taxes under alternative assumptions. In our illustration, we will work with the net income figures of our couple as they exist before the divorce, but you should carefully calculate your present net income per month. If you are paid weekly, remember to multiply by 4.3 (the number of weeks in a month). If you are paid twice a month, multiply your net pay by 2. If you are paid *biweekly,* it is not the same as twice a month because you are paid 26

times a year, not 24. In that case multiply your net pay by 26
to get an annual figure and then divide by 12.

Weekly pay of $767.67 × 4.3   = $3,301
Twice Monthly pay of $1,650.50 × 2   = $3,301
Biweekly pay of $1,523.53 × 26 = $36,565 divided
  by 12   = $3,301

RECONCILING INCOME AND EXPENSES

The next task is to compare your net income to your budgets. You will do this for each of the two budgets and for the
total of both your budgets. Don't be surprised if you have a
deficit.

Alan and Joan have a problem. Like the majority of middle-
class divorcing couples, their total budgets ($7,000) exceed
their total net income ($5,274) by the sum of $1,726. Although tax considerations may reduce this deficit by a few
hundred dollars, they still have a substantial deficit to resolve.
Let's look at their situation individually and together.

Joan's Total Budget $3,800   Alan's Total Budget $3,200
Joan's Net Income $1,973   Alan's Net Income $3,301
Joan's Deficit $1,827   Alan's Surplus $101

At this stage, the task is simply to understand the situation.
If you have deficits in either your individual budgets or in your
combined budgets, you will have to resolve them. It will take
a combination of things, including child support, alimony (if
it is appropriate), budget reductions, and, when feasible, increased income. Do not panic just because you see deficits.
This is only the beginning, not the final result.

CUTTING BUDGETS

In most divorces, there is not enough income to fund everything you have included in the budgets. This means that you must systematically consider reductions. The first thing to remember is that your job is to reduce *your* budget, not your spouse's budget. Let your spouse work on his/her own budget, at least initially. The second thing to remember is that you are looking for alternatives and that writing something down is not the same thing as doing it. Considering cuts is not the same as deciding to commit to them. This is a process of planning and exploration. The purpose is to try alternative solutions to the problem of a shortage of funds. It is an exercise in "what if." What if I repair this car instead of replacing it? What if the kids go to public school instead of private school? What if I spend half of what I budgeted on clothes for me or for the children? What if I take a different kind of vacation or what if I donate less to the church or take up a less expensive activity than skiing? The object is to establish priorities so that you can decide what is most important to you and what is less important. This is why you must concentrate on your own budget initially and not on your spouse's budget. When you tell your spouse what is important to him, or when he or she tells you what should be important to you, the only possible outcome is fighting. You stay in control of your divorce by taking responsibility for yourself. This is a time when you need to do so.

One way to establish your priorities is to make three revisions in your budget. In the first revision, reduce the total by 10 percent. Then do it again and reduce it another 10 percent. Finally, do it a third time and reduce it yet another 10 percent. In this way you will decide what your priorities truly are. This may also help you make some important strategic decisions. If, for example, you are trying to decide whether to sell your house, you can try out various alternatives here. If I sell the house, what will be the cost of replacement housing? Do I end up with more or less? Does my spouse end up with more or less income or expense? Does it make life easier or harder? What expenses does it eliminate? Will I have more or less to spend on other things I want?

You can develop three or four alternative budgets as preparation for negotiating child support and alimony with your spouse. If you do this well, you will be prepared to negotiate efficiently. You will be able to maintain control because you will know the consequences of the proposals your spouse will raise and you will each be able to discuss alternatives from a knowledgeable perspective rather than speculation. This budgeting process can be taxing and tedious. But it is one of the most worthwhile tasks you can do to insure the success of your support negotiations.

THE MARITAL HOME—TO SELL OR NOT TO SELL?

A house of your own is part of the American dream. For most middle-class Americans, particularly those with children, home ownership is synonymous with a sense of well-being and security. Whether it is a detached house, a townhouse, a condominium, or a co-op in the city, owning your own home is an important value. It is no surprise, then, to learn that this is often one of the most difficult issues to resolve in a divorce. One spouse, typically the wife, wants to stay in the house with the kids at least until they have graduated high school and left home. The other spouse, the husband in this case, wants to sell the house for one or two reasons. First, he believes that the house consumes too much of the monthly family income. Second, the equity in the house, the difference between what the house would sell for and what is owed on the mortgage, is the biggest part of total family savings. By selling the house and dividing the equity, he hopes that he will still be able to own his own home, or that both of you will be able to own your own, smaller homes.

It is a difficult issue because there is no simple solution, and both spouses have valid and important concerns. The wife does not want to move because she already feels too much stress from the divorce and because she feels that moving will be harmful to the children. The husband, too, has a valid concern. Keeping the house for a long time will preempt him from reestablishing his own life in a satisfactory manner. Often the best a couple can do initially is to acknowledge that each has valid concerns and then explore the alternatives. In many cases a thorough exploration of alternatives will reveal the sensible thing to do. It may become obvious to both that the house should be sold now or soon. In other cases, it will become obvious that it should be kept until the kids finish high school.

An important question is whether you bought the house on the premise of one or two incomes. For example, many younger couples who recently bought their first home were both employed at the time and had to stretch, even on two incomes, to qualify for their mortgage. They decided to be "rent poor" for a few years in order to own their own home. The mortgage and tax payments each month required 30 percent of their joint gross income but about 43 percent of their net income. Even if they were to equalize the income of two households now, the mortgage payment will represent 80 percent of the income of that household.

In such cases, it is possible to hang on to the house *only* at the expense of completely impoverishing both new households. No house is worth it. If this is your problem, your house should be sold as quickly as possible.

For many divorcing couples the situation is different. If you bought your house five or more years ago, it may be worth twice or three times what you paid for it. The equity in the house is probably the core of your life savings. The decision to sell the house now becomes more complicated. The parent who will remain with the children looks at the relatively low mortgage payment and concludes that alternate housing would actually cost more. The mortgage that was taken twelve years ago requires a low monthly payment by today's standards. Compared to current rents, it appears to offer a savings.

From an economist's perspective, this conclusion is not quite true. What that parent overlooks is that the real cost of keeping the house must also include the *opportunity costs* on the equity tied up in the house. That is, if the equity in the house were turned into an interest-bearing investment, it would produce income. Forgoing that interest income is the opportunity cost of the equity. If, for example, you own a house worth $150,000 and there is a mortgage of $50,000, you have equity of $100,000. Although your mortgage payment may be $600 per month and your taxes might be $200 a month, your real cost is actually higher than $800. If you sold the house and put the $100,000 in a savings account that yielded 8% interest, your annual income would be $8,000 a year, or $666 a month. So theoretically, your monthly carrying cost is not $800, but rather $1,466, when you add your opportunity costs. In actuality, it would not be quite so dramatic because the selling costs and capital-gains tax might reduce your equity substantially and the interest you receive would also be taxable income. The point is that keeping your equity tied up in the house is not cost free, and it is not necessarily the most economic route.

You need to examine all the financial consequences and alternatives. If it is only a few years until the last child is emancipated, keeping the house may be a good idea. But if it will be a long time and all the family savings are tied up in the house, you may want to consider selling. I have seen some couples successfully sell the marital home and buy two smaller houses in the same neighborhood. Others have used the equity liberated by the sale to achieve educational goals or to provide a subsidy that alleviated the economic squeeze of supporting two households. There is no automatic right answer. Each alternative proposal should be explored and budgeted thoroughly so that you can both assess all the consequences and advantages.

Also, remember that the decision is not whether to sell but rather, is *when* to sell. Do we sell this year, next year, in five years, or ten years? Also, remember that if this is your primary savings it is likely to be the *only* savings for years to come. If the cost of two households is a financial strain, it is unlikely that either of you is going to be able to save very much out of your income in the years ahead. In the economy of the 1990s, it is also unlikely that we are going to see the rapid appreciation of real estate that we saw in the 1980s. So, if you are proposing to sit on your spouse's only savings for the next ten years, and if your spouse will have to live without access to those savings, don't be surprised if his or her reaction is negative. Nor is your concern that the children not be disrupted the only factor to be considered. It may well be that a year from now you could sell the house and move to another home without overwhelming the kids. And it may be that such a move would provide a significant advantage for all of you that contributes significantly to the overall adaptation of the entire family.

CONCLUSION

Divorce forces you to take responsibility for all aspects of your life, whether you want to or not. Even the initiating spouse will be apprehensive about handling unfamiliar aspects of family and household management.

The budget process, although demanding, is also reassuring. By researching your expenses and defining your needs, you will fill in the "great unknowns," those areas of ignorance that trigger your fears and insecurities. By working through successive budgets you will find yourself controlling the process, not being controlled by it. As you develop real numbers for those unfamiliar budget lines, your dread of the unknown will disappear because you will have turned it into something known—and manageable.

As I said at the beginning of this chapter, budgets are mandatory for your negotiations. They are practical tools to help you and your spouse reach the agreement best for you. The side benefit of the budgeting process is that it will also build your self-confidence. As you work through your budgets, you will learn how much control you actually have over your life.

Chapter Eleven

NEGOTIATING CHILD
SUPPORT

*H*ow *you negotiate* child support will predict more than how much money will be paid as child support. It will also measure how well you will cooperate as parents and, ultimately, how well your children will adapt to the divorce. Few lawyers seem to understand the tricky emotional undercurrents of child-support discussions.

Child support often brings out all the disagreements you had as a couple about sharing, giving, power, trust, and control. The practical problem of *How do we pay for the kids?* may be inadvertently translated into a rehash of marital issues that are really unrelated to child support. Many couples damage their post-divorce relationship because they allow financial issues to become hopelessly entangled with the unresolved emotional issues of the marriage. Take care that this does not happen to you.

CASE STUDY: BRIAN AND KATHY

Kathy and Brian are halfway through their negotiations and have reached the point when it is time to negotiate child support. Although their early discussions have gone well, they are beginning to feel a rising level of tension as they grapple with the hard economic realities.

They did not need much time to decide that the children would reside principally with Kathy. Brian is a marketing director with a job that requires almost weekly travel. It was not practical in their case to even consider an equal parenting arrangement because there was no way Brian could have done it without a complete change of jobs. Kathy has always been the primary caretaker for the kids and both want that to continue. They have also decided that the kids, Stacy, age twelve, and Joanna, age eight, would be better off staying in the house a few years although they are in general agreement that it should be sold when Stacy graduates high school.

Each parent has prepared a budget and is alarmed because it appears that there is not enough money. Kathy is particularly upset about some comments that Brian made when he saw her budget. He said that Stacy and Joanna did not need both piano lessons and dance lessons. He also criticized her clothing budget for the girls saying that there was no reason that the girls couldn't get along with less. Kathy is angry because Brian seems to be indifferent to what growing kids cost and because he does not realize how hard the divorce is on the girls. Brian just seems to be interested in establishing his own life and is not paying enough attention to the financial needs of the kids. When Kathy tried to talk to him about starting to save money for the girls' college education, he refused to discuss it, saying that there was no way he could make such a commitment right now.

SOME DANGERS INHERENT IN CHILD SUPPORT NEGOTIATIONS

Brian and Kathy are in danger from one of the most common pitfalls of child-support negotiations. Kathy is assuming the role of exclusive bargaining agent for the children. This role for the primary caregiving parent, most often the mother, is unwittingly encouraged by judges and lawyers to the detriment of all concerned. In most divorces children reside primarily with their mothers. It is the mother who makes most child-related expenditures, and therefore it is to the mother that child support is most often paid. If the mother is able to convince the father to pay more child support, there is more for the children. If she is unable to convince him to pay more, there is less for the children. This definition of the role of each parent can create a dangerous process that aligns the children emotionally with their mother and produces a distorted perception of their father as a stingy ogre or, just as bad, as a sugar daddy.

Both Kathy and Brian contribute to this "mother in the middle" syndrome. Fathers easily lose the distinction between money they pay for the children's support and alimony so that their resentment about alimony contaminates their ability to be generous with the children.

Mothers can sometimes lose the distinction as well, so that they demand in the name of the children something they are trying to preserve for themselves.

When this happens, we find the mother arguing for an expansive definition of what the children need, while the father argues that the children can get along with less. Because most families *are* going to have to get along with less, the children will have to tighten their belts along with their parents. Unless both parents take equal responsibility for the economic discipline of the family, these negotiations quickly fall apart. Typically, the father is accused of neglecting his children, and the wife is accused of being insensitive and indifferent to the husband's needs.

The problem is exacerbated when one of the parents does not want the divorce and wants to shield the children from its consequences. The need to impose economic cutbacks on the children feeds the anger of the spouse who didn't want the divorce and provides further proof that the departing spouse is a villain.

When the *needs of the children* become this hot emotional issue, you are in trouble. The children show up for a weekend with Daddy and say their shoes don't fit because Mommy doesn't have enough child support to buy new ones. The wife tells the kids that Daddy has decided that they cannot go to summer camp. The kids begin to shake down their father for extra goodies their mother tells them she can't afford. The financial alliance between mother and children reinforces an emotional alliance between them. In turn, this may sour the time that the children spend with the father, and eventually reduces the father's desire to spend time with his children. When this happens, everyone gets hurt.

AVOIDING THE PROBLEM

The best way to resolve the problem of child-support negotiations is for mother and father to make the difficult economic decisions about the children jointly. Kathy and Brian will have to discuss piano and dance lessons with each other and with the children. If these items are to be reduced, Brian must be part of the process and not just leave it to Kathy. And if there is to be less money for the kids' clothing, it should be decided only after Brian finds out for himself just what it really costs to clothe the girls.

It is not productive for the mother to play the exclusive role of child advocate. The object of the negotiation is for the children's parents to make joint parental allocation of family resources for the children. That requires both parents to determine (as objectively as possible) what the kids need, how those needs relate to the family resources, and which needs have priority. Intelligent child-support negotiation requires that both father and mother know the real costs of the children and solve problems jointly when budget cutbacks have to be made. It may be true that they no longer can afford summer camp. But it does not automatically follow that the mother is responsible for providing supervision and entertainment for the kids through the summer. The problems created by the decision to forgo camp fall on both mother and father, and together they must decide what to do.

Both parents may have to compile a list of all the clothes the kids need for a year and then find out what those clothes will cost. If they make joint decisions, they avoid putting the primary residential parent in a position of having to convince the other parent. By keeping this a mutual task they avoid the problems that frequently afflict child-support discussions.

THE CHILDREN'S STANDARD OF LIVING

Reducing the children's standard of living is one of the most painful tasks of the divorce. Some people feel so guilty or so angry about the divorce that they vow the children will not be affected economically no matter what happens.

If you are wealthy, this goal is not difficult to achieve. But if you are like most middle-class people, it's unrealistic, and the sooner you let it go the better. It is not in the interests of your children that their parents sacrifice all so that they never notice the divorce. It *is* in the best interests of your children that two viable households be created. It is in their best interest that both of you adjust well to the divorce. And it is in their interests that their vital needs be met in a reasonable manner.

Most important, you must not make the children a conduit through which you express your own disappointment with the divorce. You may not be able to afford fancy summer vacations with the children. You may have to buy their clothes on sale; they may get one new pair of sneakers at a time instead of two. None of this will harm them. They may have to live in a smaller house. And, although no child likes to move, that won't harm them either.

Many people get stuck because they have to give up *their* dreams for the kids. You may have wanted your child to attend a private high school, but she will get educated at a public high school. It may have been a terrific idea to get your son a car as a high school graduation present. It is disappointing to you both that you can't, but he will not be harmed by waiting a few more years to have his own car.

There is no money for highly discretionary expenditures for the middle-class children of divorce. You will only be able to make such expenditures by sacrificing your basic needs or those of your spouse. And since few people are prepared to sacrifice their own basic needs, you may find yourself proposing that your spouse make sacrifices so the kids can go on exactly as before. It is an unnecessary and foolish way to get into a battle.

Make a distinction between what kids need and what you desire for them. Focus on the *needs*. Just because something might be good for them or fun for them does not mean that they must have it or that you must have it. Children should end up with about the same standard of living as their parents. A large discrepancy either way suggests that something went wrong.

ALLOCATING CHILD SUPPORT

Once you have a good idea what your children are going to cost, you need to divide the responsibility for providing it between you and your spouse. How you do that depends on how each of you defines fairness. Let's review some of the principles you should consider.

First, the children's budgets should be fully funded. That is, every item in the children's portion of both your budgets should be either funded or eliminated by budget cutting.

Second, both parents are responsible for contributing to the support of the children. Just because one earns more than the other does not mean that only that spouse must contribute.

Third, your child-support contributions should be based on your relative ability to pay. The parent with the greater income should contribute more than the parent with the lesser income. This should also be related realistically to the costs of each parent. There are three ways to allocate the child support between you: state guidelines, straight ratio method, and ratio of discretionary income.

STATE-MANDATED GUIDELINES

In the early 1980s the federal government reacted to data suggesting that low child-support awards and poor enforcement in the state courts were leaving millions of divorced women and their children in poverty. The resulting federal legislation required each state to establish minimum standards of child support to be applied in the courts that handled divorce. Although some bar associations resisted, the states complied, prodded by the risk of losing federal assistance. Although each state was allowed to establish its own guidelines, the overall result was an improvement over those in the past. Consequently, one of the items of information you should investigate is the child-support guidelines for your state.

In some states, child-support guidelines are expressed as a percent of net family income that is to be allocated to the children. In other states it is expressed as a percentage of gross income. In my home state of New Jersey, for example, if total net family income is less than $57,000 and there is one child, the guidelines call for between 19 percent and 21 percent of net income to be allocated to the children. For two children the range is 29 percent to 31 percent, and for three children the range goes up to 39 percent to 43 percent.

If you are unable to agree on child-support allocation using the other methods discussed here, or if you are deadlocked on your differences about child support, by all means use your state-imposed guidelines. In most cases these are the guidelines that will be applied by the judge if you go to trial. It is better to apply the guidelines and have the issue resolved than to drag things out. However, using the state guidelines is not always the best or the fairest way to go. These guidelines are based on statistical assumptions that may not apply to your family. In many cases they have not been calculated to include expenses such as day care or summer camp. You are better off working through the budgeting process and then using one of the following two methods.

STRAIGHT RATIO

To compare the two ways of allocating child support, let's look at Kathy and Brian. He earns $70,000 a year and brings home, after taxes, $4,200 a month. Kathy earns $35,000 a year and brings home, after taxes, $2,000 a month. The most common method for allocating child-support responsibility is to use a ratio of the father's income to the mother's income. Using this simple ratio, Brian with $70,000 annual income earns 66 percent of total income, and Kathy with $35,000 earns 33 percent. In other words, Brian has two-thirds of the family income, or twice what Kathy has.

They have calculated the combined cost of the children in both households to be $1,500 a month. Using a straight ratio, this means that Brian will contribute two-thirds, or $1,000, while Kathy contributes one-third, or $500. This is the way most court-imposed child-support guidelines operate, and it appears to have broad acceptance among lawyers and judges. But that does not mean that it is a fair way of allocating child support.

Brian and Kathy have calculated their budgets as follows:

Kathy's total budget	$3,100	Brian's total budget	$2,900
Children's portion	1,200	children's portion	300
Kathy's net expense	1,900	Brian's net expense	2,700
Kathy's net income	2,000	Brian's net income	4,200
Kathy's discretionary		Brian's discretionary	
income	100	income	1,500

Discretionary income here refers to how much money each has after he/she covers his/her own personal expenses. Kathy has net income of $2,000 per month and has a personal expense for herself of $1,900 per month. This leaves her with discretionary income of $100 per month. Brian has personal expenses of $2,700 a month and net income of $4,200. This leaves him with discretionary income of $1,500 per month. It is from this discretionary income that each can contribute to child support.

The combined total allocated for the children in both households is $1,500: $1,200 in Kathy's home and $300 in Brian's home. When we apply a straight ratio to Kathy and Brian we are immediately faced with a problem. If Kathy is to pay her one-third, where is it going to come from? She needs $1,900 for herself and has only $2,000 total net income. If she pays her one-third of the children's support she must come up with $500. This leaves her with a $400 per month deficit.

If this deficit is not redressed by more income, it means that Kathy will have to come up with her child-support contribu-

Kathy's net income	$2,000
Kathy's expenses	1,900
child support	500
total needed	2,400
deficit	(400)

tion by reducing her own level of basic need by $400. That is, she will have to reduce her personal expenses from $1,900 to $1,500 per month, a reduction that may mean serious deprivation.

Now let's look at Brian. He has budgeted his own expenses at $2,700 per month, a level considerably higher than that budgeted by Kathy. But even with this higher standard of living, he has a surplus of $1,500 per month. If he now contributes $1,000 a month, he is still left with $500 a month extra income—what is generally called discretionary income.

Brian's net income	$4,200
Brian's expenses	2,700
child support	1,000
total needed	3,700
extra money	500

Thus Brian has $500 extra and Kathy has a $400 deficit. Given these numbers, all of which are very typical, one must conclude that this straight-ratio method for allocating child support can produce unfair results.

RATIO OF DISCRETIONARY INCOME

A fairer approach is to allocate child support on the basis of a ratio of discretionary income rather than a ratio of gross income. If we apply this ratio to Kathy and Brian we get different results.

We know that Kathy has $100 of discretionary income and that Brian has $1,500. This means that there is a total of $1,600 of discretionary income of which Kathy has 1/16th or 6.25 percent and Brian has 15/16ths or 93.75 percent. Applying this ratio to the total child cost of $1,500 we get a contribution of $93.75 per month for Kathy and we get a contribution of $1,406.25 for Brian. Now let's look at the results.

Kathy's net income	$ 2,000	Brian's net income	$ 4,200
Kathy's expenses	1,900	Brian's expenses	2,700
child support	93.25	child support	1,406.75
total needed	1,993.25	total needed	4,106.75
left over	$6.75	left over	$93.25

In this second approach Brian ends up with almost the whole child support responsibility because he has most of the discretionary income. Kathy, after meeting her child support responsibility, has $6 left each month, hardly a fortune, but much fairer to her than a $400 deficit. Brian has $94 each month left over, not as much as he had before, but still more than Kathy. I believe that this second approach, although generally rejected by other lawyers, brings you closer to a fair result, and therefore to a better settlement. To see how it applies to your divorce, you will have to perform similar calculations. If you and your spouse have generally equal incomes, the straight-ratio method will work fairly. But if you do not, the straight-ratio method, notwithstanding its common acceptance, produces unjust results. Calculate child support both ways and compare. It is worth the effort, and you should make it.

CHILD SUPPORT AND JOINT CUSTODY

Because joint custody has become more popular than in the past, its impact on child-support arrangements requires some special attention. Our concern here is not with the symbolic joint custody discussed in earlier chapters, but with genuine joint parenting arrangements in which the parents share the parenting responsibilities more or less equally. Here is the problem: If each parent maintains a home for the children and each one has the kids about half the time, why should either pay the other toward child support? Perhaps it may be more convenient for one to buy the clothes, or to pay the bill for day care or summer camp. And for these purposes there may need to be a joint fund to which both parents contribute. But beyond these expenses, is there justification to negotiate conventional child support to pay for routine household expenses? The answer is: maybe.

Joint custody—genuine joint parenting with equal-time provisions—is a more expensive arrangement than sole custody or symbolic joint custody. It will not work well unless there is some semblance of parity between the two households. If one household is the "rich" one and the other the "poor" one, cooperation will break down before long. This does not mean that income must be equalized in order for joint custody to work. However, both households must offer something resembling equal amenities to the children. If Daddy's house is the one with the Nintendo game while Mommy's house has few toys and no games, I can almost guarantee disruptive resentment.

In true joint custody there is generally a higher rent cost. Both households will require a more-or-less equal amount of space. Each child will probably need his or her own bedroom, whereas they could share if it were an alternate-weekend-only arrangement. Transporting clothing is inconvenient, so some clothing will be purchased in duplicate and left at each house. Certain toys will be duplicated. Things like bicycles will be duplicated. Child-care arrangements will tend to be more complicated—and more expensive. In sum, the total cost of the children will increase.

If you are the parent with the greater income, this means that child support may not be decreased as much as you might have expected or hoped. In one sense it is true that you might end up paying for certain things twice, once at your house and again, through child support, at your spouse's house. The way to handle this problem is to consider the total cost of the kids in both dwellings and to negotiate child support to achieve your goal of equitable and effective joint parenting.

A word of warning: There are a few lawyers who advise fathers to pursue joint custody as a way of justifying reducing or eliminating child support. This is a misguided strategy.

SOME SECONDARY ISSUES

In addition to negotiating the basic amount you each will contribute, there are a number of secondary issues that need to be resolved. Doing this now will save you problems in the future. At the very least, you should begin to consider each one now.

COLLEGE EXPENSES

College tuition has become a serious problem for middle-class families in the past few years because tuition has increased much faster than the rate of inflation. If it is a problem for intact families, it is an even bigger problem for divorced families. Many private colleges and universities charge $20,000 or more annually for room, board, and tuition. Even state schools can charge as much as $8,000 or $9,000 a year. All this must be paid with after-tax dollars. This means that an annual cost of $18,000 for college would require approximately $24,000 of pretax earnings. If you're already stretched, this added expense may become impossible. As we all want the best for our children, the negotiation of who pays for what can become not just difficult but also one of those symbolic issues that carries emotional weight having nothing to do with college.

The solution is to approach this issue pragmatically and simply, just as you would any other issue.

First ask yourselves: What would you be doing right now about this if you were not getting divorced? If you have young children and college is a long way off, you might be doing nothing about it, planning to think about it sometime in the future. In that case, you probably should do the same now. If your ability to save money now is nonexistent, there is nothing to be done. Nor is there any use trying to determine who will pay for it later. Too much can happen in the intervening years that cannot be predicted right now. What I usually advise is to include a clause in your agreement that you will each contribute to the college education of your children, assuming that they are capable of and desire a college education, that you will contribute according to your relative ability to pay, and that you will further discuss the matter as each child enters the junior year of high school.

What about starting now to save for college? Kathy has proposed to Brian that they start saving now for this purpose rather than leave it for later. She thinks they should either start a separate savings account or dedicate some of their assets to be reserved for college expenses.

But in their case there is no money available for saving. If there was substantial discretionary income available it might be realistic, but for Kathy and Brian it is not.

Even when there is discretionary income available, opening savings accounts for the children may not be feasible. There is little tax advantage to saving money in your child's name. You may be reluctant to commit a major portion of your savings so that you lose any choice about its disposition. If you decide to pursue such a program, you will need to agree how and by whom the money will be managed. If you agree on a schedule of contributions, be sure you can live up to the commitment. I have seen such savings accounts become the object of bitter power struggles; you should resolve these issues in advance.

One issue that frequently arises when parents agree to help kids with college is the range of choice the child will have in choosing a college. I think it is a mistake, unless you are wealthy, to obligate yourselves so that you must pay for any college the child chooses whether you can afford it or not. This abrogates your parental authority as well as control over your own finances. I know that this can be a delicate issue. I also know that most state universities offer an excellent education. Furthermore, many of the nation's future leaders will be trained at colleges and universities that do not cost $20,000 a year. What matters is that the child gets an education that fully develops his or her intellect, not one that meets some expensive status need. You should specify in your agreement that the standard of cost you are committing to is that charged for room, board, and tuition at the state university in your state. You can always choose later to pay for a more expensive school if you wish to and can afford it.

Do not forget that what you spend need not be proscribed by your separation agreement. The agreement addresses the obligations you bind yourselves to in a contractual relationship with each other. Each of you will undoubtedly spend additional money on your children—not because you have to but because you choose to—as a product of your parent/child relationship. Do not fall into the trap of assuming that you are the exclusive bargaining agent for your child to the other parent. Your child will have an independent relationship with each of you. It is appropriate for your child to take your ability to pay into account when choosing a college.

MEDICAL EXPENSES AND INSURANCE

Your agreement should specify who provides medical insurance for the children and how uninsured medical and dental expenses will be shared. Most employers provide medical insurance for employees as a fringe benefit. Only some employers provide free coverage for family members. If you both are employed, make sure that you compare the plans carefully to pick the best one for the children.

Unreimbursed expense may be a problem depending on the plan. Many plans provide for a deductible or co-insurance requirement for each family member. You should calculate what the maximum deductible would be for each child and compare that to the average medical bills for each child over the past year or two. Some children seldom require medical treatment, and, except for emergencies, you can predict pretty closely what medical costs will be each year for routine care. For children with allergies, asthma, or other chronic conditions, the cost will be much more. You should budget based on your experience. Unreimbursed medical and dental expenses should be treated like any other item. However, there are some expenditures like psychotherapy and cosmetic surgery that may be only partially covered or not covered at all. These extraordinary expenses can't be budgeted because we do not expect them to be routine. These expenses are an unknown risk that must be apportioned between you and your spouse in some reasonable fashion. Usually, agreements provide that such expenses will be shared according to some formula (50/50, 60/40, 70/30, etc.) that reflects the ability of each parent to pay. The agreement also provides that the parent authorizing the expense will not do so in non-emergency situations without first consulting the other parent.

LIFE INSURANCE

Most support agreements include provision for life insurance in the event that a parent dies. I think it is a good idea, if done correctly. Generally one wants to provide enough insurance so that the interest, figured at the usual prevailing rates, would replace the contribution of that parent to child support. Many people have life insurance as a fringe benefit through employment. If you don't have it, you should consider buying term life insurance, and I would recommend amounts of at least $100,000 per child. Term life insurance is the lowest-cost life insurance because it pays only upon death. Other forms of life insurance such as whole life or universal life insurance accumulate cash surrender value over time. Some people find them attractive as forced savings plans. I think that anything but term life is a waste of money for divorcing couples who are tight on cash.

The children should be named as the beneficiaries of these policies—but who should be named as the trustee for the children? Unless there is a dramatic reason not to do so, your spouse should be named as the trustee for the children. If you die, your spouse will become solely responsible for the children. If you were the surviving parent, you would not want to have to get the approval of a former brother-in-law or other third party before spending money on your children. Without some clear historical evidence that your spouse cannot manage money, it is your spouse who should be named trustee.

COST-OF-LIVING ADJUSTMENT

A common cause of disputes after the divorce is disagreement about the impact of inflation on child support. In the past few years, inflation has ranged from 3 percent to 5 percent. However, in the early eighties the annual inflation rate exceeded 10 percent. Over three or four years, inflation can seriously erode the value of child support, if unaddressed. You should solve this problem in advance by incorporating a cost-of-living adjustment into your agreement.

Parents who pay child support have some predictable—and justified—concerns about cost-of-living increases. First is the fear that their incomes will not keep up with inflation. If this happens and the child support is linked to the inflation rate, they fear that ever larger portions of their paychecks will go for child support. The second objection is that just because there is 5 percent inflation this does not mean that the cost for *their* children rises 5 percent.

The first fear is easily addressed. You provide that child support will be adjusted annually according to the annual change in the consumer price index as published by the United States Department of Labor. You *also* provide that the actual dollar increase will not exceed the annual increase in the paying parent's income. This puts a cap on the increase and is an adequate, if not perfect, safeguard against unfairly burdening the paying parent. The second objection is not so easily addressed. After all, you cannot engage professional economists each year to compare the consumption patterns of your children to those of the general population. This is when simple common sense must apply. You may be right. Your kids' consumption pattern may be less than the annual inflation rate for a particular year; it may also be more. It is not worth what it will cost to find out exactly. If you are paying $1000 a month and inflation is 5 percent, it means that you will increase support by $50 a month. To apply complex and time-consuming procedures to perfecting the formula might change the support one way or the other by $10 a month. It is not worth it. I have helped many clients attempt to devise elaborate systems. My suggestion is that you use the Consumer Price Index and get on with your lives.[14]

EMANCIPATION

Emancipation marks the economic boundary between childhood and adulthood and the end of your financial obligation to support your children. When emancipation occurs and what it means for child support can differ. Although the law varies from state to state, emancipation generally occurs upon graduation from high school or when a child reaches the age of eighteen—whichever occurs last. However, as you might expect, there are some complications. As a practical matter, most middle-class kids are not emancipated upon high school graduation because they are going to college, and few children will support themselves through college.

Many state courts have now adopted a policy of delaying emancipation up to four years if a child goes to college full time. What these courts are saying is that emancipation in the real world is not a simple mechanical event. For most families, college education is an assumed and necessary prerequisite to economic independence, and these courts are unwilling to declare a child emancipated just because he or she graduates high school. Today, the trend is to recognize that the obligation of the parent extends past high school and through college. Settlement agreements often include language providing that emancipation will be delayed if the child attends college full time immediately after high school.

This raises another issue. What should happen to child-support payments when a child is attending college, particularly if the child resides at the college? The parents of new college students are often surprised to learn how much time college students actually spend at home. With summer vacation, winter vacation, spring vacation, and others, a live-away college students can easily spend five months a year at home. This means that you still need to have a room for them, they still drive your car, still eat your food, and, in general, cost you money in addition to college costs. Consequently it is not unreasonable that the parent who resides with the children will seek some continuation of child support even though the child is away at college. For the parent paying support, this demand comes as a rude shock because he (or she) thought that having paid for college, he would not also be expected to pay for the same child at home.

In such a case, both parents have reasonable problems that ought to be addressed in the agreement. Child-support payments should not necessarily end just because the child lives away at college, but neither should they be maintained at pre-college levels. You should look at the actual impact on expenses and deal with it realistically, as you would any other change in circumstance. The child support should be adjusted downward to reflect the reduced costs of having the child at home only part time. You can do this either by formula or by agreeing to a renegotiation of child support at the time the child goes to college.

If emancipation is delayed for college, what about graduate school? Are the parents responsible for supporting their child through law school or medical school? I am not aware of any courts that have imposed such a responsibility on parents except in very unusual circumstances. As a practical matter, if the child desires a postgraduate education, your contribution, if any, will be negotiated directly between each of you and the child and will not be a part of your contract with your spouse.

There are many fathers who after paying child support still go on to spend large sums of money on their children, not because they have to, but because it gives them pleasure. Similarly, if your child wants to go to law school and wants parental assistance, that child is old enough to seek such help directly from you and his/her other parent. Just because it isn't provided for in the agreement does not mean that both parents will not provide assistance.

THE IMPACT OF EMANCIPATION OF THE FIRST OF SEVERAL CHILDREN

If you have more than one child, child support will be reduced when the first child is emancipated. But the emancipation of the first of two children does not mean that child support is reduced by half. The cost of housing and utilities stays the same. The cost of family medical insurance and auto insurance for young drivers also stays the same. Accordingly, to reduce support by 50 percent upon the emancipation of the first of two children is unfair and unrealistic. A reduction of one-third is more appropriate for the emancipation of the first of two children, and a reduction of 20 percent is appropriate for the emancipation of the first of three children. These details should be considered in your agreement to avoid problems later on.

KEY POINTS TO REMEMBER

Negotiating child support can be taxing on both your time and your emotions. A large dose of common sense helps a great deal. We have considered a number of key points in this chapter, including:

- Don't let one parent (usually the mother) become the bargaining agent for the children.
- For most middle-class families facing divorce, it's unrealistic to attempt to maintain the children's standard of living after the divorce without some change.
- Child support can be allocated between you and your spouse according to state-mandated guidelines, a straight ratio of gross incomes of you and your spouse, or the ratio of discretionary income of you and your spouse. The last method seems to be the fairest, all things considered.

- Joint custody is more expensive than traditional single parent custody.
- If your children are near or at college age, college selection and expenses should be included in the child-support agreement. If they are still young, it is better to defer the college decisions until a later time, such as the child's junior year in high school.
- How medical expenses and insurance will be handled should be included in child-support agreements.
- Term life insurance is also a good idea. The children should be named beneficiaries, with your spouse named as trustee.
- You should include a cost-of-living adjustment in your agreement. It should be based on a simple index, such as the consumer price index.
- The time of emancipation of a child may vary depending on your state's law and on whether your child goes to college.
- Child support for children away at college may have to continue, but perhaps at a reduced amount.
- The emancipation of one child (where there are two or more children) should not reduce the child support proportionately; it should reduce the support by a smaller amount. These costs should be reviewed in detail.

Chapter Twelve

NEGOTIATING ALIMONY

CASE STUDY: MICHAEL AND JULIE

Michael came to see me in a state of indignation. After a fifteen-year marriage, his wife, Julie, had told him that she didn't love him any more and wanted a divorce. When Mike refused to leave the house, Julie had taken their two children and moved to her mother's house. Now she was demanding three things from Mike. She wanted to live in the house with the kids, she wanted Mike to support the kids, and she wanted him to support her.

After some thought, Mike had decided that it probably made more sense for Julie and the kids to live in the house. It would cost much less to find an apartment for him than for Julie and two kids. And of course he would support the kids— they were his kids, and he had always been a good provider. But that was where he drew the line. If Julie thought she was going to get one red cent in alimony, she was dead wrong! No alimony—no, not one damn cent! *"She* left *me*. It wasn't a bad marriage, not like some others I've known," he said. "There was no reason to get divorced. Ever since she went back to college, her damned professors have put all sorts of ideas in her head. She said she wanted more independence. She said she wanted a career and that she wasn't spending her life doing housework anymore. Well, if she wants independence, I'll give her independence. Let her work for a living, then she can tell me about independence." I've heard outbursts like Mike's many times. At best, men feel ambivalent about alimony. At worst, alimony is a red flag that triggers instant belligerence. For Mike, alimony is salt rubbed into his wounds of rejection. His wife doesn't want him, but she wants him to support her. "The nerve of that woman," he says.

It was a long time before Mike could look at the issue dispassionately, even though he was basically a fair person. He was reasonable about the house and about supporting the kids. But when I asked him to take the same approach to support his wife, his anger was in the way.

Julie was not able to support herself. She was in her third year of college, majoring in business. In a year and a half she would graduate and be able to get a well-paying job. If she quit now, her income-generating ability would be very limited.

In time Mike realized that supporting his wife *now* would enable her to earn much more *later*. That would reduce his child-support burden. Alimony in his case was not only appropriate, it was in his own interest. But it was not easy for Mike to separate his feelings of rejection and anger from the economic necessities of the divorce.

ALIMONY AND EMOTIONS

Alimony is the most complex issue to be negotiated in divorce. In some states the legal system connects alimony to fault, giving divorcing spouses an economic incentive to engage in mutual finger pointing about who is to blame for the failure of the marriage. Alimony is the "victim's" favorite issue. The victimized wife regards alimony as reparation payments; the victimized husband regards the denial of alimony as the just deserts of the woman who abandoned him. "Let him pay—he deserves it!" "Let her starve—she deserves it!" are reciprocal variations on the same theme.

The emotional whirlpool surrounding alimony is paralleled by the legal system's confusion about it. Nationwide, only 14 percent of divorcing women get any alimony.[15] Texas does not require alimony at all. Consequently there is little consensus among lawyers about alimony. Standards for alimony have changed dramatically in the past twenty years as a result of several reforms within divorce law. Most states have adopted some form of equitable distribution of the marital property. The essence of the reform was to permit the courts to award part of the husband's property to the wife, who up to that point was foreclosed from receiving the property because it was inevitably in the husband's name. Although equitable distribution enhanced women's position relative to the marital property, it introduced the assumption that the receipt of such property reduced the wife's need for alimony. Equitable distribution laws generally require the court to link the alimony determination to the property determination.

The second historical influence in the decline of alimony has been a paradoxical response to the women's movement itself. As a consequence of the increasing movement toward economic equality, there is a growing expectation among judges and lawyers that women can and should be employed and support themselves. The expectation that women become economically independent results in both lesser and shorter awards of alimony. This has led commentators to observe that the position of divorcing women has actually worsened as a result of these reforms, particularly for women in their forties and fifties, who tend to get caught in the midst of change. These women were raised with traditional sex-role assumptions, but they matured during a time of great flux in the roles of men and women. Many are not prepared to be economically independent and are indeed being victimized by changes

in the rules that are appropriate only for women who are
prepared for them.

ALIMONY FOR MEN

In this chapter I discuss alimony in the context of women
receiving and men paying. But in the interests of sexual equality some disclaimer is necessary. In truth, most statutes are not
written with this assumption made explicit. Statutes discuss
spousal support, maintenance, or alimony (different terms for
the same thing) as payable by and to either spouse. But for all
practical purposes I discuss women as recipients because the
payment of alimony by women to men is an unusual and
extraordinary event. It is true that the incidence is increasing
slightly as more women rise to high-paying positions in management and the professions. It is no longer astounding to find
a wife making significantly more money than her husband. It
is also no longer astounding to find couples in which the
husband has chosen to be the primary homemaker while the
wife pursues a high-paying career. And given the relative increase in the incidence of such arrangements, it is inevitable
that we get a few more divorces in which alimony payments by
the wife to the husband are likely.

The growing incidence of such cases, however, must be
kept in sharp perspective. In my last 200 cases, I have had only
one that fit this profile. The wife, a successful corporate lawyer, earned $300,000 a year while the husband, a teacher,
earned $30,000 a year. The wife had left the husband and it
was he who was staying in the marital home and providing
primary care for the children. Their settlement provided for
five years' alimony as part of a package of alimony and child
support to maintain the household until the youngest child
graduated high school. This case, however exemplary, is but
the exception that proves the rule. Accordingly I discuss alimony as something men pay to women.

ALIMONY AS A PRAGMATIC ISSUE

The first step toward making alimony manageable is to remove the symbolic heat from the concept. Alimony is not an expression of marital fault, nor is it a way of punishing either husband or wife. Alimony is simply part of the financial package necessary to bring a marriage to a just conclusion. If alimony is to be paid, it is because the wife is economically dependent on the husband's income.

I strongly urge men not to worry about the *idea* of alimony. Alimony becomes a battleground only when you turn it into an abstraction that carries all the emotional burdens of the divorce. The obligation to pay alimony becomes the symbol for everything the husband thought was bad in the marriage. His wife took too much, expected too much, argued too much, complained too much, and gave too little. She thought only of herself, didn't love him enough, didn't have sex enough, didn't pay attention enough, or any of the hundred other deficiencies that we find in our divorcing mates. Whatever grievances there are boil down to the feeling that "she doesn't deserve alimony!"

For their part, many divorcing women have strong feelings of ambivalence about alimony. On one hand, they need the money and are entitled to it. On the other hand, alimony represents a continued dependency on a man they do not wish to be dependent on, or a man they feel is less than reliable.

IF ONLY I HAD KNOWN THEN

One way to think about fairness with regard to alimony is to imagine yourselves the week before your marriage and negotiating a prenuptial agreement. This is one of the few occasions when hindsight can actually serve you well. Assume that each of you as a single person can choose to marry or not. The topic you are going to negotiate is alimony—specifically, what will happen if the wife agrees to have children. The facts are simple. For each year out of the workplace, her potential to earn income at age fifty is reduced about 3 percent.[16] So if she is twenty-five years old, and child rearing will take her away from a career for fifteen years, her permanent income loss is about 45 percent measured at age fifty. If she stays out of the workplace for twenty-five years, her permanent income loss is about 75 percent.

She thinks about this and says the following: "There is a fifty-fifty chance that we will get divorced by the time I am fifty. That is a very high probability. Although I am willing to marry you, I am afraid that if I take time off to have children and take care of the family, I will be penalized in the event we get divorced. What can you say to reassure me?" Her question, considering the probabilities, is far from outlandish. In fact, many young women today are asking questions very similar to this. It would seem that the husband-to-be has a limited number of possible responses. Let's try them out.

The first possibility is to offer nothing. In effect, he says, "If you marry me and if you choose to take time off to have children, that is the risk you assume." Now the bride-to-be has a choice. She can choose not to marry him or she can assume the risk and go forward with marriage and a family. If she takes the risk, she now has other choices to make. She can reduce her risk by taking off the minimal time necessary to have children and can limit the size of the family to one child. In other words, she can put her career on a par with his and give it priority. To protect her career she must minimize the time off for maternity leave by either hiring someone to stay and care for the child or by taking the child to day care outside the home.

Now the choice is his. Is this an acceptable arrangement? He thinks about it and decides that a small family isn't so bad, and, in fact, it might be okay to have a wife with a career. At least the money will come in handy. But now he seeks some reassurance. "But who will clean the house and cook and shop?" he asks. "Well," she replies, "if we can afford it, we can hire a full-time housekeeper. It may consume all my after-tax income, but at least it gets the chores done. Or, if we choose to, or if we can't afford the full-time housekeeper, we'll divide the work between us. One week I'll do the laundry, the next week you do it. I'll cook on one night, you cook the next. By alternating, we'll get all the chores done." This arrangement is not only fair, it is one that thousands of couples are currently making.

"But wait a minute," he may say. "This is not quite what I had in mind when I proposed marriage. I don't think I like this choice. I always thought I'd have a real family—two, maybe three, even four children. I'm on my way to a good career; we'll have enough money. I want a wife who enjoys being a mother and taking care of her family and her husband. I can't do laundry and I hate cooking. And my boss won't be very understanding if I have to take off from work to take the children to the dentist or go to a parent-teacher conference."

"Well," she may say, "that's what I want, too—at least while the children are younger. Once they're in high school I'd want to go to work at least part time, but I had always planned on being a full-time mother and wife. The trouble is, it's just too risky. Fifty percent is a very high probability of divorce. I'm sure it wouldn't apply to us, but still—it's just too big a chance. Isn't there anything you can do to reassure me?"

Now it's his choice again. He can have what he wants and what she wants, too. But to get it he'll have to agree to share the economic risk if the marriage fails. So he decides to take that risk. He proposes that if she takes time off from a career and the marriage fails, he will share some of his income with her to at least partially restore her to where she would have been if she had not taken time out to be a homemaker. How much compensation will he offer? And for how long? Will they just keep negotiating until they have a deal they both can live with? If they don't come to an agreement, they just won't marry, and if they do, they'll have already negotiated a fair alimony agreement.

WHAT WAS YOUR CONTRACT?

The exercise just described may seem artificial but it serves a useful purpose. It is a disciplined way to impose fairness on the negotiation.

If we take current practice as our standard, the law generally does not require men to be fair. A husband, of course, has that choice. But if he wishes to maintain even the pretense of fairness, he needs to look at what their contract really was. Whether it was explicit or implicit, there *was* a contract. Alimony may seem one-sided, but it is not. For most men, marriage facilitates careers. A man's economic position in the world is not injured by the marriage, and in many cases it is enhanced. In most cases, however, any time off from a career has reduced a woman's earning capacity. If the husband benefits from the domestic activities of the wife, I suggest that there is an implicit contract that requires him to reduce the economic penalty she pays for devoting her years to the family rather than to a career.

This contractual obligation is much easier to work with than the amorphous legal obligations in most statutes. Wife and husband together can determine how long the path to a job was closed to her and what that impact is on her now. A fifty-three-year-old woman, for example, who has not been employed for thirty years and has no special credentials has only the most marginal economic position in the marketplace. In some cases, any income-producing expectation may be grossly unfair, depending on family income and assets.

HOW ALIMONY BENEFITS WIVES

Alimony is best viewed as a transitional source of support to help the wife achieve independence. If she has initiated the divorce, with alimony she has had more time to think through where she's going and what she wants to achieve. She probably has a clearer understanding of her economic needs. If she is established in a career or has begun preparing for a career, her income needs and expectations are already defined, and alimony can be identified as a supplement for a limited time.

If the wife did not want the divorce or if she sees herself as abandoned, she perceives her need for alimony as even greater. Alimony will be an even more important issue if she has not thought about a career and is not established in a job or on her way to one. Except for the wealthy, most divorcing women will *have* to become employed if they are not already working. Alimony is the sole source of support in only a small number of divorces.

Before negotiating alimony, the wife should take careful stock of her resources and plans. If she is a mother of young children and needs to stay home with them for a time, she must decide when she can return to work. She also must decide what her work will be and if she needs further training or credentials. She needs to look at her property and assess its income-generating capacity. In other words, she must focus on her present and future income potential. Only then will she be able to decide where alimony fits into her plans. For example, she may decide to waive alimony if her husband agrees to give her a greater share of the marital property. She might do this because she prefers the security of owning income-generating property to income paid by her ex-spouse. Or she may expect that in five years her own earned income will be sufficient to meet her needs. She can use that expectation in her negotiation. The better defined her interests are, the easier it will be for her to make an intelligent case for her alimony proposals. Even if getting a job is not a realistic alternative, the wife's negotiating position will be stronger if she has explored this option along with her other financial resources. She may well have a legal entitlement to alimony. But a woman's best strategy for negotiating is to stress needs and interests first and entitlement second. The more concrete her plans and proposals, the better she will negotiate.

HOW ALIMONY BENEFITS HUSBANDS

In the long view, alimony can serve many of the husband's interests. Believe it or not, it is in *his* interest that his wife views the alimony agreement as just. Bitter ex-wives get even. Intentionally or not, they can and often do poison a father's relationship with his children. They can look for ways to take husbands back to court to improve their position. Alimony can buy you peace—an important asset in post-divorce life.

A gross disparity in living standards between father and mother may affect the children's feelings for their parents. Children's sympathy for their mother's plight sets the father up as the bad guy. The kids' perception that their father has the money also sets him up for their anger. When children live with their mother, it is difficult for them to separate concepts of child support and alimony. In fact, that distinction is meaningless to them. All they know is that their father is gone and living well, and they are not. With such inequality, both the kids and their mother become adept at continually maneuvering the father into spending more on the children. It doesn't end, and it produces nothing but rancor and resentment.

Many men fear that alimony will make their wives reluctant to remarry because remarriage terminates alimony. However, I have often found the case to be just the opposite. Alimony doesn't encourage women to remarry, but a fair settlement that leaves the wife with a decent standard of living helps insure her adjustment and her success as a single person. Miserable, bitter women are not attractive prospects to single men. It is in the husband's interest for his wife to remarry and do well. Whatever enhances her ability to function well, to feel that she has been treated fairly leaves her more, not less, prone to risk marriage again. I have met very few women who have turned down opportunities for remarriage simply to preserve their alimony.

Having alimony as a safety net makes the wife more secure and enables her to take professional and social risks. If a husband is still worried that alimony will inhibit his wife's willingness to remarry, he might provide that if her remarriage fails within one year, his alimony will resume. This takes the risk out of remarriage for her and makes it easier for her to take a second chance. If a wife wants to change careers to one with higher-paying potential, giving her the security to do so can be traded for reduced alimony as her income increases.

HOW LONG DOES ALIMONY LAST?

In the traditional divorce, alimony was paid indefinitely but was never really *permanent*. Truly permanent alimony would be paid until a wife died. Most men die before their wives, and if alimony hasn't ended before that, it certainly ends when the husband dies. In some agreements the man's life is insured to cover part or all of his alimony obligation, but insurance is expensive for older men and can be prohibitive if there is a history of illness.

Today, alimony is viewed most often as a transitional supplement to a woman's income—a way of tiding her over until she can support herself. It is often referred to as *rehabilitative* alimony, designed to support her until she can be economically rehabilitated. I see this as an unfortunate term when the condition from which a woman is to be rehabilitated is being a mother. I prefer to call this *limited* or *temporary* alimony that is generally related to some event or set of events, such as a wife's graduation from an educational program, her employment at a specific salary level, the end of infancy of the children, or the expiration of a negotiated period of years.

This does not mean that permanent alimony is not necessary in some cases. It is appropriate in long-term marriages involving traditional homemaker wives who cannot reasonably be asked to develop a career late in life. Permanent alimony, however, is becoming a less prevalent part of divorce settlements. Actually, the term "permanent" is a misnomer because alimony is terminated by the death of the payor and also by remarriage unless the couple has negotiated to the contrary.

EQUALITY

In American society, popular notions of fairness and justice are dominated by the issue of equality. However, there is no legal presumption that the incomes of husband and wife must be equalized. Few judges would award a nonworking wife half her husband's income as alimony. But despite the absence of a legal rule, the premise of equality is a powerful emotional issue. A woman who has shared a life with a man for many years does not calmly accept the notion that he will now live far better than she will. The closer a divorcing couple come to equal living standards, the easier the settlement will be. If there is a substantial difference between the husband's and the wife's income, then all the other factors must be analyzed.

Women should remember that the law does not require men to pay alimony to help women achieve equality.

CASE STUDY: MARY AND BENNETT

Years ago I represented a woman who had been married to an investment banker for nine years. Mary and Bennett had struggled financially during the early years of the marriage and had begun to live much better in the last two years. Mary had begun work on her doctorate in psychology four years earlier, combining her part-time student life with being a mother and homemaker. She had three more years of school to complete the degree. For Mary, the most difficult part of the divorce was accepting the fact that her husband was going to be much wealthier than she was. His six-figure income was increasing rapidly. Yet, permanent alimony was not realistic because of her young age and short marriage. Mary was thirty-one years old and on her way to a professional degree and eventually a substantial income as a psychologist. She was leaving the marriage with enough money to buy a house, although clearly a less expensive one than she had had. Mary negotiated five years of alimony and child support. Her husband agreed to a genuine attempt at shared parenting of their child.

Mary's anger that "he would live so much better" was, for a time, a major threat to settlement. It required long discussions and hard work on her part to let go of what really was an attachment to the past. When Mary was able to look forward, she realized that she was actually in an enviable position. At a relatively young age she would have the career she had always wanted, enough income to cushion her while she established her practice, and a comfortable home. That her husband would have more money than she was really irrelevant.

WHEN IS ALIMONY LIKELY?

If both husband and wife earn similar incomes, alimony is not an issue. But if there is a disparity, alimony *may* be appropriate. The first consideration is whether the husband has significantly more income than the wife after paying whatever child-support obligation he has agreed to. Disparity in living standards does not automatically entitle a wife to alimony, however. A short marriage, for example, rarely produces much alimony. If there are no children, if the wife never interrupted her career, and if she has not been economically disadvantaged by the marriage, she does not have a great claim to alimony even though there is a disparity in incomes.

The second consideration is the length of the marriage. Marriages of less than ten years generally will not create a substantial alimony obligation. But in a marriage of thirty years, a substantial disparity in income invariably raises the question of alimony. The longer the marriage, the more pressure for parity. In very long marriages, the issue of equality becomes stronger and the duration of alimony longer. A shorter marriage will, at best, promote temporary or rehabilitative alimony for a period of a few years.

THE ECONOMIC ROLE OF WIFE AND HOMEMAKER

When a woman takes time out from her career to perform homemaking duties or when she makes homemaking her primary role instead of a career, her ability to generate income declines. A fifty-year-old woman married thirty years who has not been employed for twenty-five years has little likelihood of building a career with substantial income. She needs permanent alimony and will quite reasonably press for parity of living standard with her husband. On the other hand, a thirty-five-year-old woman, married ten years and out of the work force for eight years, has a much better chance of resuming her career and achieving substantial income. Of course, in some cases, the disparity in income may be due not to the wife's homemaking activities but simply to her career choice.

The expectation that women support themselves when possible must be tempered by the impact on careers of time out. It has been estimated that on the average every year out of employment reduces a woman's earning capacity by about 3 percent. Thus, ten years away from a career would, on average, reduce her earning capacity by about 30 percent. Longer marriages create a stronger premise of alimony because they typically have a greater impact on a woman's ability to earn. If a wife's income-earning capacity has not been adversely affected by a long marriage, duration of the marriage is not so important a factor. In each case, the woman needs to assess where she would be in her career if she had not taken time out. Fields such as advertising have a much more dramatic income ladder than teaching. While a senior teacher may earn twice what a beginner earns, a senior advertising executive may earn ten or fifteen times what a trainee earns.

LIVING STANDARD DURING THE MARRIAGE

Traditionally, alimony was supposed to keep a woman in the "style to which she had become accustomed." Today that standard has little credibility. Divorce, if done with fairness, requires about a 30 percent cut in living standard across the board. If done unfairly, it will produce greater reduction for part of the family and less reduction, or even an increase, for others. Thus, maintaining the standard of living enjoyed during the marriage is for most people an unrealistic objective in the years immediately following the divorce.

A wife's claim to alimony, assuming a disparity in incomes, will be influenced by six factors:

- the size of the disparity
- the reasons for the disparity

- the duration of the marriage
- the age of each spouse
- the standard of living during the marriage
- the ability of each spouse to generate income

Let's look at some examples of how these factors interact to determine the amount and duration of alimony.

CASE STUDY: BEN AND PEGGY

After twenty years of marriage, Ben and Peggy were divorcing. When they married they were both twenty-three and first-year employees at the same advertising agency. They had graduated college the same year as marketing majors. Peggy left work two years later when she was pregnant. At that time, she and Ben were earning the same salary. Over twenty years, Ben had made several well-timed moves to other agencies and was now a vice president earning more than $100,000 annually. A year before the separation, Peggy decided to return to work. The best offer she found was an entry-level position in an advertising firm paying about $22,000. The couple's two children, ages seventeen and fifteen, lived with Peggy. Although Ben was very cooperative when negotiating child support, he was resistant to alimony.

There was a very large income disparity between Ben and Peggy even though they had started in the same field at the same time with the same credentials. I asked Ben his opinion, as a knowledgeable executive, what Peggy's salary might be today had she not left her job. He replied that, although she might not have matched his current salary, she certainly would have earned far in excess of $22,000. I then asked Peggy if she thought she had time to rebuild her career. "Forty-three is not

that old," she said. "I can do it in about five years." Ben agreed
with her assessment.

I asked Peggy whether she felt she should receive alimony.
Her response was a vigorous "Yes! Why should I be penalized
for taking care of the family? Why should I have to scrimp
while Ben doesn't even have to economize?" I asked Ben if he
could explain to Peggy that it was fair for them to have very
different living standards. Ben replied that he didn't see why
he should be permanently responsible for Peggy. He was worried that between college expenses and alimony he would
never see relief. I asked both to prepare proposals for our next
session that addressed each other's concerns.

At our next meeting Peggy proposed that Ben pay alimony
for seven years. She felt that would give her time to get her
salary up to where she could maintain her present standard of
living. She felt that Ben should pay enough alimony to equalize their net incomes. Ben initially proposed alimony of
$10,000 per year for five years, pointing out that Peggy al-
ready agreed she could earn a comparable salary within five
years. I asked her to calculate how much she would need to
meet her present budget, pointing out that standard of living,
not equality, was her objective. I asked them both to continue
thinking about the issue until our next meeting. The next week
they settled the alimony issue. They agreed on alimony for five
years at $20,000 per year. With Ben paying child support,
their net disposable income was less than $10,000 apart after
calculating alimony. They agreed that after three years the
alimony would be reduced one dollar for each two dollars of
increase in Peggy's income. The alimony agreement acknowledged the long duration of the marriage and Peggy's capacity
to earn a satisfying income in time. The settlement brought
their respective living standards into the same range, although
Ben retained a higher income than Peggy. Their formula for
reducing alimony was a recognition that both should share the
benefits of Peggy's raises.

CASE STUDY: JOHN AND MARIAN

John and Marian were married thirty-two years when he decided he wanted a divorce. John, age fifty-seven, earned $72,-000 a year as a senior engineer. Marian was fifty-five and had not been employed since their marriage. She was a traditional homemaker and raised the couple's three children, by now all grown. Marian had devoted herself to making a home for John and the children and had been looking forward to John's retirement at age sixty-two. She was surprised by his decision to divorce.

John and Marian had a difficult situation. There was little reasonable expectation of substantial employment for Marian. She could, at best, get minimum-wage employment part time. The second difficulty was John's age. If he deferred retirement to age sixty-five, he would still have only eight years of employment remaining. The reality for this couple is significant belt tightening. They negotiated an alimony agreement that provided Marie with $32,000 a year from John's income until he retired. John agreed to retire at sixty-five instead of sixty-two. Marian would receive 50 percent of John's pension, which would be her primary means of support.

CASE STUDY: BILL AND SANDRA

Bill and Sandra had been married for eight years. Bill, a school principal, earned $55,000 a year. Sandra worked as a teacher for the first three years of their marriage, until their child was born. One year before the divorce, Sandra enrolled in a part-time MBA program. Continuing part time, she could complete the program in two and a half years. As a full-time student she could finish in one and a half years. Bill thought she should quit school and immediately return to teaching to support herself.

Bill was relieved when I explained to him and Sandra that their short-term marriage did not suggest long-term alimony. It was true that Sandra could immediately return to teaching and earn a living. But she could double her income potential by completing her graduate degree. The incentive for Bill to agree to the latter was twofold. First, by supporting Sandra's completion of her MBA, he would avoid a disgruntled, perpetually angry ex-wife. Second, her enhanced earning power would allow her to assume greater responsibility for child support and, ultimately, for college expenses for their child.

After thinking things over, Bill agreed to pay alimony for three years: $20,000 a year for the first one and a half years, $10,000 a year for the balance to launch Sandra's career. Sandra agreed that child support would be reviewed after three years with an eye to adjustment in Bill's favor. Sandra also agreed to pay one half the college expenses for the child.

Although every marriage has its unique characteristics, these cases incorporate the common problems addressed by alimony. In each case there is an income disparity related to the wife's domestic role. In the shortest marriage—Bill and Sandra's—alimony is used as a short-term tool to help the wife achieve higher income for the long term. In the case of Ben and Peggy, alimony is used to partially reduce the income difference while Peggy reestablishes her career. In the case of John and Marian the alimony acknowledges the long-term contract of the marriage and the fact that the wife now has no real options for employment at substantial income. She has that choice, of course, and if she does go to work her earnings combined with the alimony will give about the same as her husband's. Both will be working; both will have the same living standard. That was their contract for thirty-two years.

CHANGE OF CIRCUMSTANCES

Alimony, like child support, should be subject to change when the basic premises that produced the alimony agreement change. If, for example, a woman inherits a lot of money after a divorce and now has far more income than her ex-husband, it would be fair to reduce the alimony, and most state courts would agree. If a man becomes disabled and can no longer earn an income, it would be unreasonable to expect him to pay the same alimony as before. Much post-judgment conflict arises from attempts to modify alimony and child support because of changed circumstances.

It is not practical to create a support agreement that is adjusted each time one of you gets a raise. Although alimony reduction can be linked to a wife's increased income to reflect increased independence, it is generally not a good idea to try to link alimony to every change in the income of either spouse. It is common to increase alimony to reflect inflation by linking it to the consumer price index, but otherwise you should avoid complex formulas.

Renegotiation should be limited to unanticipated and significant changes, such as a sudden and unanticipated reduction in income through illness or job loss. Most states provide the right to request relief if such a misfortune befalls either spouse. Do not attempt to anticipate each possibility. This creates too much risk of fighting over relatively remote happenings. You should have a mediation clause in your agreement that provides an alternative to court action if a change of circumstance occurs. In my experience this is usually adequate.

CASE STUDY: BARRY AND SARAH

Barry and Sarah had successfully negotiated most of their separation agreement. They had resolved child support, property distribution, and, for the most part, alimony. Barry, an accountant, was fifty-two. Sarah, a florist, was fifty. They had agreed that Barry would pay Sarah alimony until he retired, at which time his pension would provide supplemental income to both. However, the income from the pension would be significantly less than Barry earns now, reducing both their incomes.

Barry and Sarah were stuck on two issues. First, Barry wanted to retire at age fifty-nine, as soon as he was eligible to collect his pension. Sarah found this alarming. She had always thought Barry would retire at sixty-five. The difference to her was six years of alimony and six more years for her interest in the pension to accumulate. But Barry wanted to live a simple life and was eager to trade a lower standard of living for the freedom to do what he wanted.

The second disagreement concerned what would happen if Sarah lived with another man or remarried. She felt that neither cohabitation nor remarriage should affect her alimony. However, Barry and Sarah lived in New York, one of the ten states where cohabitation by the wife causes alimony to be reduced or ended. New York law also provided for the termination of alimony upon the remarriage of the wife.[17]

I asked Barry why alimony should end if Sarah lived with another man. "Why should I support another man?" responded Barry. "If Sarah uses my alimony payment for rent, I end up supporting that other man, and it's not fair. Besides, if she lives with another man, she'll have no incentive to get

STATES IN WHICH COHABITATION ENDS OR MODIFIES ALIMONY

Alabama
California
Georgia
Illinois
Louisiana
Maryland
New York
Ohio
Pennsylvania
Tennessee

Source: *Family Law Quarterly*, Volume XXIV, No. 4, Winter 1991, pp. 355–356

---

married, and the law says that alimony ends when the wife gets remarried." I agreed that was true but told him that couples could agree to continue alimony after remarriage.

I then asked Sarah for her thoughts. "Look," she said, "I earned the right to alimony by working hard for the twenty-seven years of our marriage. My right to alimony from Barry has nothing to do with my future relationships. Besides, what makes you think that the available men out there have the money to support a wife?"

SHOULD ALIMONY END UPON REMARRIAGE?

Barry's and Sarah's disagreement is a common one. The issue is actually a throwback to the days when most middle-class women did not work outside the home. Alimony ended upon remarriage because it was assumed that the new husband would support the wife. It also ended upon remarriage because of fear that single men without income would ask divorced women to marry in order to live off their alimony.

Although most states automatically terminate alimony upon remarriage, this social policy isn't logical. After all, most women today, married or divorced, are expected to work and contribute to their own support. Today's economic realities suggest that remarriage does not necessarily improve the economic position of the divorced woman. If termination of alimony upon remarriage is of questionable social justice, then termination of alimony because of cohabitation is even more dubious. Just because a divorced woman lives with another man does not mean that she benefits economically. Moreover, there is no assurance that the relationship will last. Shouldn't she have the same opportunity as her former husband to experiment with a relationship without economic sanctions? It is not a good idea to write a contract that has an ex-husband looking over the shoulder of his ex-wife, waiting for her new relationship to mature so he can claim that it has become cohabitation. These clauses tend to cause far more trouble than they are worth. They sour the negotiation, and when enforcement is attempted they sour the post-divorce relationship.

Barry and Sarah ultimately resolved the issue by postponing it. They agreed that if Sarah lived with a man or remarried, neither event would automatically terminate alimony. However, they also agreed that in such an event they would return to mediation if Barry believed that Sarah's new circumstances significantly reduced her need for alimony. The agreement to return to mediation was not an agreement to reduce alimony; it was an agreement to discuss whether there was a reduced *need* for alimony. Presumably, if they agreed that Sarah's need for alimony was reduced, they would also agree on a reduction.

RETIREMENT

It is entirely appropriate that alimony be reduced or cease entirely when the husband retires. No one is required by law to work until he dies just to pay alimony. As a couple, you will be dividing whatever retirement-oriented assets you have. If a man is nearing retirement age, he may have accumulated a substantial pension, which, combined with social security, may be sufficient to support both spouses. If he still has many years to work, then each spouse has time to prepare financially for retirement.

The most common issue concerning retirement and alimony is the age at which the husband retires and, based on his reduced income, seeks a reduction or elimination of alimony. I recently saw a couple in which the husband, a physician, wanted to retire at fifty-five to pursue a lifelong fantasy of sailing around the world. After a thirty-year marriage in which his wife had played an exclusively domestic role, he wanted alimony to cease upon his early retirement. Understandably, his wife objected strenuously—an objection also fueled by the fact that his fantasy was a major factor propelling him out of the marriage.

The standard here must be one of reasonableness. There is nothing inherently wrong with early retirement, depending on the consequences for each party. Most people treat sixty-five as an acceptable retirement age although many retire at sixty-two when they become eligible for early social security.

Retirement at a younger age would generally raise some obligation for the man to cushion the consequence for his wife. In the case of the physician, there were sufficient assets so that he was able to provide his wife with more income-generating property to reduce the consequence of an earlier reduction in alimony. However, most couples do not have that much wealth, and, for most, retirement at age fifty-five is not feasible.

I suggest using age sixty-five as a standard. If there is to be a substantial deviation from that, and if permanent alimony is appropriate, the burden of making it work should rest on the husband.

CASE STUDY: BARRY AND SARAH (CONCLUSION)

Barry and Sarah still had to resolve the problem of Barry's early retirement. This was a particularly sore point with Sarah because she felt that Barry's dream of leading the simple life was one of the reasons their marriage fell apart.

After lengthy deliberation, Barry finally agreed to delay his retirement to age sixty-two. He also agreed that if he decided to retire earlier, he would guarantee Sarah the same income as if he were working to age sixty-two.

NEGOTIATING YOUR ALIMONY AGREEMENT

Negotiation of the alimony provisions of your agreement, whether using a mediator or through lawyers, should follow a step-by-step process. You do not want to be reduced to simple horse-trading: "I'll pay you two hundred a month"; "I won't take a cent less than five hundred," etc. This just becomes another futile power struggle. Instead, what you do is relate alimony, if it is appropriate, to your interests and objectives and then make proposals to each other that help you achieve those interests and objectives.

A fruitful discussion of alimony begins with assessment of your needs and resources. You negotiate in terms of your interests and objectives to maximize the success of your new life. You approach alimony like any other issue, with an eye to the future and the successful transition for all members of the family.

STEP ONE: MEASURE THE DISPARITY

The central question is whether there is a disparity between your incomes that produces significant differences in living standards. Child support should first be deducted from the husband's income before his income is compared to the wife's. But child support should *not* be added to the wife's income; it is for the *children's* support, not for hers. Thus, assuming a case where the children are living with the mother and the father is paying child support, husband's income minus child support minus wife's income = disparity.

STEP TWO: IDENTIFY INTERESTS

With no disparity, or a negligible one, alimony is easily resolved. If the disparity is big enough to produce significant differences in living standards, the premise of alimony arises. The next question is one of duration, that is, how long will the husband pay alimony? To determine this, the couple must identify both husband's and wife's needs. They must discuss the length of the marriage, the wife's earning capacity, and her age. A long-term marriage combined with the wife's reduced earning capacity should move the negotiation toward a permanent alimony agreement, tempered, of course, by our previous discussion about retirement and change of circumstances.

If a marriage was not long term, that is, if it lasted less than fifteen years, and if the wife has substantial earning potential, you both should be prepared to consider less than permanent alimony. Again, there is no formula, no absolute rule of thumb. The key is for both of you to state your objectives and to understand each other's goals.

Questions for the Wife:

- Are you embarking on a new career or resuming an old one?
- How long do you need support from your husband?
- What do you worry about?
- What do you need to feel secure?
- What information have you acquired on future employment prospects?
- How do these prospects relate to your child-care responsibilities?
- Are there anticipated events such as a child beginning full-time school that will alter your employment possibilities?
- Do you need training to enhance your income potential?
- If you are already employed, what opportunities or job changes do you anticipate over the next few years?

Questions for the Husband:

- How secure is your income?
- What job changes or opportunities can you anticipate over the next few years?
- What standard of living is realistic?
- How much will it cost you to live?

As husband and wife talk, they may discover that the wife truly wants to be economically autonomous and has no desire to live off the husband's income. They may also discover that the husband under- or overestimated the wife's economic prospects. Asking questions about the needs and interests of your negotiating partner are the heart of principled negotiation. It moves you away from the distinctive dialogue of "You owe me," or "You don't deserve it," to "What do you need?" and "How can we solve that problem?"

Don't be surprised when some of your questions evoke questions from your spouse. Both of you need to know each other's aspirations and needs so you can formulate proposals to each other. Ideally, you will ask each other what these needs and aspirations are. If one of you doesn't ask, the other can volunteer the information. Remember that the proposition "I need" or "I would like" is not the same as "I insist," "I must have," or "I demand."

Avoid blaming statements, fault statements, and victim statements. They simply derail the negotiation. If your spouse makes such a statement, don't take the bait. Treat it as an expression of anxiety, anger, or worry, but *not* as a proposition to be denied or rejoined. These occasional lapses, if acknowledged and left behind, need not poison the discussion. Insist on the task at hand—identifying interests and needs. Only after you have done this will you both be ready to make concrete proposals about the amount and duration of alimony. When you get stuck, use a mediator or a lawyer to move the dialogue along. But remember: The more you take the initiative, the better.

STEP THREE: STATE YOUR THEORY OF CONTRACT

Alimony should be paid only if there is good reason to pay it. But when there is good reason, it should always be paid. The reasons have to do both with need and with fairness. At this point you should review first by yourself and then with your spouse just what your contract was. Did the wife take time off from a career to devote to a family? Was her income-generating capacity harmed? Had she not done this, how would life have been different?

When you make your alimony proposal, you should be able to complete a sentence beginning "This proposal is fair because . . . ," and not be embarrassed by the result. If your proposal means that you will be able to live better than your wife, why is that fair? It may well be fair, but you both should be able to relate it to your history and your contract. I recall a divorce I mediated in which the husband was a very successful architect before he married. His wife, a struggling artist when they met, was subsidized by him for the five years of the marriage, during which they had no children and she pursued her career. At the end of the marriage he proposed that there be no alimony. It was fair, he said, because his wife had never been economically disadvantaged by the marriage. Alimony, seen as a form of compensation for economic disadvantage suffered by the wife to benefit the family, was simply not required and hence not fair in this case. Whether it is in yours will depend on your particular history, on the present, and on the future, as defined by you and your spouse.

STEP FOUR: MAKE YOUR PROPOSALS AND NEGOTIATE

If you have gone through these steps conscientiously, you should be in a position to make a reasonable proposal. You should propose how much alimony will be paid and for how long. You should state why you believe it is fair—that is, how it relates to your contract, how it relates reasonably to your interests, and how you believe it relates to your spouse's interests. If your spouse does the same, you will have two propositions to compare and negotiate. It is unlikely that the first proposals will be the same. Don't be discouraged. After all, it is quite understandable that each of you sees your history and contract differently.

A difference in position should not lead to an immediate rejection. Explore each part of both proposals. How far are you apart? Are there some areas where you are closer? If so, work on these first. Create agreement before you work on disagreement. You do not have to reach a final agreement in one session, and you do not have to reach final agreement on alimony before going on to negotiate the division of property.

Get as close as you can, and stop. Your mediator or your attorneys may have some helpful suggestions for closing the gap. Sometimes the remaining alimony issues get resolved during property negotiations, when you can better see how your cash flow relates to your assets. However, in most cases you will be able, through these four steps, to negotiate your alimony agreement.

Chapter Thirteen

NEGOTIATING THE DISTRIBUTION OF THE MARITAL PROPERTY

*N**egotiating the* distribution of property between you and your spouse is a three-step process. The first step is to identify the marital property. This may be a little more complicated than you think because in divorce, property is not always treated the same as in other situations. The second step is to value the property, that is, to determine what each asset is worth. Finally, when you know what you have and how much it is worth, you are ready for the last step: negotiating the division of the property.

This chapter includes some technical discussion about property and how to value it. Readers who get anxious about arithmetical calculations may feel that it is too complex for them to understand. But if you don't learn to understand this material, eventually you will have to trust someone else to make decisions for you. That is not informed decision making. At the least, this chapter will empower you to use professional help effectively so that you understand every aspect of your settlement.

CASE STUDY: BEN AND HELEN

Ben and Helen have been married for eighteen years. Following several years of escalating discord, Helen decided that she wanted a divorce. Ben, though resistant at first, has finally realized that it's probably for the best. They have two children, ages eleven and fourteen. Ben is a chiropractor. They married just after they graduated college, and Helen worked to support them while Ben went to chiropractic school and then built a practice. During the early years of his practice Helen did all the secretarial work at night. Now the practice is successful, and Ben has a clerical staff. After staying home with the kids for five years after the oldest was born, Helen resumed her teaching career.

Ben and Helen have pretty much resolved the issues of custody, alimony, and child support. Now they have to divide the marital property. They own the following assets:

- The house, purchased sixteen years ago for $40,000, is now worth about $270,000. It has a first mortgage of $21,000 and a second mortgage of $20,000. The net equity is about $229,000.
- Ben's Keogh plan, started about ten years ago, now has a present balance of $94,000.
- Helen's pension plan is worth $13,500.
- They each have individual retirement accounts (IRAs) worth $22,000.
- A sailboat that is Ben's most prized possession is worth about $20,000. Five years after they married, Ben bought the boat with a $3,000 inheritance from his grandfather. When he bought the boat it was a mess, and he has devoted

years of painstaking work, as well as thousands of dollars, to restore it.

- Helen has jewelry worth about $30,000, including her engagement ring now worth about $10,000, a pair of diamond earrings inherited from her mother, also worth $10,000 and an emerald pin she bought before she ever met Ben.
- They have two cars. Ben's 1990 BMW is worth $22,000, and Helen's 1987 Ford station wagon is worth about $6,000.

We shall follow Ben and Helen through this chapter on property division to help you to understand some of the concepts.

STEP 1: IDENTIFYING THE MARITAL PROPERTY

In practically all states, marital property is defined as that property acquired during the marriage that is not exempt from distribution. If it was earned during the marriage, it is clearly marital property. The money in Ben's Keogh plan, for example, was saved from income earned during the marriage. It is clearly subject to distribution between him and Helen.

IS PROPERTY EXEMPT?

Property can be exempt from distribution for several reasons. In most states property inherited by one of the spouses remains the personal property of the spouse who inherited. Thus, Helen's diamond earrings are hers alone and are not regarded as marital property. Property also may be exempt if it was owned before the marriage and is still owned at the time of divorce. Helen owned the emerald pin before the marriage. It is still hers and is exempt from distribution.

What about Ben's boat? It was bought with money he inherited and that he brought into the marriage. Doesn't that make the boat exempt property? If you think about it long enough, you realize that most of the value in the boat was created *during* the marriage. Ben's labor during the marriage, combined with a lot of money earned during the marriage, gave the boat its current value. Thus, the boat is marital property and is subject to distribution. Had Ben put his inheritance in a bank account and left it there, the money in that account would have been exempt. But in this case, Ben mixed or *comingled* the premarital property with marital property (his labor and their money). As a result, the property is not exempt.

Exemption refers to the specific asset, not simply to the source of the money that was used to buy it. Specific items like the jewelry were exempt. The only thing that might suggest exemption for the boat is that it had originally been purchased with exempt funds. The boat itself is no longer exempt because it has been comingled with non-exempt resources.

WHAT IS PROPERTY?

Ordinarily, we use a common-sense definition of property. That is, property is something that we own and something of value. Because we own it and it has value, we can, if we choose, sell it to someone else. Using these criteria, we can easily identify most of the property of the marriage. It includes the house and all the furnishings and possessions in it. It includes the automobiles we own, the bank accounts we have, any stocks and bonds we own, and our other tangible possessions.

There are also less tangible forms of property that may play a role in divorce. These must not be ignored. Certain legal rights may have great value as marital property. Suppose, for example, that during the marriage your spouse had written a book or music that had been copyrighted and for which he or she is still receiving royalty payments. The economic value of such "intellectual property" might be an important marital asset. The same would apply to patents for inventions. Other rights may also be important. Consider Helen's pension, for example. It is not something that she can sell. It is only a right to receive income in the future. The present value of that future right is a marital asset if that right was earned during the marriage. We will discuss valuing these rights shortly.

There is a third category of property that is unique to the world of divorce. Let's consider Ben's chiropractic license. The license cannot be bought or sold. Yet, in some states, Ben's license would be regarded as a marital asset subject to equitable distribution. In other states the legislatures have taken a less expansive view and do not consider personal credentials such as licenses and degrees to be property subject to distribution. However, in these states Ben's chiropractic practice would be regarded as a business subject to equitable distribution. Even though his practice is based on his personal reputation, it would be appraised and considered in the distribution of the marital assets. It is possible to sell a professional practice in some cases. But salability is not the sole criterion.

It's worth a few paragraphs to understand the logic that influences this area of law. Ben acquired his credentials during the marriage. In fact, Helen worked to put him through school and helped him build his practice. Consequently Ben has a business that produces substantial income. His income is far greater than Helen's. To ignore this enhanced earning power that is itself the product of the marriage may result in an injustice to Helen. She will be left in an economic position that is inferior to Ben's, even though she invested considerable time and effort in helping to create that income-earning capacity. It is to redress potential injustices of this type that divorce law has evolved its own definition of marital assets.

In the case of Helen and Ben, Ben's practice, his license, or even his degree, depending on the state, would be given a value using a methodology similar to the appraisal of any other income-producing asset. Helen's share would be negotiated and paid to her in some fashion from the other assets of the marriage.

STEP 2: VALUATION OF THE ASSETS

Each asset should be valued by using an appropriate appraiser. If an asset is of negligible value, it may not be worth the cost of appraisal. If the two of you can agree on the value yourselves, that is sufficient. Automobiles, for example, are easily valued by reference to "blue books" and other similar guides available to people in the lending business. If you live in a townhouse community and last week three townhouses exactly like yours sold for $100,000, then you can be pretty sure that yours is worth about the same. But if either of you is in doubt, you should have the property appraised. Nothing is worse than getting to the end of your negotiation and then turning the agreement upside down because one of you belatedly decides that he or she should have obtained an appraisal.

USE PROFESSIONALS

A few words are in order about appraisals. First, use a disinterested professional. This is not the place to save a few dollars. Most realtors will give you an opinion of your home's value for free in the hope that you will list the house with them if you sell. These values tend to be unreliable because they may be influenced by what the realtor thinks you want to hear. If you need to have the house appraised, use a professional who does this work full time. It will cost you a few hundred dollars, but it is worth the peace of mind.

CHOOSING AN APPRAISER

There are several ways to choose an appraiser. Lawyers tend to have multiple appraisals, with each side getting its own. It is not unusual for these appraisals to be influenced by the outcome desired by the client. Thus, if the wife is likely to keep the house as part of the settlement, one would expect that the appraisal obtained by the husband's lawyer to come in high, and the appraisal obtained by the wife's lawyer to come in low. One way to get around this cynical state of affairs is to get a *third* appraisal by a neutral party and then average the three. Frequently a judge will be frustrated by the broad divergence of the adversary appraisals and will appoint the court's own neutral appraiser.

My own preference is to have a single neutral appraiser. I have not found that three experts, two of whom have vested interests, are more accurate than one neutral appraiser. Appraising is not a science, and one appraiser can indeed be wrong. But the risk of some error in the appraisal is less costly than the cynical manipulation of a threesome in which two are biased. There are several ways you and your spouse can choose. Together you can attempt to choose one person. If you inquire, you can probably find out whom the local courts use when they need a neutral appraiser. Your lawyers may also be of some help here.

A second way is for one of you to compile a list of five appraisers. The other chooses the appraiser from that list. In any event, decide which assets require appraisals, choose your appraisers, and get the job done.

Let's return to Ben and Helen. They chose a real estate appraiser for the house. They found an actuary to appraise the present value of Helen's pension. They considered a jeweler to appraise Helen's jewelry but decided that, as most of it was exempt from distribution because Helen had inherited it or had owned it before the marriage, they would estimate the market value of the remainder themselves. They had to hire a forensic accountant to appraise the value of Ben's chiropractic practice. Finally, they hired a former yacht broker, who now devoted full time to the appraisal business, to appraise Ben's beloved sailboat. From the time they began until they had all their appraisals in hand, the procedure took six weeks.

FIXING THE CUTOFF DATE FOR DIVISION OF THE ASSETS

Whether you live in a community-property state or in an equitable-distribution state, you need to determine what date will be used for a cutoff of further equitable distribution. What this means is: What is the date after which property that each of you acquires is no longer considered marital property subject to distribution? Ordinarily that date is fixed by the filing of a complaint for divorce. But if you are attempting to negotiate an amicable settlement before either of you files a complaint for divorce, you need to agree on a date that, for purposes of distribution, marks the end of the marriage.

This can be a problem only if you ignore it. I have seen couples who were separated for years before negotiating their agreement. When it came time to fix the cutoff date, one wanted it to be the time of separation while the other wanted it to be the time of negotiation. As a result, what started amicably ended as a rancorous divorce. If you are separating, you should agree on a cutoff date even if you are not ready to negotiate the agreement. If one of you wants to set the date and the other resists, the resisting spouse creates the necessity for the other to file a complaint in the court or to risk an unfair result later. It is not a happy choice and should be avoided. This is a topic for which the counsel of your attorney is invaluable in avoiding problems.

TAX CONSIDERATIONS

There are two important tax considerations that affect the value of your assets. First is the issue of capital gains tax, and second is the deferred taxation of pensions, other retirement accounts and corporate profit-sharing plans. Although you will want to consult your accountant, these are not difficult to understand.

Capital gains tax is the tax you would have to pay on the appreciated value of an asset if you were to sell it. For example, Ben and Helen paid $40,000 for their house, and it is now worth $270,000. If they were to sell it without a realtor for $270,000, they would make a profit of $230,000. That profit is their capital gain. If they did not buy another house and just kept the money, they would have to treat that gain as ordinary income on their income tax returns. Depending on a number of other factors, the tax could be as much as $75,000. The house in which you live is subject to a number of exclusions that might reduce or eliminate the impact of the capital gain tax, and that is something you should review with your accountant. What you should be aware of is that the net equity in your assets may be substantially *less* than you think it is. In this case, the house has a value of $270,000 and current mortgages of $41,000. This means that equity (value less mortgage) is $229,000. However, if the capital gain tax were to be imputed, the net equity (equity less accrued tax) would be closer to $190,000.

The second tax factor is the tax that was never paid on various kinds of tax-deferred employee benefits and retirement plans and accounts. Consider Ben's and Helen's individual retirement accounts. Each has $22,000. These retirement accounts contain income that was never taxed. If these plans were to be cashed in, Ben and Helen would have to pay substantial tax plus a penalty of about 10 percent. Consequently, cashed in, these accounts would have an after-tax value of about $14,000 rather than the $22,000 face value of the accounts. The same analysis would apply to Ben's Keogh plan. It has a pretax value of $94,000 and an after tax-value of about $66,000 ($94,000 less a tax of 30 percent).

This does not mean that these assets are going to be sold or that they ought to be cashed in. The importance of understanding the tax implications is that the real value of some assets may be less than you think, and it is vital that you understand the real values when you negotiate. Compare, for example, a certificate of deposit worth $10,000 with an IRA of $10,000 and $10,000 worth of IBM stock that was originally purchased for $6,000. All three assets appear on a financial statement as $10,000. However, the after-tax values differ greatly.

Certificate	$10,000	IRA	$10,000	IBM Stock	$10,000
less	0	tax	4,000	cap gain tax	2,000
net value	$10,000		6,000		8,000

These figures are estimates and may vary from case to case, but for purposes of illustration, they are close enough. The point is that in reviewing and evaluating your assets you must account for potential taxes. This is when you use professional assistance to inform and guide you both. There are a number of strategies that can be employed to reduce potential tax impact. Most lawyers are not particularly sophisticated about taxes, so I strongly suggest that you use accountants to evaluate your assets.

The significant difference between the gross values and the net values will play an important part in Helen and Ben's negotiation. Some items will be traded off based on pretax values. For example, if Ben keeps his IRA and Helen keeps her

CASE STUDY: BEN AND HELEN—AFTER APPRAISALS AND AFTER TAX

ASSET	GROSS EQUITY	NET EQUITY EXCLUDING EXEMPT PROPERTY
House	$229,000	$154,000
Keogh	94,000	66,000
Helen's pension	13,500	14,000
Ben's IRA	22,000	14,000
Helen's IRA	22,000	13,500
Boat	22,000	22,000
Jewelry	30,000	10,000
BMW	22,000	22,000
Ford	6,000	6,000
Ben's Practice	130,000	91,000
total	590,500	412,500

IRA, it doesn't matter whether they use pretax or after-tax values because they offset each other either way. But when they negotiate Helen's share of Ben's practice, Ben will want to negotiate based on after-tax rather than pretax figures because he wants the tax burden distributed with the asset.

WHAT ABOUT THE MARITAL DEBT?

There are two types of debt to resolve in most divorces. The first is relatively easy because it is specifically attached to one asset. Most common is the mortgage on the house. When an asset serves as collateral for a loan, we call the loan a secured debt. Your house secures the loan you took to buy or to refinance the house. If you have a car loan, that too is a secured debt; the car serves as collateral and secures the debt. Secured debt is easy to negotiate about because you subtract the debt from the market value of the asset to determine your equity in the asset. If your car is worth $12,000 and the car loan balance is $9000, then your equity in the car is $3,000. If one of you takes that car, and the loan that goes with it, you are taking equity of $3,000. If the house is worth $200,000 and the mortgage is $120,000, then the equity is $80,000 for purposes of calculating and dividing the assets. The offset of debt against value to produce net equity is a generally accepted principle that should cause you few problems.

The problems tend to arise around unsecured debts of two types. Unsecured debt has no specific asset as collateral. Your credit-card debt is the most common form of unsecured debt. Ordinarily, credit-card debt should not be a problem if you use your credit cards as a convenience. Such use of credit cards means that you have the money in the bank and will be able to pay the entire bill at the end of the month. Many people, however, use credit cards because they do not have the money and are using the card as a source of borrowing. When credit cards are used (or abused) in this manner, the result is the steady accumulation of high-interest debt.

Divorcing couples frequently are in financial disarray at the time of their initial separation because they have not yet worked out an agreement and have not yet come to grips with the economic realities of financing two households. These couples often use their credit cards to cover the deficit and quickly run up large balances with heavy monthly interest payments. When it comes time to resolve this issue, they tend to attack each other for using the cards and incurring the debt. "I didn't tell you to spend that money. It's your debt, you pay it!" "If you hadn't been so stingy I wouldn't have had to use the credit card to buy clothes for the kids—you should pay that bill!" This can become a problem that derails your negotiations.

Debt that is incurred during the divorce transition should,

in my opinion, be treated as marital debt. It was necessary to establish two households. There was a lack of ready cash, and you used deficit financing to accomplish a necessary task. You should try to avoid making your credit card debt another reason to replay the emotional issues that led to your divorce. This short-term debt should be treated as an offset against your assets and paid accordingly. Sometimes it pays to take a debt consolidation loan against your home equity as a way to lower your monthly payments and make your cash flow problems more manageable. If you treat the credit card debt pragmatically, you can avoid a major problem. Of course, you also must stop running up the short-term debt. You both should immediately agree on a cutoff date after which any debt incurred "belongs" to the person incurring it.

DEBT TO IN-LAWS

The second troublesome problem is money that was loaned to you by one of your families. Typically, one of your parents gave you money for the down payment on the house with the caveat that "Someday, when you can afford it, pay it back." There is no promissory note, you have paid nothing back, there have been no interest payments, and it does not particularly look like a debt. But either one of you, or the parent that provided the money, now gets worried that the debt will not be honored and demands payment. If you end up in court, you might even have difficulty proving that it was a loan rather than a gift.

Loans from in-laws are also tricky because sometimes in-laws get involved in the divorce conflict, trying to protect their child from the other spouse. This is an unhealthy situation and to be avoided. Whenever possible, money that has come from one set of parents should go back to them unless it was explicitly clear that the money was a gift to both of you. If it was a long-term loan and if it was to help purchase the house, it should be treated as a mortgage to be paid when the house is sold just like any other mortgage. On the other hand, you should not be pressed to pay it off right away, just at the time you are most strapped for cash. You should each explain to your parents that this is a time of great difficulty for you both and that their forbearance and noninvolvement would be most helpful. With appropriate reassurance, most in-laws will be cooperative.

STEP 3: NEGOTIATING THE DIVISION OF ASSETS—EQUITABLE DISTRIBUTION AND COMMUNITY PROPERTY

There are two different systems for dividing marital property in the United States: equitable distribution and community property. Community property is the simpler system. In principle, all marital assets are equally divided between husband and wife in community-property states. If you live in one of the eight community-property states, your task is considerably simplified. The community-property states are: Arizona, California, Idaho, Louisiana, Mississippi, Nevada, New Mexico, Texas, Washington, and Wisconsin. However, in some of these states equal division is only a presumption subject to override if the result would be fair.

All the rest of the states have adopted some variation of equitable distribution. This concept, unlike community property, does not assume an equal division between husband and wife.

Specifically, equitable distribution was developed as a reform to insure that women were not deprived because their husbands had been the primary economic contributors to the marriage. The primary impulse served by the early equitable-distribution laws was to convert the noneconomic domestic contribution of the wife into a claim on the economic assets owned by the husband. The law made it possible for judges to ignore the fact that title to an asset was in the name of the husband and to give the wife some money as her "share" of the husband's property. Even though this requires the creation of categories of property that are not salable in the traditional sense of the word, it promotes a more equitable recognition of the contribution of the wife.

Equitable distribution, from a woman's point of view, is an improvement over the title systems that awarded the property to whichever spouse had title, most often the husband. It is not superior to community-property systems from a woman's perspective because women rarely get more than half the assets under equitable-distribution systems and often get less. With a community-property system, on the other hand, women are more likely to receive an equal share of the marital property.

EQUALITY AND OUR SENSE OF JUSTICE

One of the most persistent ideas in our sense of fairness is the notion of equality. That is, most of us have been raised to believe that the fair way to divide anything is to divide it into equal portions. Because it is so pervasive in our common sense of justice, equality invariably plays an important role in negotiations about dividing marital property.

Many divorcing couples do indeed decide to divide their property fifty-fifty, and, in many cases, it is the appropriate thing to do. When there are few assets, it's often the easiest thing to do. If you have been married a long time and all your assets were accumulated during the marriage, it is also probably the most appropriate. But it is not always the fair thing, and the law of equitable distribution specifically rejects fifty-fifty as a *required* standard for division. Let's look at an example in which fifty-fifty would be unfair by any standard.

Husband and wife have been married two years. They bought a house the year they married and made a down payment of $50,000 of which the husband put up $5,000 and the wife put up $45,000. Assume for purposes of our example that the value of the house is the same now as it was when they bought it. It is difficult to see how anyone could regard it as fair for the husband to get one-half the equity in the house. It would be a $20,000 windfall for him and a $20,000 loss for her without any apparent justification for either. Here, "equal" would be unfair.

This is a good time to remind you of two principles: First, equitable distribution does not mean equal distribution; there are many situations in which equal would be unfair. Second, just because an asset is subject to equitable distribution does not mean that it gets divided equally between the spouses. In this case, the house is clearly subject to equitable distribution. It was purchased by both of them during the marriage. Even though they used funds that they owned prior to the marriage, the purchase comingled those funds and so the house was subject to distribution. But that does not mean that the house gets divided equally. This is important to remember when you are discussing whether an asset is subject or exempt. Just because you concede that it is subject does not mean that each spouse gets half.

PRINCIPLES THAT SUGGEST UNEQUAL DISTRIBUTION

There are a number of things that would justify unequal distribution of certain assets or that would justify net distributions that are other than fifty-fifty.

1. Unequal Contribution

An analogy often applied to equitable distribution is that a marriage is similar to an economic partnership and divorce should be seen as the dissolution of the partnership. Accordingly, if one partner has contributed more, as in our example above, it is fair that the dissolution reflect that unequal contribution and return to each that which each has contributed. In this sense, equitable distribution constitutes the return of capital to investors proportionate to their original investments.

When one partner brought significantly more money to the marriage than the other, it is often fair to take that into consideration in dividing the assets. It may also be appropriate to consider this when, during the marriage, one spouse made a greater economic contribution than the other. This position may not be easily accepted by your spouse. In fact, your insistence that you made a larger contribution than your spouse could trigger a very emotional fight. Many marriages break up precisely because partners fight over who is contributing or not contributing emotionally or financially. When you suggest that you should get more because you gave more, your spouse may see that as your attempt to vindicate your own position in the marriage.

I am not suggesting that you ignore issues of fairness you think are important but that you realize that some of these issues have tricky emotional pitfalls. Raise them *only* when you really believe them to be important.

Business assets and employment-related assets frequently generate discussions about who contributed more. I find that many people have difficulty with the proposition that they should share their pensions with their spouses. "This is something I earned all by myself. Why should I have to give it to her?" This attitude also arises about professional practices and family-owned businesses in which one spouse did all the work. If this applies to you, you will have to look at the contributions your spouse made directly to your business, as well as the non-economic contributions your spouse made to the family, that may offset your efforts in building your business.

Consider, once again, Ben and Helen. Ben built his chiropractic practice through many years of hard work and sacrifice. "What I built should be mine," he says. "Why should Helen get it"? In fact, Helen contributed to that business in several ways. She worked to put Ben through school. She worked as Ben's clerical helper during the early years of the practice. And it was Helen who stayed home taking care of the kids while Ben went to the office. All of those contributions increase Helen's claim to a share, perhaps even half. That is what Helen and Ben will have to negotiate.

Just for example, let's change the script and see if it makes a difference. Suppose that Ben and Helen were supported by Ben's parents while Ben was in school. And suppose that Helen did not help with the practice because she preferred to spend her time playing tennis. Also suppose that the couple has only one child who was cared for by Ben's mother while Helen played tennis. Would you still believe that Helen should get the same portion of Ben's practice?

You cannot simply apply a simple mechanical formula to equitable distribution. It takes some serious thought.

2. Unequal Needs

The most common case of unequal needs is substantial difference in the earning power of the spouses. If one spouse earns $100,000 per year and the other earns $30,000 per year, it may be appropriate for the lower-earning spouse to get a greater share of the marital assets to bring him or her somewhat closer to parity with the living standard likely to be enjoyed by the spouse with the greater income. In particular, this may become relevant around the issue of savings and long-term security. The spouse with the greater income will probably have a greater ability to save for retirement. That spouse is better situated through employment to make larger contributions to pension and other retirement plans than the spouse with less income. If both are young, long-term retirement may be less of an issue; each will have plenty of time to accumulate long-term security. But when the couple is older—late forties or more—career patterns are usually established and the long-term economic chances of each are in general apparent.

To some extent, this differential in earning power can be dealt with through alimony. But because of all the limitations inherent in alimony, many couples—particularly those with substantial savings—prefer to distribute more property to the wife in lieu of alimony.

Differences in need can also be based on other than earning power. Spouses may have substantial differences in age or in health. These differing needs may suggest that one has a short time remaining in which to earn income while the other has a long time—or that one can expect expenses to rise as health deteriorates. There are no formulas that can be applied. You must look at need as dispassionately as possible. And you must remember that the law does not say that differing need is the exclusive basis for dividing property. Rather, it is but one factor that should be weighed along with others.

3. Unequal Exempt Property

Suppose that the wife of a divorcing couple has an inheritance of $2 million in a state that exempts inherited assets from equitable distribution. Suppose, also, that the marital property totals $400,000, of which $150,000 is the husband's Keogh plan. Finally, suppose that both spouses are fifty-five years old. Does it seem fair to divide the marital property equally in this case? The exempt property of the wife suggests that her long-term security is far more predictable than her husband's and that an equal division of his pension would feel patently unfair. This is not a common situation. But for people who do have significant amounts of exempt property, fairness requires some recognition of unequal financial status.

4. Short Marriage

Suppose a couple is married three years and has no children. Suppose that the husband is a struggling artist who has produced little income but, subsidized by the wife, has pursued his career. Suppose, also, that the wife is a big-income earner who has saved substantial money during the marriage. Does it strike you as fair to divide the savings equally between the two?

As the length of the marriage increases, most judges and divorce lawyers begin to recognize a more mutual claim to the savings even if one spouse has contributed all or most of the income. In short marriages, that claim tends to be much weaker. Just because people are married is not in itself the basis for one to get a windfall at the expense of the other.

5. Emotional Investment

Consider Ben's beloved sailboat. It was his hobby and his passion. While Helen played tennis, he worked (played) on his boat. He has never thought of the boat as an economic asset. He is more likely to think about the boat as an extension of himself. He has no intention of ever selling it. He also cannot imagine that Helen is entitled to any part of the boat. She never liked it. In fact, she despised everything about it and refused to set foot on it. She said the boat made her seasick and that when Ben was on the boat she thought he was unbearable. As property goes, the boat is an object of very intense feelings.

Sometimes when you are dealing with an asset that is not a major portion of the marital estate and that one of you feels strongly about, it pays for the other spouse to tread lightly. Helen may want to consider that she will win concessions in other areas by letting go of her claim on the boat or otherwise reducing her claim. Less than equal division on this asset is common sense because it avoids a struggle over an outcome that is not worth the cost. That does not mean that the law says that Helen's claim should be less. Rather, her own judgment leads her to conclude that her claim is best made on some other asset.

HOW TO NEGOTIATE THE DISTRIBUTION

After you have identified and valued the assets, each of you should develop a comprehensive plan for division. You may choose to approach this one or both of two ways. First, you can look at all the marital assets in gross. That is, look at the total net worth of the marriage. In the case of Ben and Helen, for example, the after-tax net worth of the marriage is about $412,000. Now, propose what overall percent of the marital estate should come to you, and then list the bundle of assets that should make up your portion. The second approach is to proceed asset by asset, identifying the percentage of each asset that should come to you. In this approach, your focus is on each asset, not the final percent allocation.

Your proposal should incorporate all your reasons for the division you propose. What principles of fairness do you want your spouse to consider in discussing your proposal? You should itemize the elements that you believe play a role: how long your marital partnership was, what each of you contributed economically and emotionally to the creation of the assets, etc. Discuss any other principle that you think is fair to apply.

Your proposal should also incorporate what you have learned from your lawyer about local standards in the courts— recognizing all the limits of such prognostications. If it is nearly universal in your jurisdiction that the house gets divided equally but the pension gets divided one-third/two-thirds, say so. Such predictions are helpful mostly when the distribution proposed by either of you radically departs from what appears to be the norm.

HOW TO DISAGREE

You should not be surprised if the two of you have different opinions on the division of marital property. Nor should that discourage you. You may be lucky and agree from the beginning. That happens most frequently when both spouses agree on an equal division because neither spouse can think of a compelling justification to convince the other to accept less than half. But many divorces are settled on other than fifty-fifty divisions.

The first thing to do when you find yourself in disagreement is to identify the areas of *agreement*. Many couples who find themselves in furious disagreement are actually quite close to agreement. Some of the worst litigation I have seen has been between people who were actually within 5 percent of each other's positions. If the marital net worth is $300,000 and you proposed fifty-fifty while your spouse proposed sixty-forty, you are actually in agreement on $270,000. You both agree that you should get at least $120,000 (you think it should be more), and you both agree that your spouse should get at least $150,000 (your spouse thinks it should be more). The scope of your disagreement is the $30,000 that you think should go to you and that your spouse thinks should go to him/her.

It is much easier to carry on a negotiation over the $30,000 than it is over the $300,000. Your disagreement concerns only 10 percent of the marital assets. Your negotiation becomes more focused, and it is easier for you to find compromises, when you look at the common ground first and consider the disagreement second.

FINDING THE RANGE OF REASONABLENESS

There is no precise formula for determining what is fair in any particular divorce. In fact, in most divorces there is more than one possible resolution that is fair. If you live in an equitable-distribution state, you will have to negotiate until you identify with a package that you both feel is reasonable and fair. Avoid struggling over a few dollars; it really is not worth it. If the agreement is within the range of what is reasonable, if you are close, go with it. The amounts involved when couples are stuck are often not worth the aggravation and delay that result from trying to fine-tune your agreement. Be practical—and be finished.

BEN AND HELEN

Let's go back to Ben and Helen to see what we mean by the "range of reasonableness." After they had listed and valued the assets, each one proposed the way he/she thought the assets should be divided.

Ben felt that the house should be divided fifty-fifty. He felt that his business should be divided one-third to Helen and two-thirds to him because he had, after all, been the one to build the business. He acknowledged that Helen should get something for the assistance she gave, but was adamant that she did not deserve half. He felt that the same principle should apply to the work-related tax-deferred assets like the IRAs, the pension, and the Keogh. The person who had generated the asset should get two-thirds while the other should get one-third. Finally, he felt that certain personal assets should stay as they were. He conceded all the jewelry and Helen's car to her but wanted the boat and his own car for himself.

Helen rejected Ben's proposal as unfair and self-serving. They had had a long-term partnership, she had done her part in good faith, and there was no reason that she should accept less than half the marital estate. She wanted half the value of each and every asset that was subject to equitable distribution. She should keep the $20,000 worth of jewelry that was her exempt property, but everything else should be split right down the middle, fifty-fifty. At first glance it appears that Ben and Helen are in trouble because each seems to have such a different position. But, in fact, both have reasonable positions. Ben's position is not unreasonable in the sense that the doctrine of equitable distribution does indeed recognize that property ought to be distributed with some recognition of who produced it. So his desire to get more of the property because it was his efforts that created most of the value is not an inherently unreasonable position. Further, if this couple was to go to trial, a result consistent with Ben's position would not be surprising.

On the other hand, exactly the same thing can be said for Helen's position. There is a commonly held belief among lawyers and judges that in long-term marriages the assets should be divided equally. The philosophical assumption seems to be that if people have spent enough years together in a partnership the distinction between what he did and what she did has become too fuzzy, and the safest way to do justice is to split the equity 50-50. So if they were unable to settle and went to trial, it would also not be surprising if the judge ordered an equal division of assets.

This is not as contradictory as it appears. First, divorce negotiations and divorce litigation are not an exact science. There is always a range of variability. The same case negotiated by two different teams of lawyers will not produce exactly the same results. The same case tried before two different judges will not produce exactly the same results. There is a range of variation for any case and that range is what I refer to as the range of reasonableness. Both Helen and Ben have positions within that range. When Ben and Helen compare the numbers each one proposes, they find that the difference between them is not very dramatic.

ASSET	VALUE	BEN'S PROPOSAL		HELEN'S PROPOSAL	
		BEN	HELEN	BEN	HELEN
House	229	114.5	114.5	114.5	114.5
Ben's Keogh	94	63	31	47	47
Helen's pension	13.5	4.5	9	6.75	6.75
Ben's IRA	22	22	—	22	—
Helen's IRA	22	—	22	—	22
Boat	22	22	—	11	11
Jewelry	30	—	30	5	25
BMW	22	22	—	11	11
Ford	6	—	6	3	3
Ben's practice	130	87	43	65	65
totals	590.5	335	255.5	285.25	304.25

The real difference between Ben's position and Helen's position is only $50,000 in pretax dollars (in after-tax dollars it is even less, but for the sake of simplicity we look here only at pretax dollars). Out of a total marital estate of $590,500 they are $50,000 or 8.5 percent apart. A variation of less than 10 percent suggests that they are both within a range of reasonable outcomes.

How did Ben and Helen settle their case? Ben agreed to share all the pension and Keogh money fifty-fifty. Helen modified her demand for half the value of the practice to 40 percent, and Ben, feeling that his extra contribution had been recognized, accepted. Helen agreed that Ben would keep his boat and BMW because these were so important to him, and that she would keep all the jewelry and her car. As a result of this, Ben had a total of $312,250 or 53 percent of the assets and Helen had $278,250 or 47 percent of the total assets. He felt that he had been acknowledged by getting more; she felt that she had been acknowledged by getting essentially half. This is how divorces get settled.

Chapter Fourteen

PULLING THE AGREEMENT
TOGETHER

W*e have now discussed* the major components of divorce settlement—dividing the marital property, custody and financial support of the children, alimony—and the emotions that affect the entire process for everyone in your family. The time is near for you to put into practice the techniques I have outlined. However, before you begin, I have some additions to your list of items to negotiate.

SECONDARY ISSUES

There are three issues that do not fall within the five issues of divorce we have discussed that I will consider briefly here. Although they are secondary, they should be negotiated so that they do not cause misunderstanding later.

INCOME TAXES

There are two questions to be dealt with. The first is how you will file your tax return if you are not divorced by the end of the calendar year. If you are divorced before December 31, you cannot file joint returns; you must file as single persons. However, if you are still married, you may have a choice of filing either single or joint return. It almost never pays to file as "married-separate"—a category that puts you in an unfavorable rate table—but it may pay to file a joint return. What often happens is that the spouse who earns less money—most frequently the wife—concludes correctly that she would pay less in taxes if she filed as a single person, or even in the married-separate category. Although this is true, it may mean that the other spouse pays far more tax than he otherwise would pay, and more tax than the wife saves by filing alone. I have seen this produce some very sour results.

Have your accountant project your taxes both ways and then choose the way that produces the least *total* taxes paid. If this disadvantages one of you, the other should compensate that spouse accordingly. This is an opportunity for cooperation that should not be missed.

The second question is: Who gets the exemptions for the children? The entitlement to the exemption is controlled by residence, not by who pays child support. If you do not stipulate otherwise, the parent with whom the children live more than half the time automatically is entitled to the exemption. However, you can negotiate anything you want to as long as both of you do not try to take the exemption for the same child. If you are in different tax brackets you should arrange for the parent in the higher bracket to take the exemptions and then to share part of the savings with the other parent. It makes no sense to pay more tax than absolutely necessary. Specify which parent gets the exemption for each child. If there is only one child left unemancipated, you may wish to alternate, each of you taking the exemption every other year. Tax planning should not be ignored. Properly done, it can save you considerable money.

LEGAL FEES

Another minor issue that arises is who should pay the legal fees and other expenses associated with the divorce. Because most divorcing people detest each other's lawyers, the suggestion that you contribute to your spouse's legal fees may be infuriating. Even so, this is a commonly negotiated issue that must be addressed, even if you find it distasteful.

If you have had a litigious divorce with frequent court appearances and numerous motions to the court for prejudgment relief, your legal fees could run into many thousands of dollars. On the other hand, if you have had a cooperative negotiation with a settlement prior to filing for divorce in the court, your total costs should not exceed $5,000 or $6,000. In addition to the lawyer's fees, there may be fees owed to an actuary for pension appraisals, to a real estate appraiser, and to an accountant. Depending on the complexity of the divorce, the fees could range from $500 to $5,000 or more.

Ideally, in an amicably settled divorce, the total legal costs should be paid from some joint marital asset. If your premise is truly a no-fault divorce, then the legal fees and expenses are a transaction cost to end the marriage. Difficulty often arises when one spouse, usually the non-initiator, demands that the other pay all the costs because "You wanted this, and you should pay for it." As I have said throughout this book, such a punitive posture is neither productive nor persuasive.

One alternative is for each to pay his or her own fees. Assuming that each of you has hired a moderate-priced lawyer, the fees ought to be about the same. But what if one of you went to a very expensive lawyer who collects a large retainer from all clients, even those who will settle amicably? Should this expense be imposed on the other spouse? It can be a nettlesome question because the other spouse may already harbor substantial resentment toward that lawyer. To have to contribute to what is perceived as an unnecessary expense may be unbearable. Another alternative is to treat this as an expense to be borne relative to your incomes or other indicator of ability to pay. The best advice I can give you here is to suggest that this is one of those emotional issues in which what you feel is often not a reliable guide to what you should do.

Do not let this sabotage your agreement. Try to resolve it with the same pragmatism and fairness you have employed throughout your negotiation.

DISPUTE RESOLUTION

If you have negotiated a good agreement, you have significantly reduced the probability that you will get into post-divorce fights that drag you back into the courts. But there is no way to completely insulate yourselves from the possibility of a disagreement that you cannot resolve yourselves. One way to reduce the cost of possible future conflict is to incorporate a dispute-resolution clause in your settlement agreement. Your lawyer is unlikely to suggest this because most divorce lawyers have had very little contact with mediation or arbitration. Regardless of your lawyers' attitude, give serious consideration to both mediation and arbitration provisions.

Dispute-resolution clauses require that you engage in some form of dispute resolution for post-divorce conflict other than going to court. You may choose one or both of two techniques: mediation and arbitration. In mediation you use the services of an impartial third party to help the two of you negotiate a resolution. If you have used a mediator to negotiate your settlement, he or she will probably suggest such a clause. If you have not used a mediator, you should consider this anyway. You should also consider designating a particular individual as mediator. The purpose here is to have someone readily available when a dispute arises. It is preferable that this person be known in advance so that you can get into mediation quickly, before the conflict escalates.

The second provision to consider is binding arbitration of

the dispute. Although arbitration has not been used much in divorce, its use is growing. In arbitration, the impartial third party hears both sides and then decides the matter just as a judge would. If you have agreed to arbitration in your agreement, the arbitrator's decision will be binding. Generally, arbitration in agreements is used as a sequel to mediation. That is, you first go to mediation, and only if mediation is unsuccessful do you go to arbitration.

The advantage of an arbitration clause is a quicker and less costly resolution of the conflict. Arbitration is less formal than a hearing in court, and if you reside in an area where the courts are very busy, the arbitration may occur much sooner than a court hearing. The other advantage is that you can also designate a particular individual to serve as arbitrator so you do not have to worry about who will arbitrate. I do recommend that the arbitrator be a lawyer. Although I do not believe that the mediator must be a lawyer, I think that anyone empowered to make binding decisions should be an expert on the law that applies to the dispute. For that reason, the arbitrator should be chosen from the ranks of divorce lawyers, retired judges, or law professors who are experts on family law. In most parts of the country, the yellow pages will list several possibilities. Your lawyers or mediator may also be helpful here.

COMPLETING THE NEGOTIATION

There will come a time in your negotiation when you are ready to finish, although this is not always obvious. One of you will begin to suggest that you have resolved just about all the issues between you. This may not always be a mutual conclusion, as one of you may regard the unfinished details as more critical than the other does. One way to test your degree of completion is to prepare an outline of your agreement as it stands at that point. You should be able to do this whether you are using your lawyers to do the negotiating, whether you are using a mediator, or whether you are doing it yourselves. If you are unable to prepare such an outline, you are dangerously out of touch.

Consider the outline prepared by Beth and Don, a couple on the verge of completing their negotiation.

OUTLINE OF TENTATIVE AGREEMENT
BETWEEN BETH AND DON

1. Parenting

a. We agree that we will have joint custody of the children in that we will make all important decisions about the health or education of the children together and by consensus.

b. The children will have their primary residence with Beth. They will spend the following time with Don:

(1) Alternate weekends beginning at 5 P.M. on Friday and ending Monday morning when Don will take them to school.

(2) Every Monday night through Tuesday morning when Don will take them to school.

(3) Every other Thanksgiving, Christmas, Easter, Labor Day, Memorial Day, and other holidays to be discussed in the future.

(4) At least one full week of vacation during the summer.

(5) If a child must stay home from school due to illness, Don will stay home with the child half the time even if it is a day when the children would be with Beth.

2. Child Support

a. Don will pay Beth $1100 a month for child support for Kathy and Debbie.

b. *Cost of living increase—undecided*

c. We agree that we want the children to go to college but will discuss it further when they enter high school.

d. Beth will provide medical insurance for the girls through her employment because it is free. If this changes, we will discuss it further to see who provides insurance. We will share equally in any uninsured medical or dental costs for the girls.

e. We will each maintain $100,000 of term life insurance with the girls as beneficiaries and the other parent as trustee.

3. Alimony

a. Don will pay Beth $500 a month alimony.

b. *We are not in agreement on the duration of the alimony. Beth seeks seven years, Don is not willing to pay more than three.*

c. *Cost of living increase—undecided*

d. Alimony will end if Beth remarries. *We are not in agreement on what happens to alimony if Beth lives with another man.*

4. Distribution of the Assets

a. We are agreed that Beth will stay in the house until Debbie graduates high school. During that time Beth will be responsible for the mortgage and tax payments as well as routine repairs. We will share major repairs fifty-fifty.

The house will be sold when Debbie graduates. The net proceeds will be shared fifty-fifty. The house will also be sold if Beth remarries. *We are not in agreement on what happens if Beth lives with another man in the house.*

b. Beth will keep her pension. She will also get 25 percent of Don's pension but will not get it until he retires.

c. The Citibank savings account will be split fifty-fifty.

d. Beth will keep the Toyota. Don will keep the Buick. Don will be responsible for the car loan on the Buick.

e. Beth will be responsible for paying off the Bloomingdale's balance of $430 and the Visa bill of $322. Don will be responsible for paying the American Express bill of $870, the Sears bill of $234, and the MasterCard bill of $653.

f. We are in agreement on the furniture, and the attached list shows who gets what.

g. *We are not in agreement on Beth's diamond ring. Beth thinks she should keep it, Don thinks it should be sold and the money divided.*

5. Income Taxes

We will file joint federal and state tax returns in 1991. We do not expect a refund. Don will be responsible for paying any taxes due. After 1991 Don will take Debbie as an exemption and Beth will take Kathie.

6. Legal Fees

We each will pay our own.

7. Dispute Resolution

We think we agree on having both a mediation clause and an arbitration clause but want to find out more about this.

Beth and Don agree on most issues and at this point are in disagreement on only a few. The theme running through their disagreements reflects Don's continuing resentment about the divorce. Don is angry about the possibility of Beth's developing a new relationship. His desire that alimony cease and the house be sold if Beth lives with another man is evidence of that. So is his focus on the ring he gave to Beth. It has sentimental value for him, and he doesn't want her wearing it if she is with another man. Although Don acknowledges that Beth needs alimony, he resents having to pay it. That is why he presses to shorten the length of alimony. He also resents the suggestion of a cost of living adjustment because he feels it protects Beth from inflation but leaves him exposed.

Outlining their area of agreement is helpful to Don and Beth because it puts their disagreements in perspective relative to the whole. It also reinforces the idea that it would be folly to litigate their case when they are so close to an agreement. This perspective enables them to negotiate a conclusion. They agree that the cost of living increase will not exceed the increase in Don's salary. They agree that the cohabitation by Beth will end alimony and require the sale of the house only if the cohabitation exceeds a year. And they compromise on the duration of alimony at five years. Neither one is particularly pleased with these compromises. But each one recognizes that the few concessions are worth it so they will be finished with negotiation and able to get on with their lives.

PROBLEMS WITH CLOSURE

As you reach the end of your negotiation you may find yourself getting stuck on little things. This end stage can give you unexpected and surprising headaches, and I want to prepare you for them. It is not uncommon for fighting actually to increase as you near the end of negotiating your separation agreement. Be careful—this sudden escalation could ruin your settlement.

CASE STUDY: MARYBETH AND TONY

I recall a couple I had seen for what started out as a very difficult divorce. Marybeth and Tony were moderately wealthy and had one small child. At first this case had all the appearances of a custody fight that promised an all-out war. However, they were able to break through the hostility and negotiate a cooperative parenting agreement and a very fair economic settlement. But at the very end, after dividing a marital estate of more than $600,000, they almost went to war over a $300 bracelet.

Here's what happened: Tony was an orderly man who planned ahead. When he saw an appropriate gift for Marybeth, he would buy it to save until her birthday or some other occasion. Sometime before they decided to divorce, Tony had purchased a gold bracelet and had put it in their safe-deposit box. Although he had not given it to her, Marybeth knew it was there. At the last negotiating session Marybeth demanded that she get the bracelet. Tony refused. She insisted, arguing that it was intended for her and she would be damned before she let his girlfriend get it. He would not budge, Tony said, even if hell froze over, etc. "She has gotten too much as it is. There has to be an end, and this is it." Try as I might, I was unable to move them.

Why were Marybeth and Tony stuck on a trivial item? When they started negotiating they had been very angry. In order to reach their settlement, each had suppressed a lot of anger. They had done exactly what I have suggested you do—they had put the anger aside for one hour a week in order to negotiate an agreement. But now, as we moved toward closure, each felt safe to act out the anger and resentment they felt. And they had chosen a small and unimportant issue to be the symbolic repository of the anger that they still carried.

However, as long as the problem is recognized for what it is, it can be dealt with.

After trying—and failing—to help them find a reasonable way out, I made a proposal. It was too ludicrous, I said, for this agreement to fall apart over such a trivial issue. But in view of the fact that each one was determined that the other not win on this issue, I proposed that the bracelet be cut into two pieces and divided between them. They agreed, and we were finished. As I was mediating this divorce, I drafted a memorandum of understanding for their lawyers to use when preparing the separation agreement. In the section on personal property I included a clause that provided for them to choose a jeweler to cut the bracelet into two parts.

When they came back for the final review of the memorandum and read this section, Tony and Marybeth were embarrassed. Rather than destroy the bracelet, they decided to give it to their daughter for her tenth birthday.

WHAT IS YOUR SYMBOLIC ISSUE?

Many couples manage to find their equivalent of the gold bracelet. It may be an issue relating to the children, to alimony, or to an item of property. It doesn't really matter. What does matter is that, relative to the settlement as a whole, the outcome of that particular issue is not critical. What is important is the symbolic weight that you put on it, and the liberties you take in acting out your anger. It is easy to lose your perspective and endanger your entire agreement.

Caution is in order as you approach completion. If you were the non-initiator of the divorce, your ambivalence toward it can be aroused by imminent settlement. If you are fearful about the future, if you have trouble making decisions, and if you worry that maybe you are not getting the best deal, this is the time when your anxiety can sink the agreement. Pre-settlement jitters are commonplace, but you need to hold on.

This is the time to reconfirm your pragmatism about the divorce. It is the time to review the problems you are solving. You may have to do a little practical horse-trading to get the deal finished, but—by all means—get it finished! The problem may not be yours but your spouse's. He may be trying to push your button one last time. She may be trying to extract one more concession before letting go. If you feel that you have conceded up to your limit, this may seem intolerable to you.

Sometimes the best thing to do is nothing. You just wait it out. If you really have reached your limit and cannot go even one inch more, you may have to say so. But don't back yourself into corners with no face-saving escape routes. Suggest another meeting that allows you time to think more about the issues. It is almost never productive to use ultimatums. They just provide justification for your spouse's hesitance about finishing the settlement.

LETTING GO OF THE ROPE

In divorce negotiations I frequently use the imagery of a tug-of-war. There are two ways to win a tug-of-war. The first is to pull your adversary over the line and win by sheer force of will. The second is to drop the rope. At a minimum, you end the game and get on to other things. Most often, in the little power struggles that mark the completion of the agreement, you win by letting go of the rope. That is, you concede on the little symbolic issue that is holding you up. But, you ask, "Doesn't that mean I've been defeated?" "Defeated on what?" is my response. If it's a symbolic contest, it has no real or substantive impact on the settlement. It just serves to hold you in the marriage that you are seeking to end. Your concession on that final little issue says that you are ready to be finished with negotiations, and that you are done with the marriage. The struggle is over because you are no longer available to struggle.

It is not appeasement to walk away from a contest that is symbolic. It is only common sense.

USING YOUR LAWYERS TO WRAP IT UP

As you and your spouse approach agreement, the role of your lawyers as technicians increases. If your lawyers have played a dominant role in negotiating the agreement, they should be prepared to draft and revise your final separation agreement. If you have done most of the negotiation, with your lawyers in advisory roles, you will need to explain clearly to each one what your intentions are and how you arrived at each aspect of the agreement. Tell them what trade-offs you made. Tell them the assumptions you made at each stage so that they know you fully understood what you were doing.

Several problems may be encountered at this point. First, your lawyers may be as capable of getting stuck in the details as you are. If they have difficulty agreeing on the fine print, make sure that the issue is really worth the legal fees and aggravation it is costing you. Sometimes lawyers get into disputes over how to resolve disputes that may arise in the future but are not a problem now. One that we discussed earlier is the impact of cohabitation on alimony payments. We know that remarriage ends alimony—but what happens if the wife lives with another man instead of marrying him? I have seen agreements endangered by this issue even though cohabitation by the wife was unlikely and the alimony was for a short duration. Other favorite sticking points are the impact on support payments if a job is lost, or what happens to child support or custody if the parent with primary residential responsibility wants to move. Although these are all contingencies that may occur, you do not have to resolve them in advance, and indeed it may be impossible to resolve them in advance.

How far to push on the fine details is a decision that should be made by you and not your lawyer. Lawyers are in a difficult position. They are there to protect you, and they know you want them to protect you. But sometimes they have difficulty reading just how far they should go in pursuit of the goal. Most contingencies are covered in the statutory and case law of divorce. That is, the court is available to resolve post-judgment disputes when they arise. Changes in circumstance that require changes in support or changes that require modification of parenting agreements are all subject to court intervention. You need not negotiate a resolution to every contingency that may arise.

GETTING DIVORCED

Once you have settled on what your separation agreement will provide, the actual drafting and signing of the final agreement should not take more than a month. If it drags on, find out why and fix the problem. Sometimes the lawyers are busy attending to more urgent matters. If they do not have time for you, get other lawyers. If they do have the time, tell them to get it done. Once the agreement is signed you are "economically" divorced. The next step is the legal divorce—the actual dissolution of the marriage by the court. I recommend that you do this as soon as possible.

States vary in the procedures required for an uncontested divorce, and within states some courts may be more backlogged than others. This is something to discuss with your lawyers, making clear that you want it done as expeditiously as possible. There are several good reasons for this. Finality is good for everyone. If your marriage has ended, the quicker you redefine your social status the better. I also think that it is better for your children to put a formal end to the marriage as soon as possible lest you support their continued fantasy that their parents will reconcile. If either of you harbors some remaining ambivalence about the divorce, the formal divorce helps to provide emotional closure.

The actual divorce hearing is generally undramatic and anticlimactic. A few states do not require either of you to appear; the decree is issued based on the documents submitted by your lawyers. Others require that only one of you appear to testify. Even if you both appear, it is usually a ten-minute affair that is the reverse of a civil marriage ceremony. Attended by your lawyers instead of the best man and maid of honor, you get unmarried by the judge. The ceremony is nothing to fear and should be completed as soon as possible.

Chapter Fifteen

SOME FINAL THOUGHTS
FROM THE COACH

*D*ivorce is difficult. It challenges you in ways that, perhaps, you have never been challenged before. But it is possible for most people to survive this difficult time and emerge with the ability to build a new life informed by lessons learned. The most important point of this book is that you have choices to make. You will make them consciously and explicitly, thereby retaining control, or you will make them unconsciously and by default, thereby giving up control.

In a book like this, writer and reader must both struggle to simplify complex and arduous tasks. Parts of what you have read look foreign and difficult. Laws about equitable distribution, custody, and support seem complicated and hard to understand. You may well be thinking, "Wouldn't it just be easier to put this in someone else's hands and let him/her worry about it (worry about me) so that I don't have to?" The answer is that it will not be easier. It will only make your life more difficult. You can do this, and you can do it well, if you take it one step at a time.

Two important concepts I hope you take from this book are worth a brief review here. First is that divorce is a transition. And second, the key to good divorce is good negotiation. If you can master the implications of these two concepts you can exercise great influence on the outcome of your settlement agreement.

DIVORCE AS TRANSITION

The message here is that what you feel today is not what you will feel tomorrow, and certainly is not what you will feel five years from now. And if what you feel today is not what you will feel then, it is probably not a very good guide to how you should *behave* today.

The relationship between what you feel and how you act is the first puzzle you must solve to make sense of your divorce. Popular thought encourages us to express our feelings rather than to bury them; to "let it all hang out." And as we have seen, divorce is a time of powerful feelings of anger, fear, and resentment. Certainly you must acknowledge these feelings and talk about them. But do it in the right place and at the right time. Talk to a therapist or, within limits, talk to your friends. But be very careful not to *act out* your feelings in ways that actually injure your own long-term interests. Remember, most of what you do by instinct in divorce is wrong.

When we behave instinctively, or reflexively, we are responding to the present based on our experience of the past. There is nothing inherently wrong with this as long as it is appropriate and logically related to the task at hand. The reason it backfires in divorce is that little in your past experience prepares you to anticipate and solve the problems of divorce. So when you act reflexively, you are choosing from alternative solutions that have little to do with your real problem.

You need to shift your focus from the past to the future. Your disappointment in the failure of your marriage, your sadness, loneliness, anger, resentment, sense of betrayal, and all the other feelings associated with the end of your marriage do not provide you with a guide to the future. Your future is based on a life without your present spouse, and therefore a life that is essentially different from the life you have had during the marriage. The steps you take now must be oriented to the tasks of that future life rather than to the marriage that you are leaving. Bad divorce involves people who get trapped (or trap themselves) in futile attempts to vindicate the past and to rewrite a history that for most purposes is already irrelevant. Good divorce is possible only when you take an accurate inventory of the resources that you have today and then use them efficiently to achieve the goals you have set for the future.

The desire to vindicate the past is perhaps the most dangerous of all the things you do by instinct. It sets up an inevitable regression of the divorce toward a permanent adversary relationship between you and your spouse so that the each of you is forever in the other's way as you try to adjust and adapt. We are all trained from early on to protest our innocence and find the blame in those around us. The illusion that your troubles have their origin in the behavior of others, but not in yourself, is one of life's short-lived comforts. So in divorce, as you experience the pain of marital dissolution and transition, it is natural to blame your spouse and your spouse's deficiencies. But you pay a twofold price for this indulgence. First, you justify the same type of behavior in your spouse so that you also waste valuable energy defending yourself from your spouse's reciprocal attacks. Second, you waste valuable opportunities for cooperation that would serve you better if devoted to designing, and achieving, your future objectives. In other words, you give in to your instincts at the price of losing control.

When you lose control you get bad divorce. When you retain control you have the possibility of good divorce. The only person whose behavior you can control is you. All of your ability to influence the outcome of your divorce settlement through negotiation will ultimately be derived from your own self-control. That will be the basis of your power. Conversely, if you choose to give up self-control, that will be the basis of your powerlessness.

NEGOTIATION AS CRITICAL TASK

Negotiating your settlement agreement is the central organizing task of your divorce. We have seen that nearly all divorces are resolved with a negotiated settlement and that only a small percentage of all divorces actually goes to trial. But notwithstanding that almost all divorces settle, many of those settlements leave people feeling emotionally and financially drained because the quality of the settlement process has been so defective. So, again, you have some important choices to make.

You must decide what role you will play in negotiating the divorce agreement. If you choose to be an active participant and to stay in control, you improve the chances of a good agreement. If you choose to be passive while someone else takes charge, you abdicate responsibility as well as control. You are the world's foremost expert on the topic of your life. Only you can decide what is in your best interest, only you can decide what your goals are, and only you can make the judgments necessary to achieve those goals. No lawyer can know as much about those things as you already do. The greater the role you play, and the smaller the role played by your lawyer and other experts, the greater the possibility that the agreement will genuinely fit your needs.

But the advantages of being your own negotiator come at a price. In my opinion, the price is a bargain for what it gets you. Nevertheless you must be willing to pay it. The price consists of the hard work you will have to invest to learn the legal and financial information that you need, the time it takes to complete a negotiation process, and the patience and forbearance required to work cooperatively with your spouse for the one hour a week you spend negotiating.

You need to learn something about the law as it applies to divorce in your state. If you have children, you need to consider parenting issues of custody and visitation. You will have to learn about child support and spousal support laws. Finally, you will have to learn what the law allows to the distribution of the marital assets. Although much of the law appears daunting at first, there is nothing in it that cannot be mastered by anyone with a modest education and willingness to learn. You will use your lawyer to help you understand your rights and obligations, but you will need to make sure that your lawyer is willing to support your need to know and decide.

Next, you will need to become very knowledgeable about your family finances. You will need to engage in a comprehensive budgeting process in order to establish your priorities. This is probably the most difficult task of all. Economic retrenchment is almost a guaranteed requirement of a middle-class divorce. Deciding what to do without is always a painful process. And deciding what your children can do without is even more difficult. But it is precisely this task that will measure how well you will do in the negotiation and divorce. Indeed, it is this task that will reflect whether you have truly decided to take responsibility for yourself and for the divorce. Along the way you will use this task as the occasion to assess your financial resources and your personal resources. You may be surprised that this process may trigger some creative problem-solving and decisions to move in new, more satisfying directions.

Finally, you will learn new skills for negotiation that you will use to negotiate the settlement agreement. You will learn how to keep the discussion focused, how to identify your interests and your spouse's interests, and how to keep the negotiation moving forward. You will learn how to set the agenda, how to handle the inevitable anger that accompanies negotiation, and how to resolve disagreements about the issues. Of particular importance, both of you will learn how to balance your divergent interests with your many convergent interests. Despite the divorce, you and your spouse retain much in common and many convergent interests that can be the basis of forging a cordial and cooperative relationship, particularly around the tasks of parenting your children.

Having learned all these things, you can then negotiate your settlement agreement and do it well. This is when your hard work will begin to pay off. And it will continue to pay off for years after. The well-negotiated settlement agreement will become a document reflecting the most efficient accommodation of your financial and personal resources to the needs of all family members. It will maximize the chances of building new lives for you, your spouse, and your children.

The premise of the book is that you serve your own enlightened self-interest by maintaining control over the process of the divorce. Such control is best achieved when both you and your spouse are determined to avoid the damage of acrimonious and adversarial divorce. Paradoxically, you will each do this well only if assisted by the other. Particularly if you have children, your successful adjustment to your new life will be determined in part by whether or not your spouse is successful in his/her adjustment. In fact, most of what this book suggests is paradoxical. You get power by taking responsibility and "owning" the divorce. You obtain your spouse's cooperation by offering your own, even though you are angry and disenchanted with each other. And you negotiate your way to a good divorce even though you feel like fighting.

The ultimate measure of the good divorce you seek will not be clearly evident for five years. That is the period in which all members of the family can be expected to have completed the transition. By then, your own new life pattern should be complete as should your former spouse's. One or both of you will probably be remarried or will have found a companion or potential mate. Or one of you may still be single. In any event, how you will be living will be the result of affirmative choices you have made. If you have chosen well, the divorce will not be a continuing important influence on your life. Rather, it will have been an important chapter in a book now closed, and you will be well on your way to successful new lives. The choice is yours to make.

ENDNOTES

1. Salvadore Minuchin, *Family Kaleidoscope* (Massachusetts: Harvard University Press, 1984), 48.
2. Judith Wallerstein and Sandra Blakeslee, *Second Chances: Men, Women and Children a Decade After Divorce* (New York: Ticknor and Fields, 1989).
3. Lenore Weitzman, *The Divorce Revolution* (New York: The Fare Press, 1985), 283.
4. *Ibid.*, chapter 10.
5. Wallerstein and Blakeslee, *Second Chances.*
6. *Ibid.*
7. Weitzman, *The Divorce Revolution.* 204.
8. Robert Mnookin, "Bargaining in the Shadow of the Law" (*Yale Law Journal,* Vol. 88, 1979), 950–997.
9. *Family Law Quarterly,* Vol. XXIV, No. 4, Winter 1991, 328–329.
10. *Ibid.*, 335–336.
11. *Ibid.*
12. You may contact the Academy of Family Mediators at P.O. Box 10501, Eugene, Oregon 97440.
13. Wallerstein and Blakeslee, *Second Chances.*
14. Annual changes in the Consumer Price Index may be found in most annual almanacs.
15. Weitzman, *The Divorce Revolution.* 144
16. *Ibid.*, chapter 7.
17. *Family Law Quarterly,* Vol. XXIV, No. 4, Winter 1991, 555–556.

INDEX

Uncontested divorce, 91–92, 301
Unequal contribution, 278–80
Unequal distribution
  contribution and, unequal,
    278–80
  emotional investment and, 282
  exempt property and, unequal,
    281
  needs and, unequal, 280–81
  short marriage and, 281–82
Unequal exempt property, 281
Unequal needs, 280–81
Unsecured debt, 274
Upheaval, 45

Vacations, 173–74
Victim role, 37–38, 48, 66–67
Vindication, 63, 304
Visitation, 29, 171
  See also Custody
Visiting parent, 171

War of the Roses, 22
Women
  alimony and, 237, 241–42
  children and, as rescue source,
    60–61
  dating and, 60
  divorce experience of, 27, 58
  domestic chores and, 175–76
  emotional dangers for, 59–61
  employment and, return to, 60,
    75–77
  equal incomes and, 105–6
  as lawyers, 122–23
  lawyers and, as rescue source, 60
  "mother in the middle" syndrome
    and, 213–15
  poverty and, 29–30
  remarriage and, 60
  as single parents, 60

"Zoo daddy" syndrome, 174–75